THE COMPLETE BOOK OF MOTOR CAMPING

Editorial Staff

Don O'Reilly
George Engel
Marla Ray

Produced by Lyle Kenyon Engel

Revised Edition, 1973
Published by ARCO PUBLISHING COMPANY, INC.
219 Park Avenue South, New York, N. Y. 10003

Library of Congress Catalog Number 75-103075

Printed in the United States of America

Contents

Foreword

By Bob McCurry, Vice President
U.S. Sales and Service Chrysler Motors Corporation

□ The wonderful world of motor camping, a phenomenon of the 1960s and and the '70s!

Travel trailers have been with us since the 1930s–you can find commercial proof of this in old copies of *National Geographic* which carried travel trailer advertisements in the mid-30s–and there have been home-built conversions of old school buses, hearses, city buses and even Greyhound-type buses for several decades.

The wonderful world of motor camping, as we see it today, is the result of an explosion of interest within the last few years, although it has been building steadily since 1960.

The nation's economy has boomed–a few valleys mixed with the peaks, as you well know–and millions of families have been enjoying the increased leisure time and the larger spendable income in all forms of recreation.

Thousands of those families have turned to the recreation vehicles and the more readily available camping facilities as a means of travel and sightseeing within the budget.

For many, motor camping solves a fundamental economic problem, permitting them to see the country, see what it has to offer, without the accompanying high cost of motel lodging and restaurant meals, especially those with large families.

There are benefits other than economic. Camping opens the gates to a whole new sphere of influence many never experienced.

Also, in many sections of the country, certainly true in the West where much of the area is public land–national, state and local parks and forests–there are limited motel accommodations even for those who do have the fat wallets.

In motels, you can't be close to what you want to see and live with.

Motor camping is pioneering . . . pioneering in comfort.

Once the initial investment is behind you, it can be an inexpensive way to enjoy a full family vacation, year after year.

Ten years ago, it wasn't much of an industry, especially in the area of self-propelled campers.

As recently as 1960 there were only about 55,000 recreation vehicles, 20 per cent self-propelled, but by the end of the decade, 1970, the total was estimated at more than three million vehicles.

The problem is, no one really knows what the actual growth is. There is no way to break it down and it becomes frustrating at times.

For the benefit of the neophyte, it is best to classify the recreation vehicles in five groups:

1. Tent campers or pop-up campers, the lower slung trailers which can be quickly opened to private sleeping quarters, possibly sleeping and eating quarters;
2. Travel trailers, the hard tops;
3. Slide-on campers, easily loaded and mounted on pickup trucks;
4. Conversions or cutaways, from compact vans, wagons, larger vans or panel trucks;
5. Motor homes.

There is a category beyond these, with which we are not involved here, the large mobile homes, 10 and 12 feet wide and 55 feet long, in which many families live, year round.

Generally, for the purpose of motor camping, the motor home is the largest and the most deluxe vehicle in use.

Of course, a recreation motor home may come in king size, if you choose, as described by one of our company executives:

"At Springdale, Utah, we saw a family of five people and a dog in a converted Greyhound Sceni-Cruiser, diesel-powered, air-conditioned, deluxe–at least a $100,000 vehicle.

"It was probably pretty good living, once you parked it, if you could find a parking space."

Not everyone wants to be a bus driver . . . you know what they say, "Leave the driving to us."

It is dangerous to try and generalize the recreation vehicle market.

The American family, the American individual, still has a very basic need to get back to the primitive life, but by degrees.

He wants to get out and feel he is in tune with nature.

For each family, for each person, it is a different need, the degree to which he will do that depends on the individual.

You can get any degree of comfort and convenience you are willing to pay for.

The recreation vehicle market is about as individual as the people who are using them.

Everybody can satisfy his own best interest and do it as he wants it to be done.

I think you will find more individual initiative and ideas in this area than anywhere else.

We are witnessing the growth of a sophisticated kind of camping which can appeal to those who want the luxury of living at home, while at the same time enjoying the open road and the great outdoors.

Of course, the more expensive motor homes provide this sophisticated comfort, but so do the self-contained slide-on campers and the better-equipped travel trailers.

Those luxury-seeking travelers have caused a developing market today for 10 to 15 to 20 thousand dollar vehicles, a market which certainly did not exist two decades ago.

The most important group in this recreation vehicle market are those average families, even the affluent families, with varying interests. The versatility of the designers and builders serves them well.

It may be well to point out that the automobile and truck manufacturers neither build nor sell campers and motor homes.

The industry builds the truck vehicles which serve as the base and the camper builders buy their chassis from dealers, not from the factory.

The industry builds trucks and vans for many uses, one of which is motor camping, and we work closely with the hundreds of camper builders to be sure we build the vehicles best suited to this need.

It is to our industry's advantage, to be sure, that you, the camper owner, are able to get good maintenance service and that area is rapidly being strengthened.

Introduction: The Wonderful World of Motor Camping

□ There are three major problems in the buying of a camper, a recreation vehicle—known from here on as "RV"—whether it be a trailer or a motor home:

1. Which to buy? We will try to help you answer that question in these pages.
2. How to pay for it? That, dear friend, you must answer.
3. Where are you going to take it? We can help you on this one.

A good friend who has had extensive experience in the RV field, as a key man in the industry and as a family camper and user of long standing, told us:

"In your book, if there is one piece of advice I could give, it would be this:

"Carefully determine the type of vehicle which suits you best. This is a very important decision. Get acquainted with the equipment you need.

"Don't get stars in your eyes and get carried away gung ho with the first one you see, because there are those to whom the pop-up camper is the ideal solution. For those who do not have a vehicle capable of towing a large trailer, the little ones tow easily.

"For others, the hard top trailer has appeal, from little to big, from inexpensive to very expensive.

"The real key here is the floor plan. Which floor plan suits you best? There are 1000 different floor plans, so determine your needs before you buy.

"In the self-propelled field, the slide-on camper is great. The real plus here is if you already own a suitable pickup truck, use it during the week in your business.

"Then there are the conversions, all the way from minimum equipment to maximum equipment.

"The vehicle with the most is the motor home. People who worry about wheeling a 27-foot bus in city traffic can forget it, because within fifteen minutes of driving you will get over that.

"Today's motor home is equipped with automatic transmission, power steering, power brakes and Mama can also learn to drive it in fifteen minutes."

Another industry expert, one who also has a long eight-year history of personal family motor camping, voiced a similar warning:

"It is most important to determine in advance the way the vehicle should be equipped, the type of springs, type of shock absorbers, the steering, the load-carrying capacity.

"If he doesn't do that, the customer is going to be very unhappy because it will be extremely costly to maintain, because some things will constantly be breaking.

"Our biggest concern, as a manufacturer, is the guy who bought a pickup truck without any idea of putting the camper on it, and later puts a fairly heavy rig on top of it and wonders why he's having so many problems."

Most self-propelled RVs are, in reality, trucks. They have the appearance, the comfort, the ride of an automobile, but as to the work load, they are trucks.

Every vehicle has its limitations, not only to run down the road, carry the load, but to stop.

You get this thing going and you have to stop it. The bigger the load, the bigger the brakes.

The salesman may tell you, "If it's big enough, it will carry it."

That is not true.

A half-ton truck with an eight-foot box will accept a 3000 pound camper, but the axle won't carry it, the tires won't support it and the brakes won't stop it.

First, you must start with the load you want to carry, then determine the equipment you need to carry it.

If you are buying a slide-on camper, determine the weight of the camper, then weigh everything you are going to put in it. The total must not exceed the rated maximum payload of your pickup.

Dodge publishes a handy free booklet, "Discover America . . ." which lists this type of helpful information.

For example, four people–two adults and two children–weigh 600 pounds, clothing for four people 100 pounds, food 200 pounds, even the spare LP fuel tank, extra water, spare storage battery, aluminum boat and outboard motor, golf bags and other sports gear are listed.

It's not hard to put 2000 pounds of people and gear in a camper, plus maybe a motorcycle strapped on the rear.

Some of these units sleep four, five and six people, are loaded with kitchen facilities, toilet, shower- and that means hot water–and, as mentioned, many campers carry a spare motorcycle for off-the-road transportation.

As vacation camping units become more sophisticated, they get heavier.

Consequently, the use of trucks as tow vehicles for travel trailers is also increasing.

Too much trailer weight can lead to frightening experiences.

One fellow set out on a trip with a large trailer, the weight apparently properly balanced, but as he got up to speed on the busy interstate freeway the trailer started swaying, first gently, then vigorously, the arc growing wider and wider.

Although inexperienced, the driver had the good sense to stay off the brakes and gently eased off the throttle, but it was too late.

The trailer whipped into a three-quarters turn, 270 degrees, dragging the auto in the arc and stopping broadside across the two lanes of highway, stretching from center guardrail to the outside banking.

Fortunately, the drivers behind had seen the swaying trailer and had fallen back to a safe distance.

Twenty minutes later, after much jockeying in the small turning area, the shaken motorist was once more slowly on his way.

The near disaster could have been prevented if the trailer hitch had been equipped with straight line sway control attachments, but the trailer renter wasn't sufficiently informed to offer that advice.

Today, there are more do-it-yourself home handymen who buy the minimum van, with all the front seats removed.

Perhaps you are a craftsman or tradesman with special carpentering or metal working skills. You can install most facilities at a big saving.

In some cases, the finished camper may be crude, but it gets the job done.

There is more of this do-it-yourself activity now than ten years ago, in aggregate numbers, although the percentage is down.

Because of the do-it-yourselfers, the industry statistics on the number of RVs are unreliable, as mentioned earlier by Bob McCurry.

"The camper business is without question much bigger than we can count," another auto executive told us. "Just stop in any hardware store on a weekend and you can quickly see how many men are buying tools, equipment and material for home projects."

The major growth in the camper business is taking place among the city suburban dwellers who want to get away from the noise and dirt of the city.

That is over and above the major market among farming folks, where families already own a pickup truck.

They have the base vehicle and you see many home-made shell campers, perhaps the minimum kind of unit, but they are being used constantly.

Then there is the compact station wagon, used as a passenger car most of the year. Come vacation time, you strip out the bench seats, hang some curtains at the windows, build up some relatively inexpensive bunks and storage cabinets and you're ready to go.

Of course, you have to stop at a park where there are rest room facilities and picnic tables, but you have a travel vehicle which takes you close to nature, sleeping under the stars.

It's a great feeling.

Many retired couples use motor campers as their principal homes, traveling South in the winter, West or North in the summer, visiting relatives and friends (but not imposing) or just enjoying each other.

Some retirees, their families grown and on the wing, maintain an apartment in the home city for the sake of a permanent attachment, but the RV makes it possible to live as they wish.

Some follow a hobby, travel to the major golf tournaments or follow the sun and seasons to the prime fishing areas.

Of course, there are the business uses, the busy construction executive who travels in several states, perhaps all over the country, and has his office and necessary records with him at all times, on the job with what he needs.

A plumber outfitted one as a mobile shop and covers an extended rural route.

Other businessmen use RVs for mobile offices or display rooms, a salesman carries a line of dresses into the neighborhoods, one man operates a mobile poodle clipping service, door to door, or should we say kennel to kennel accommodations.

Many auto racing drivers use slide-on campers or motor homes, going from speedway to speedway with their families, camping in the race track pit area or infield after the race, taking off for the next track after daylight.

Leading gold cup powerboat racer Tommy Tucker Fults travels with his brother-in-law in a camper trailer, sleeping in the pit area on docks at the race sites.

Industrial companies set them up as hospitality suites at major sports events. Some slide-ons and motor homes are equipped with roof decks, great for watching a sporting event from the sidelines.

Indianapolis race car owner Lindsey Hopkins and the makers of Sprite donated a motor home which the United States Auto Club uses as a fully equipped press headquarters at major races.

Staffed with typewriters, duplicating machines, reference files, it is also equipped with telephones which are connected with the local phone system at the track, for the use of newspaper and radio reporters filing their stories.

The varied tastes of the family members can be satisfied, both for those who prefer simple travel vacations and those who like to explore.

They can get to their location in comfort, relatively quickly, and when there, the more hardy can take off and back-pack into the woods and back country. In the meantime, the living accommodations are close by.

With the more sophisticated self-contained units, your major limitation is water, probably carrying no more than 50 gallons.

Generally, you can pull into any place and stay there until the water or even gasoline is exhausted.

The waste is contained in the holding tanks and today, many service stations have complete facilities for dumping the holding tanks, sometimes called "honey dipping."

Directories of these complete service centers are available, addresses listed in Chapter 1.

Campgrounds often provide complete hookup facilities for power, water, sewage and dumping stations, as well as recreational accommodations, stores and even baby sitters.

Now, if they'll only come up with something so Mother doesn't have to do the cooking, dish washing and laundry.

Motor camping is now a year-round sport, attributed in part to the parallel growth in snowmobiling.

In the Northern and Midwestern states, one businessman flier told us, "On a Friday afternoon in the winter we see almost as many campers headed north on the Interstates as we do in the summer.

"The only difference is they are towing trailers with a couple of snowmobiles on the back end instead of boats."

With the combination of boat/snowmobile uses, it seems evident that the future of the RV industry will be bullish.

Once a family has made the original investment in the RV, the vacations become relatively inexpensive.

The operating life of an RV is much longer than the conventional auto.

Exception, of course, is the pickup truck if it is also used for business, but still the slide-on camper portion has a long life. Just back up a new truck under it and away you go.

Another factor affecting the growth of the industry, and we are including you, the family camper, under that umbrella word "industry," is the sizable increase in good camping facilities, not only the campsites but the support facilities.

Just two items–the network of truck/camper centers, sometimes called land-based marinas, plus the more than 1000 gasoline service stations which cater to campers, including holding tank sewage disposal. Truck stops, too, like veteran auto race driver Red Amick's on the Interstate near Muncie, Indiana–the "country club" truck/camper plaza, the travelers have named it.

Service station rest rooms, for example, are so much improved.

Not too many years ago, a wife would cringe at the sight of some gas station rooms, but not true today, except in rare instances.

Dodge's Phil Marriner mentioned, "My wife came out of one a couple of weeks ago commenting about the lounge chairs and carpeted floors in the ladies' john.

"It was a regular gas station, nothing special, except I noticed they had a huge parking area and I assume they want to attract campers, giving them a place to stop for a few hours, or overnight rest."

The network of free rest stops on the Interstates and turnpike highways also adds to the incentive to go motor camping.

Of course, laws vary from state to state, but while it might be "illegal to camp overnight," it is extremely doubtful if the police will bother anybody who is tired and needs a few hours nap for highway safety's sake.

After all, truckers by the hundreds use the rest stops for a sleep break, lying down across the seat for a nap.

You just happen to be luckier... you have a comfortable bed in your "truck."

The motor home fraternity has grown rapidly.

In 1964, the industry built 872 pure (not van conversion) motor homes, of which 268 were on Dodge chassis.

In 1970, 20,000 new pure motor homes were estimated, with Dodge building chassis for 17,000 of them. For comparison, 12,000 new van conversions were predicted for the same period.

It is estimated there were 55,600 pure factory built motor homes on the road in 1970 and the 1980 forecast is 251,000 motor homes, figuring an eight-year life which is conservative.

If the entire RV field grows that fast, there will be fifteen million RVs on the road in 1980.

Talk about a population explosion!

Actually, a more conservative seven-and-a-half-million RVs has been predicted for 1980.

There were more than three million RVs in the U.S.A. during the 1970 season, according to the Recreational Vehicle Institute, and growing faster than 600,000 annually, right now.

Statistics can be boring and sometimes misleading, so this will be brief, to give you an idea of the size of the camping world:

The 1971 estimated new vehicle production and the cost range:

Tent or pop-up trailers	156,500	$ 300 to $ 2,000
Travel trailers	160,000	$ 700 to $17,000
Pickup shells or caps	126,000	$ 300 to $ 1,000
Slide-ons for pickups	140,250	$1,000 to $ 7,000
—plus the pickup truck	—	$2,300 to $ 3,600
Chassis mounts	10,000	$4,500 to $ 8,500
Compact van conversions	12,000	$4,500 to $ 7,500
Motor homes	20,000	$5,000 to $20,000 and up

Perhaps this is a good spot for a disclaimer.

Conditions change, designs change, prices change. This is a fast-changing world, so your only guarantee must come from the manufacturer, the sales agency or the campgrounds.

This book is intended as a guide, to help you in your planning for camping vacations. The information is as accurate as possible at the time of writing.

Using this book as a guide, double check before you buy, before you leave home. Be certain there is space available in the Great Smokies or the Trav-L Park or whatever, be sure what services are available to you. That is our sincere advice.

I. Facilities

□ This is the "complete book of motor camping."

You know it is, because that's the name on the cover.

We have a confession. To be truly a complete book of motor camping, this would have to approach the size of an unabridged dictionary or a set of encyclopedias.

There are more than 670 manufacturers of recreation vehicles; there are hundreds of makers of supplies and accessories.

Campsites

Rand McNally's Western Campground Guide lists 7000 State, National and private campsites in the thirteen Western States alone.

So, to select your campsites for that vacation, our suggestions are:

1. Buy a campground directory for that particular geographic area you plan to travel;

2. Consult your local automobile club's tour department; or

3. Write to the tourism or recreational travel promotion department of the particular states you plan to visit. All fifty states (yes, even Alaska and Hawaii) publish complete directories, free, and don't worry about the correct name of that department. Just address Tourism-Recreation Promotion Dept., State House, the particular capital city and it will get in the proper hands.

They want your business!

There are more than 450 million acres of public domain land in the U.S.A., about a fifth of the total land area of the country and all America bids you welcome–North, South, East, Midwest and West.

Comes the time you and your family embark on your first RV trip, that will truly be the "first day of the rest of your life."

The thousands of public and private campgrounds provide excellent RV accommodations, some obviously better than others.

It is always best to make a reservation for your first overnight stop, then you can go on from there.

Public and Private Campgrounds

The several networks of franchised or syndicate-owned campgrounds, such as KOA, Kampgrounds of America, and Holiday Inn's new Trav-L-Parks, publish directories and make reservations ahead for you.

Rates run from free or $1 or $2 in the public grounds and $2 to $4 a day in the private grounds.

You can expect to find recreational facilities, electric and water connections, a store, meter wash and shower/rest rooms at many campsites.

For the self-contained RVs, many grounds provide sanitary dumping stations for the holding tanks.

The Holiday Inn's Trav-L-Park system opened at Destin, Florida, near Fort Walton Beach on the East Coast, with seven more pilot sites underway.

Destin boasted three hundred spaces on the beach or in wooded areas, with playgrounds for children, gift shops, laundry facilities, plus the reservation system which has worked so well for the motels.

All are franchised, the managers trained in the H.I. innkeepers school, with Davis Smith as the T-L-P director.

"We ran a little story in the *Holiday Inn Magazine*," editor Lois Crowe told us, "and the mail just poured in. The amount of interest shown was amazing!"

It has been mentioned here that there are three million RVs in use. *U.S. News and World Report* said forty-nine million people were on the camping trail in 1969, with an estimate of 20 per cent growth in 1970.

Obviously, to reach a figure like sixty million people camping, in three million RVs, you would have to count the same people on each of several camping trips. Regardless, it's big, big, big!

The point is, there were only 16,146 campgrounds counted in 1969, providing 578,342 campsites. Only a half-million campsites for three million vehicles!

KOA was born in 1961 at Billings, Montana to house the expected flood of RV families enroute to and from the Seattle World's Fair.

It was so successful there are now about five hundred franchised KOA installations coast to coast, with national reservation service.

The Rand McNally campgrounds guides are great. They even give post office names so you can have your mail forwarded to that particular camp area, specifics about each camp, as well as a list of sanitary dumping stations along the highways.

For campgrounds guides, see your local bookstore or write to:

Rand McNally
P.O. Box 7600
Chicago, Illinois 60680

or

Sunset Family Camping
Lane Magazine and Book Co.
Menlo Park, California

For National Park information:

"Guide to Outdoor Recreation
Areas and Facilities"
Bureau of Outdoor Recreation
Department of the Interior
P.O. Box 7763
Washington, D.C. 20240

For private campgrounds information:

Kampgrounds of America
P.O. Box 1138
Billings, Montana 59103

Trav-L-Parks
Holiday Inn National Headquarters
Memphis, Tennessee 38118

Stuckey's Camparks
Eastman, Georgia 31023

Holiday Camps, USA (for tents)
3177 Mercier
Kansas City, Missouri 64111

Safari Camps of America
East Gate Plaza
Columbus, Missouri 65201

Holding tanks sanitary disposal stations:

Rajo Publications
P.O. Box 2576
Palos Verdes, California 90274

Woodall Publishing Co.
500 Hyacinth Place
Highland Park, Illinois 60035

Bottled gas and service:

Primus Refillers Guide
Primus Sievert
47 Larking Street
Stamford, Connecticut 06906

In addition to the drive-in-today-stay-a-few-days campgrounds, a new idea has blossomed—the condominium concept of trailer camping.

You buy your own permanent campsite, use it as long and as often as you wish, and rent out the spot when you decide to take a trip away from home base.

We will explain more fully later in this chapter.

Then a step further—fly in and camp out vacations, in which you fly commercial to the vacation area and your rental RV is waiting for you at the airport, with your first night campsite reserved as you requested.

More details on this later, in this chapter.

The Great Smokies and Georgia/Alabama

It is doubtful if there is a National park more dedicated to campers than the Great Smoky Mountain Park in Tennessee and North Carolina.

Certainly the Smoky Mountain Park has the largest camper traffic, with more than seven and a half million visitors a year.

The camper is king in the Smokies, a truly great natural wonderland, yet nearby are unusual tourist attractions such as Ghost Town at Gatlinburg, where kids enjoy the daily shows.

And, if you happen to be an auto racing nut, one of the sport's top cameramen hangs out at Ghost Town, big and bearded Pal Parker.

The Smokies campsites are well populated, yes, but not overcrowded.

It used to be that you could go in and if the campground was full, the ranger would park you beside the road, or in the parking lot; but the traffic got so heavy that was cut out a couple or three years ago, the position now being, "First come, first served. When we're full, we're full, but we'll help you find a place."

The rangers have radios in their cars and on their hips.

They'll call into headquarters for you and ask where there are openings. HQ will advise "there are six spots at so and so, or three places somewhere else."

When all the public parks are full, you just have to go to a private commercial campground.

Usually, the private campground is smaller because it has to pay for itself.

For information you can contact:

Gatlinburg Chamber of Commerce
Gatlinburg, Tennessee 37738

or

Superintendent
Great Smoky Mountain National Park
Gatlinburg, Tennessee 37738

A little farther south, a progressive group of nine cities forms the "Valley," straddling the Georgia-Alabama border line.

There they are building a four-and-a-half million dollar campground and park, more than 200 acres, to accommodate tent campers and RV families.

It all began with the sixty-million dollar construction of the West Point, Georgia Dam on the Chattahoochee River, a flood control project which is creating the huge new West Point Reservoir.

To give you an idea of the size of the man-made lake/reservoir, there will be 525 miles of shoreline, with plenty of provision for beaches and boating.

With the dam nearing completion, it will probably be 1973 before that lake is full, but the first campsites will open in 1971, and plans are for them to be deluxe, with everything the camper wants.

West Point, Georgia and its sister city, Lanett, Alabama (you'll never notice where one ends and the other begins) has blossomed from a quiet rural center into a doggone nice "small town" community, just progressive enough to supply your needs, yet small town enough to be friendly.

We have seen the plans and feel that the West Point Dam-Reservoir-Campgrounds Park may well become the model for other communities to copy, if they can, in future years.

For information contact:

Mr. Vince McDonald
Valley Chamber of Commerce
West Point, Georgia 31833–or–
Lanett, Alabama 36863–take your choice

New Condominium Concept

Comes now the condominium campgrounds idea.

E. Randall Henderson was a founder of the original "condo" approach to campgrounds, in 1968, called Holiday Out.

For fairly obvious reasons, there was some flack so they changed the name to Venture Out.

Perhaps that play on words awoke the folks in Memphis, Tennessee to the idea which is now Trav-L-Park, mentioned earlier in this chapter.

Regardless, Henderson is now president of Outdoor Resorts of America, based in Nashville, Tennessee, opening at four locations, three in Florida and one at Gatlinburg, Tennessee in the Great Smokies.

Within this new concept, you buy your campsite, about 35 by 70 feet, for $5000 to $7500. You own it, pay taxes on it and can will it.

The site is landscaped with paved drive, concrete patio, patio table and benches and, in Florida, a palm tree.

The required additional $15 to $20 a month fee covers the mowing of the grass, cleaning, daily garbage collection and maintenance of the recreational facilities. It also covers the electricity, water and sewage disposal.

At some locations, telephone cables are being installed to be available at each site.

"In other of our Resorts," said O.R.A.'s Arthur Fort, "the phone companies never anticipated anything like this to happen, so it will be a year or two before they can get their main trunk lines in."

Many owners stay at their campsites about five months a year, Fort said, then travel.

While you're away, O.R.A. will attempt to rent your site at $5 a day, $30 a week and split the rental fee with you. You might reclaim $400 a year.

In the long range plans at O.R.A., there are fifteen of the condo campgrounds, "the fifteen most visited spots in the United States."

In Florida, at Nettles Island, near Stuart on the East Coast, there are 1600 campsites; at Long Key, near Marathon, 419 units available; Orlando, near the new Disneyworld, 1200 sites and Gatlinburg, Tennessee can accommodate 397 RVs.

For information, contact:

Mr. Arthur G. Fort, Jr.
Outdoor Resorts of America
Nashville, Tennessee 37201

or

Venture Out
802 South Central
Knoxville, Tennessee 37901

Fly In/Camp Out

As with most major appliances and vehicles today, there are many rental outlets for the occasional camper, the fellow who doesn't want a long term investment, nor the care and feeding of an RV year round, such as the apartment dweller with no place to park it.

Also, for the fellow who is thinking about buying an RV, it's not a bad idea to try before you buy, and you can try by renting.

Again, the rental accommodations come in all degrees from a pup tent to a motor home. You may find many outlets listed in the yellow pages of your phone book, under "camping" and "rental," or similar designations.

Travco president Peter R. Fink estimates there were at least 5000 rental motor homes on the road in mid-1970, the number growing all the time.

In fact, Travco had completed the largest single sale of motor homes, 150 Sightseer vehicles to go into a fly in/camp out rental plan in Canada, in conjunction with Air Canada airline.

One Travco motor home was enroute to Europe for display by Air Canada to kick off a planned fly in/camp out European program.

It all started with American Airlines in 1964, but A.A. gave it up.

More recently, American had a program going with Avis and KOA in which you would fly to your camping area, drive an Avis rental car to the KOA grounds and rent a tent.

Eastern Airlines inaugurated their fly in/camp out vacations with the first rental units in Tampa, Florida and Charlotte, North Carolina, the latter because of the proximity of the Great Smokies and other Carolinas mountain/lake attractions.

Eastern later expanded the program to include other Florida cities and Atlanta, Georgia, while Trans World Airlines opted a similar plan, also in conjunction with Camp America as is Eastern's.

TWA operates its camping program out of thirteen cities from Boston, New York and Philadelphia to Los Angeles, San Francisco and Hawaii, with such intermediate stops as Albuquerque, New Mexico, better known as the home town of auto racing's only Indianapolis-winning brother duo, Al and Bobby Unser.

The Air Canada Travco program is in conjunction with a Camp America affiliate, Camp Canada, what else?

Basically, you have your choice of a compact wagon conversion for about $99 a week, up to the big chassis mount camper, sleeping six, for around $250 to $300 weekly, plus 10 cents a mile and buy your own petrol.

The tour representative meets you at the airport, with your camper.

Considering that you might otherwise have to travel two or three days each way, over the highway; you can pack a normal ten-day vacation into five or six days. The cost of the plane tickets is less, or little more than the cost of travel if you rented a camper at home and did the whole ten days on the road.

What was it the man said—"Pioneering in comfort."

Speaking of plush touring, there is available an audio tape tour package.

You plug the cassette into the tape player and your tour guide instructs you to "Drive down route 66 for five miles, then turn onto state road 90, and two miles on your left you will see, etc., etc." A conducted tour at your own pace.

You can get any degree of convenience you are willing to pay for.

Contact your favorite travel agent or airline reservation office and ask for the tour department, or write:

Camp America
P.O. Box 554
Far Hill, New Jersey 07931
or
Camp Canada
880 Ouellette Avenue
Windsor 14, Canada

RV Rentals

National Car Rental inaugurated an ambitious test RV rental program for the 1970 season, offering 22-foot self-contained motor homes, deluxe slide-on pickup campers and 17-foot travel trailers.

As we discussed earlier, with the variety of numbers tossed around relative to the size of the RV population, National's Don Hesse quoted 117 million family camping trips annually, 50 million people and 25 per cent in rental units.

Hertz was also in a test program, as was a Pacific Coast Avis licensee.

RV Associations and Conventions

Are you a joiner? Do you like to travel and mix with people of similar tastes?

There are many state and regional RV clubs. There are also organizations for families which own a particular RV nameplate, the Air Stream trailer owners and the Wally Byam Caravan tours are probably the best known.

The National Campers and Hikers Association operates with state directors and often has more than a hundred chapters in any one state.

More than 31,000 people attended the 1970 NCHA Campvention at Brooklyn, Michigan, across the street from the Michigan International Speedway, where the U.S. Government's endurance test of automobile air pollution control equipment was being run.

The campsites were spread over a four square mile area in that Irish Hills resort area, about 75 miles west of Detroit.

Camping enthusiasts from as far away as England and Australia were among those in the 8500 RVs in that instant city.

Wells were dug, a mile of drinking water pipe laid and 150,000 gallons of water were trucked in daily to supplement the supply. A supermarket chain set up a store in a tent and a barn was converted to a vehicle repair shop.

One breakdown listed the community makeup as 211 tents, 1488 tent trailers, 5179 travel trailers, 830 pickup campers and 400 motor homes.

Rain which turned part of the area into a quagmire did not dampen the spirits of the campers.

One man said, "We're out to have a hell of a good time. That's why I belong to five trailer clubs and why I go to conventions. That's why I'm home only two weekends out of the summer."

It was the 11th annual NCHA affair, described by one man as a middle class, middle-age Woodstock with church hymns replacing rock music, and beer, Cokes and iced tea replacing the marijuana.

For the young folks there was an outdoor dance pavilion and lots of fun and games.

The Indiana chapters, all 118 of them, have bid for the 1972 convention at Camp Atterbury, an ex-military reservation, predicting an attendance from 60,000 to 70,000.

The first convention, in New York City, drew 100 people, and the following year in Missouri, 272 families turned out.

The attendance has been up and down since then, in 1962 at New York, 1125 families; Alabama 612; Ohio 2287; 1965 in Kentucky 3745 families; Kansas 2125; Pennsylvania 4200; Illinois 4353; South Carolina 4095 and Michigan with its almost 8000 families.

For information, write to:

National Campers and Hikers Assn.
7172 Transit Road
Buffalo, New York 14221

2. Safety Rules and Regulations

□ The wonderful world of motor camping has never been more convenient than it is today. On a roving vacation through outdoor America you are restricted only by such laws as concern public safety and welfare.

The money savings and convenience of motor camping is only half the story.

Of equal importance is the completely unfettered life free of worries . . . the ability to stop almost anywhere, at any time, retaining the convenience of home.

On trips of this nature your only contact with legal authority might well be the Park Ranger who will be helping you. A cross-country vacation on wheels usually involves less conflict with humanity than a trip to the supermarket, if you drive carefully and obey the traffic laws.

Here is an attempt to condense and collect for you the relatively few regulations which govern motor camping. There is also a chart listing certain state requirements for trailer towing.

Now and then an out of state camper may be stopped because his equipment does not conform with the local requirements. Such laws differ from state to state and it is admittedly difficult for the once-a-year traveler to keep abreast of the changes.

State Reciprocity Agreements

If your RV is legally registered in your home state, most other states will permit you to travel through without penalty. However, all states do have the right to cite you for unsafe equipment.

Check lights, brakes and hitch before leaving home. That's for your own well being also.

The state laws chart gives information about the important safety equipment each state requires.

Speed Laws for RVs

Towing a trailer? Then you have a few more problems than the family in a self-propelled camper or van, but only because towing laws are a confusing mixture of non-conforming standards from state to state.

In many states a pickup camper, housecar, small van or motor home is considered the same as a passenger vehicle.

In a few states, a pickup truck automatically is pegged at a lower speed limit unless you can convince the officer that your vehicle is a passenger carrier, which it is.

A few states do not differentiate between vehicles in that their speed laws are the vague "safe and prudent."

In almost every state, the trailer-tower is required to reduce speed from five to fifteen miles an hour below the posted passenger car limits.

In spite of this somewhat ambiguous situation, don't fret. Consult the chart on towing and hauling regulations but, always remember, local conditions take precedence.

Regardless of the figures in the chart, always observe the posted speed limits, because construction, weather, heavy traffic and other factors dictate the local interpretation of speed laws.

Observe the flow of traffic around you.

Tips on Staying Out of Legal Trouble

When you approach a state line, reduce speed and watch for the inevitable new state signs which often show the maximum speed permitted, day and/or night, and for the various type vehicles.

Sometimes the simple act of checking a detail may save embarrassment or costly problems later.

Some state boundaries are not easily recognized. Maybe unmarked signs may be old, faded or unlighted at night. The driver may think he is complying with state law, while actually being in violation.

You do not have to be reminded to carry proper identification papers, driver's license, registration and proof of ownership of the trailer, boat, cycle and all vehicles. That's elementary, but it is wise to check with your insurance man to be sure the towed vehicles are covered, especially if it is a rented unit.

And, of course, you know better than to argue with the law, even if you think you are right and are sorely tempted to argue. It is safer to politely explain you are new in that state or locale and you had intended to comply with all rules. Chances are, that approach might bring only a warning for out of state first offenders. At least, it's worth trying.

For your own welfare, make regular checks enroute of your lights, hitch, safety chains, license tag light, mirrors. Replace burned out light bulbs and keep your equipment properly adjusted and tightened at all times.

Anti-Pollution Laws

Much attention is now focused on environmental pollution.

Most states impose severe penalties for roadside littering, tossing a can or cleaning tissue out the car window. Carry a litter bag in the car, the camper, the trailer.

Put your garbage and trash in designated containers along the highway or at rest stops. How many times have you stopped along a country highway where there is a beautiful view, or on a winding road leading down from the mountain, a spot overlooking a river or lake, a scenic pull-out, and seen trash and litter which spoiled your visual picture? Don't you be guilty.

Burning of trash is forbidden at most campgrounds, except by special permit. It only takes a family a day or two to completely fill and clog public campgrounds stoves by burning trash. Use the campgrounds trash containers only.

In older days, not so far back in history, it was considered not only proper, but wise to dig a shallow hole and bury campground trash.

Ecologists now prove cans are slow to rust and deteriorate and bottles never do. Heavy rains uncover this buried trash and animals dig it up.

Future generations are exposed to pieces of metal and glass fragments, suffering cuts. The Forest Service warns that glass, catching the sun rays just right, will start a fire, it could be a disastrous fire.

So, the new rule of the '70s is "If you can pack it in full, you can pack it out empty." That's the new way of the great outdoors.

Pollution of Roadsides

Discharging of waste matter from a sanitary holding tank along any public road or highway is obviously prohibited. Even the most remote desert highways are covered by these laws.

If it seems strange, just think of the millions of vehicles using the major routes annually. It wouldn't take long to pollute every highway from Boston to Los Angeles.

It is illegal to dig "gopher holes" in campgrounds anywhere in this country to discharge the waste from sanitary holding tanks.

In State and National parks, even the discharge of sink water is often prohibited. Sometimes, campers are permitted to use drain buckets for the purpose of catching ordinary dish water, so always carry a three-gallon bucket and short drain hose and fittings.

Be sure to empty the bucket in the designated disposal before it gets brim full.

Roadside Rest Areas

The greatest aid to travelers since the advent of paved roads is the roadside rest area, strategically placed so weary motorists may stop for a rest or a nap.

Safety research has proved even a short two-hour nap can freshen a driver tremendously. Even twenty minutes or a half hour helps.

His eyesight sharpens, the reflexes quicken and the concentration improves.

The new trend is to develop rest areas on both sides of the highway at the same map location.

Once a rest area was little more than a wide turnout space.

Today's rest areas often have fully equipped restrooms; some with shower stalls, picnic tables under shade, landscaped vegetation, automatic night lighting, water faucets, drinking water, trash containers, public telephones and regular police patrols for your safety.

Some people have the misconception that the rest areas can be used as free overnight campgrounds. The design concept of a highway rest area is a place where tired motorists may safely park for a few hours' relaxation.

They were never intended to be used as campgrounds. The moment a famliy sets out camping gear, pitches a tent or starts hanging out the wash, look out.

The next patrolman will politely urge you on your way.

Overnight Parking Along Highways

Despite the fact that hundreds of thousands of campsites are scattered over the land, one night you might wind up short of your planned destination.

The simple solution is to pull off the highway at the first opportunity. After all, travel in any kind of an RV assures the family the same accommodations everywhere. It should make little difference whether you stop at a campground or a highway rest stop as long as you don't set up camping gear outside the vehicle.

Some states do not permit overnight parking alongside highways, but generally the police would agree that a few hours' rest is better than forcing an exhausted pilot onto the road.

Common safety dictates you would not park overnight alongside expressways or turnpikes, other than designated rest areas.

In rural country, where side roads permit parking some distance from the busy routes, few patrolmen would bother a napping camper, but there might be other visitors who would be less considerate, marauding vandals/robbers, for example.

A half dozen simple rules to guide you:

1. Don't park close to highway lanes. Park well off the pavement, at least 50 feet from the shoulder.

2. Don't park in driveways or intersections where you will block or impede private or public traffic.

3. Don't park on private property without permission. Even desert land is privately owned. In farm country, it's all private property. As a matter of courtesy stop and ask the farmer's permission, unless the hour is late.

4. Parking is usually prohibited in municipal parks, fairgrounds and other publicly owned sites unless posted.

5. Discharging any waste products from a holding tank, or leaving an open drain hose from the sink lying on the ground, or littering the parking area is a sure invitation to eviction and possibly arrest and fine.

6. When parking along rural highways, the least conspicuous locations are best. Folding chairs, bed, other personal equipment outside the RV is verboten.

On many roads, signs will indicate parking only in emergency, but if you are sufficiently tired and dangerously sleepy, that may qualify as an emergency, as long as you park far enough away to avoid creating a hazard.

Campground Etiquette

If you arrive in a State or National Park after dark, it is usually permissible to locate a vacant camping site on your own and wait until morning to register.

The Ranger will appreciate it if you do not wake him up in the wee hours. His morning patrols are routine and you will be contacted.

Some basic rules on entering a campgrounds after dark:

1. Drive slowly, about five miles an hour, and be alert for campers out walking in the dark.

2. Don't flash a spotlight around to disturb other campers.

3. Avoid loud talking, whether arguments or laughter. Never blow the horn. An accidental blast can be just as unnerving as one done intentionally, so be careful.

4. Don't let children run loose in a strange grounds at night. They might stumble over tent ropes, other objects, or fall into a creek or lake.

5. Be as quiet as possible when setting up camp. Postpone hammering tent stakes, if at all possible, and save major camp-making duties until daylight.

Crossing the Borders—Canada and Mexico

Entering Canada

1. No passport or visa is necessary when entering Canada if you are an American citizen. Carrying identification papers, such as voting certificate or birth certificate is recommended. Naturalized citizens should carry proof of naturalization.

2. No duty or fee is required for entering a vehicle into Canada on vacation. A permit is issued, at the border, for each vehicle, including trailers, bicycles and motorcycles. Such permits are good up to six months. Carry your registration papers with you and if using a rented vehicle, a copy of the rental contract.

3. United States driving licenses are honored in Canada.

4. Before leaving home, obtain from your insurance agent a Canadian non-resident inter-Province motor vehicle liability card, which assures your insurer agrees to abide by prevailing limits of liability in Canada.

5. If you take your dog, obtain a veterinarian certificate as proof of rabies vaccination within the past twelve months. A description of the dog should be on the certificate.

Special note: Pistols and fully automatic weapons are prohibited from entry into Canada. Rifles and shotguns are permissible, just as is fishing tackle. Provide a description of such equipment at the border crossing, which speeds up the process when you leave Canada on the return trip.

Non-resident hunting and fishing licenses are required in Canada.

Campers may bring about two days' supply of food, per person, free of duty. This includes a full tank of gasoline for each vehicle. Allowed duty free are, each person, up to fifty cigars, up to two hundred cigarettes, two pounds of tobacco, six rolls of film and most items of personal nature. Tobacco, of course, is allowed for those over sixteen years old. Also, you can bring forty ounces of liquor for each person over twenty-one.

You will have no trouble using American currency in Canada and, in fact, most leading national credit cards are accepted as identification, the charges being billed through a Canadian credit card company.

The rate of exchange fluctuates, but the dollar and cent system is used and the exchange rate published in the daily newspapers. Basically, you will find that you can buy a dollar's worth of merchandise for perhaps ninety-five cents American.

A note regarding the credit card purchases: if you are billed direct, you can pay at the lower rate of exchange, but if you are billed by your American credit card company, you pay them at the full American dollar value and you can bet they will pay the Canadian rate of exchange, and that they will make the profit.

You may obtain detailed information from:

Canadian Government Travel Bureau
Ottawa, Ontario, Canada

"Custom Hints for Returning U.S. Residents"
Bureau of Customs
Treasury Department
Washington, D.C.

Entering Mexico

American auto insurance is not good in Mexico and you must obtain insurance from a company licensed to do business in Mexico. This can be handled through agencies at the border, such as the AAA motor club offices. You can buy daily insurance from them.

All persons fifteen years and older must buy a tourist card from Mexican Customs, $3 (American). You buy it at the border.

You must keep proof of ownership in the vehicle at all times. A permit valid for six months must be obtained at any Mexican Custom Station at the border.

It is recommended that Americans carry travelers checks and exchange them for Mexican currency at any bank as the need arises, or make purchases with the checks and receive your change in Mexican money.

For travel deep into Mexico there are some inoculation requirements on which your doctor or any Mexican consulate can advise you.

You may bring in two cartons of cigarettes, fifty cigars, three-and-a-quarter pounds of tobacco, small amount of provisions and food and other personal items duty free, per person, plus a fifth of whiskey for each person over twenty-one and ten rolls of film each.

For your own protection, insist on registering any valuable cameras or jewels or other expensive items for identification, as this may save considerable argument when you leave Mexico.

You wouldn't like to pay duty on something you already owned.

Also, if you blow a tire, be sure you bring out with you the old tire, or you might be accused of selling a tire in Mexico and have to pay duty.

Do not drink Mexican water unless you are sure it has been purified or distilled. Carry bottled water or use a water purifier or buy major brands of soft drinks in Mexico. You've heard of "Montezuma's revenge"?

Mexican customs regulations are frequently changed, so it is best to consult a consulate or inquire of local authorities on the U.S. side of the border.

You can expect to be thoroughly checked on return to the United States because of the campaign to stamp out the vicious narcotics smuggling racket.

If it takes you a little longer to go through U.S. Customs, be patient, because their campaign is in a good cause—the welfare of you and your children.

And a serious word of warning, regarding marijuana or other narcotic possession or sale, Mexico is much more harsh than the United States and a few hundred Americans are serving long prison terms there. Don't carry it or buy it, even for your own use. You won't enjoy a Mexican prison term.

State Laws Chart

State	Max. Towing Limit: (night-time speed limits usually 10 mph less)	Overnight Parking? Allowed at Roadside?	Safety Devices Required
ALABAMA	70 divided 60 other	YES	Reflector flares
ALASKA	50	YES	Reflector flares
ARIZONA	As posted	YES	Reflector flares
ARKANSAS	50	YES, unless posted	
CALIFORNIA	55	Only in emergency	Safety chains, flares, external side mirrors, adequate hitch
COLORADO	60	YES	Safety chains
CONNECTICUT	As Posted	If posted	External mirrors, adequate hitch
DELAWARE	50	YES	Safety Glass
DIST. OF COLUMBIA	As posted	If posted	Safety chain
FLORIDA	As posted	YES	Safety chain, external mirrors, flares
GEORGIA	60	YES	Safety chain, external mirrors, flares
IDAHO	60	YES	Safety chain, external mirrors, flares
ILLINOIS	55	If posted	Flares
INDIANA	55	By permit	Safety chain, flares
IOWA	55	YES	Safety chain, flares
KANSAS	70	YES, unless posted	Adequate hitch, flares
KENTUCKY	60	YES	No report
LOUISIANA	45	YES	Safety chain, flares
MAINE	45	YES	Safety chain

MARYLAND	50	Only if posted	Safety chain, flares, fire extinguisher
MASSACHUSETTS	As posted	If posted	Safety chain, safety wheel-and-chocks
MICHIGAN	50	No law	Safety chain, flares
MINNESOTA	65	YES	Safety chain
MISSISSIPPI	50	YES	Safety chain
MISSOURI	65	YES	Flares, fire extinguisher
MONTANA	50	If posted	Safety chain, flares
NEBRASKA	50	YES	No report
NEVADA	Safe	YES	No report
NEW HAMPSHIRE	45	YES	Safety chain
NEW JERSEY	50	YES	Safety chain
NEW MEXICO	60	YES	Safety chain
NEW YORK	50	NO	No report
NO. CAROLINA	45	YES	Adequate hitch, flares
NO. DAKOTA	50	YES	Safety chain, flares
OHIO	60	If posted	Safety chain, flares
OKLAHOMA	50	If posted	Safety chain, flares
OREGON	55	If posted	Safety chains
PENNSYLVANIA	50	YES	Flares, fire extinguisher
RHODE ISLAND	35	YES	Safety chain, flares
SO. CAROLINA	55	YES	External mirrors, adequate hitch
SO. DAKOTA	70	YES	Safety chain, flares
TENNESSEE	65	YES	Safety chain
TEXAS	60	YES	Flares
UTAH	60	YES	Safety chains, flares

VERMONT	As posted	YES	Fire extinguisher, Safety chain
VIRGINIA	45	YES	Safety chain, fire extinguisher
WASHINGTON	As posted	YES	Safety chain, flares
WEST VIRGINIA	55	YES	Safety chain, flares
WISCONSIN	65	NO	Safety chain, adequate hitch
WYOMING	As posted	If posted	Flares

3. Truck Mounted Campers

☐ Riddle: What does a well-equipped camper sales lot or showroom have in common with Cleopatra, fabled Queen of the Nile?

Answer: Infinite variety, although in somewhat less anatomical a frame of reference.

Putting behind us thoughts of Cleopatra's admittedly fascinating embodiments, let us take up the plight of the prospective buyer of a new or used truck mounted camper, a man who has suddenly become aware of today's dazzling spectrum of types, sizes, features, accessories and prices.

His first and natural reaction is utter bewilderment.

A typical first time visit to the camper lot is usually predictable.

First, a stop at the brochure table; a guided tour through five or six different types of campers; a despairing effort to follow the salesman's well-rehearsed proud flight through such unfamiliar terms as "chassis mount," "self-contained," "cab over," "walk through," "GVW" and finally the kid-in-the-candy-store syndrome over the wide range of attractive optional equipment offered for every model, each item seeming to be a vital necessity.

It all ends in a rash of growing indecision, confused retreat and the "don't call me, I'll call you" routine.

The brochures are filed in the den drawer until "we can take a little time to get this thing figured out."

Or, even worse, it can result in the impulse purchase of the wrong camper.

This is unfortunate and unnecessary. The baffling abundance of camper styles and components exists for one basic reason—to fill the individual needs of those who use RVs for everything from portable offices to retirement homes, and especially for the uncounted thousands who use them for comfortable, independent and inexpensive travel.

As Bob McCurry said, "The recreation vehicle market is about as individual as the people who are using them."

The pickup is a great dual-purpose vehicle, with all the advantages of a passenger car and weekday truck, plus the capability of carrying a camper body.

Pickup campers make up the largest volume of the various classifications, because so many people already own the truck for business or family utility usage, and it is readily convertible to an RV.

Here, also, comes a problem. The truck now owned may really be too light for the camper body desired.

The factory-recommended heavy duty equipment, or camper package, should be added to the pickup for satisfactory performance, maintenance and safety.

It is not necessarily true of the motor camper business, as it was with the legendary mousetrap.

A man might build a better camper, but he shouldn't expect the world to beat a path to his door. The regional world of his own area perhaps, but not the wide, wide world, not even the lower forty-eight as they say in Alaska.

There are hundreds of RV builders (and there is a practical reason for this proliferation) scattered around the country. The reason: shipping awkwardness and expense.

Regular trucks are shipped on tri-level railroad cars, stacked three high, perhaps twelve trucks to a car.

Slide-on campers are bulky and there is no way to drive them onto a freight car.

The usual shipping method is to put two or three on a lowboy truck and send them on their way, at a cost of about $1 to $1.20 a mile.

Send a driver on a 1000-mile trip and you have a big freight bill.

If the manufacturer was to put $200 freight cost into a camper to get it halfway across the country to Kansas City, the local builder there would take him apart on price, because he only has about $30 in delivery costs.

Because freight is such a penalty, there are hundreds of builders to satisfy the demand, three or four in each major camping area, and thus there are hundreds of designs, floor plans and ideas.

The solution for the would-be buyer is quite simple.

First, identify your own price range and your own family travel needs and the choice of design will become relatively easy.

Carefully determine the type of vehicle which suits you best: your family size, the condition of your check book and the kind of traveling you prefer, whether open road or the wilderness.

A pickup truck is a great dual-purpose vehicle, combining car and truck advantages. This is particularly true of the new Dodge Club Cab pickup which has an additional 34 cubic feet of storage space inside the cab with optional fold down seats for two.

The least expensive, and least luxurious, way to turn your pickup into a camper is with the addition of a shell (above). For those with less spartan desires, a slide-on unit (below) offers a comparatively unlimited variety of extras.

Truck mounted campers fall into three categories–shells or caps for pickup trucks, slide-ons for pickup trucks and chassis mounts, which resemble the slide-ons in appearance, but which are permanently mounted to a usually heavier duty truck chassis.

For the moment, we will pass by the wagon and van conversions and motor homes. Although also truck chassis based, that's another department, covered later in this book.

Making a choice of the three types of truck mounts is the first and most important step and the following descriptions should help remove some of the guesswork, and speed you on your way to fun and frolic.

Selling price–approximate:

Shell, caps, canopy-type	\$ 300 to \$1000
Slide-ons	\$1000 to \$7000
. . . plus pickup truck if needed	\$2300 to \$3600
Chassis mounts, including chassis	\$4500 to \$8500

Shells or Caps or Canopy-type for Pickups

Shells, also called caps, canopy-type or sleepers are at the bottom end of the truck camper line in both price and luxury.

These are principally covers which extend straight back from the cab and cover the bed of the truck, normally sealed to the upper edge of the truck side-walls and tailgate with a thick, airtight gasket.

Most shells are secured to the body by inside clamps and entrance is from the rear by way of the lowered tailgate and a tilt-up door.

The interior is plain, if not severe, its decor usually of prefinished plywood walls, with front, side and rear windows, a dome light and the ever-present wheel wells in the truck body.

The floor and sides of the original truck may be finished to your own liking, usually a do-it-yourself project.

There is standing room height, for a midget or your young child, but not for you. The elevation is from the deck of your truck to a line level with the roof of your truck cab.

Overall design of the shell can be anything from a simple curved roof of corrugated aluminum to fully framed and stressed walls and ceiling with embossed aluminum exterior.

Optional equipment is pretty much limited to functional items like roof vents and extra windows, and one manufacturer does offer a full length double roof which slides back to become a canopy.

The shell camper is popular with sportsmen–hunters and fishermen–whose spartan accommodations are not only adequate, but considered the honorable way of outdoor life.

Ordered with the proper equipment a pickup with a slide-on can still pull a trailer.

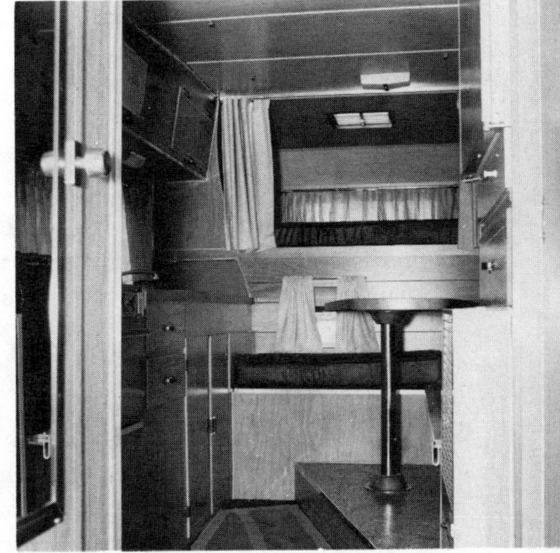

Floor plans vary with the manufacturer, but nearly all slide-ons have doors in the rear.

The tailgate makes a handy platform for the camp stove, ice box and wash basin, as well as a place to sit.

This is "tailgate camping."

Compared with the larger truck camper units, shells have certain built-in disadvantages such as the lack of headroom mentioned earlier and lack of stowage facilities for the dozens of items that fall under the umbrella term "camping gear."

The typical truckbed to ceiling interior measurement is 48 inches, which is further reduced by a mattress–hardly enough height for most indoor activities, including, to be blunt, the confident use of a portable toilet.

The sleeping area can accommodate no more than two friendly adults and a child.

However, the shell is extremely popular for some very good reasons, such as the price.

This is good value for mobile sleeping quarters, confined or not, and places the shell well below the slide-ons and chassis mounts in the cost department.

Also, a half-ton pickup is usually adequate for a shell, but a three-quarter or one-ton pickup is usually recommended for larger and heavier slide-ons.

An important favorable factor is vehicle stability. Most shells weigh well under 200 pounds and have very little effect on the center of gravity and handling characteristics of the pickup.

They can go anywhere the truck can go, with no necessity to consider top or side clearances, and the configuration is kind to gas mileage. All the truck's components, including engine, frame and drive train will prove their long-lived gratitude for the shell's light weight.

The shell is convenient. Two strong and determined men can remove one without due recourse to the truss industry and an idle shell is a considerably less imposing backyard monument than a demounted slide-on.

Of course, when you use it, you have to put up with the public facilities at the campsite. But, it is less costly.

As a brief sum-up, the shell is a good choice for two friendly people who are willing to leave the kitchen, furnace and bathroom at home and accept some spartan simplicity in the good name of economy.

Slide-on Campers for Pickups

Slide-on units are the next step up in the truck mounted camper hierarchy–a considerable step up in luxury, weight and price.

Some of the lightest slide-ons can be carried by a half-ton truck, but most manufacturers recommend at least three-quarter ton capacity, one-ton for the heavier models.

Just about the worst mistake a new camper buyer can make is to under-

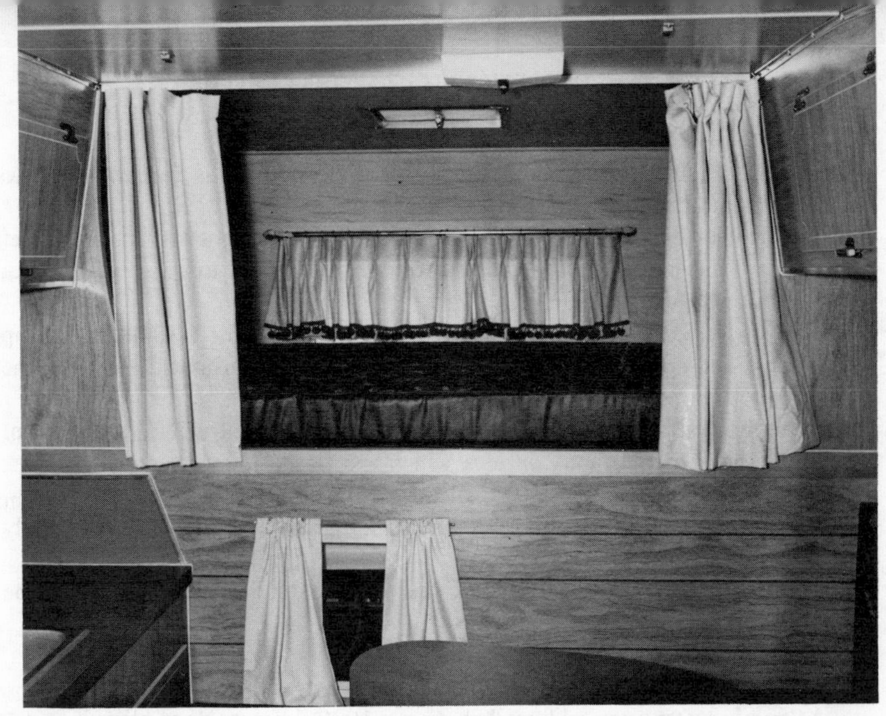

"Cab over" styles fit a bed over the cab. Small window under bed looks into the cab.

Appliances fit into small areas while large rear-view mirrors offset camper size.

specify his requirements. So many do, because nothing is free on a truck. However, that is foolish economy in the long run.

The heavier duty chassis is needed because of the weight and higher center of gravity, the latter making slide-ons more susceptible to sway than either the shells or the chassis mounts.

Slide-ons are designed, as the name implies, to slide onto a standard pickup truck bed, and are usually held fast by four heavy duty turnbuckles around the outside bottom edge.

Actually, you don't slide the camper on the truck. That would take a lot of muscle. The camper stands on legs which are raised and lowered like jacks, either manually or power-assisted, and you back your truck under the camper, crank down the jack/legs, hook up the turnbuckles and you're almost ready to roll.

Doorways are usually in the back, but some extended models can also be entered at the right rear corner.

Of the three truck camper categories, slide-ons are the most varied in design, basic configuration and in variety of interior arrangements.

As one industry exec told us, "There are 1000 different floor plans."

There are several large manufacturers who would like to come up with the production line concept, but as mentioned earlier, no one yet has devised a plan for economical loading and shipping slide-ons, so each one of the 487 manufacturers (according to the Recreational Dealer Magazine) goes merrily on his way, promoting the designs and floor plans which sell best in his area.

Depending on your budget, you can have all the luxury of a trailer with kitchen, water and electrical systems, toilet, shower (which means addition of a water heater) and storage space—a little or a lot.

At the lower end of the slide-on price range, about $1500 or so, is a unit which looks very much like a shell camper, extending only a little higher than the truck cab and giving very moderate wind resistance or side sway.

Parked at the campground, however, the top is hydraulically pumped up to give a full six feet, four inches floor to ceiling height. There are variations of this roof-raising method.

One brand comes in three lengths, eight feet, 10 feet and 12 feet, three inches, sleeping two to five people.

Interior features are the single greatest distinction between the shells and the slide-ons.

You can have a folding table, thick foam seats which convert to double or twin beds, cabinets, wardrobe, drawers for storage, full interior lighting using 12- or 110-volt current (often convertible), ice box, gas or electric refrigerator, three-burner propane stove and even the proverbial kitchen sink fed by a water tank, sometimes with a compressor for better water pressure.

Other options include intercom systems, between the camper and the truck cab, roof rack for the boat, rear rack for the cycle, even television antennas, and they come with simple portable johns or the recirculating automatic johns with the sanitary holding tanks.

As the size of the slide-ons increases, the inventiveness and luxury of their interior and exterior design become more and more pronounced.

The term "cab over" comes into its own with the forward extension of the upper body out over the roof of the truck cab.

This extension makes an excellent room, even though less than standing room height, to contain a double or twin beds, side storage compartments and an excellent forward and side view favored as a traveling observation balcony for the youngsters.

The cab over portion–of course, an integral part of the entire unit construction–is secured to the truck cab roof through the use of shock absorber mounts, for greater stability.

To the neophyte, it may seem incredible that a room measuring less than 11 feet by 8 feet can contain the slide-on's quantity of appliances, cabinets and closets, furniture and fixtures, and still provide room for four to six people in relative privacy and comfort.

Of course, the interior is designed for double duty use and you might have to make the bed before you eat, or do the dishes before you take an afternoon nap.

So far, the only method of eliminating dish washing is the use of throw-away plates and utensils.

The buyer can choose from many interior arrangements, no matter what section of the country he calls home. Even with 487 manufacturers, there is some standardization.

The family with young children may wish to have the beds close together, while a family of adults may wish them separated, divided into two or more room compartments.

One cook will want the kitchen next to the dinette for easy service, another will want it near the rear door for coolness and ventilation.

There is no difficulty in finding a satisfactory, livable layout, just a matter of deciding what you really want and the amount of money you want to spend.

It will be repetitious, but throughout this book you will find the advice to determine your needs, your family's needs, your own travel plans, before buying. It will save time and grief and money later.

One reason we may repeat some thoughts here is that all readers may not read the entire book, picking out the chapters and the factors which interest them the most. We want to be helpful.

Depending on your budget and desires you can buy such equipment as a five-gallon butane tank with regulator, stove hood with 12-volt fan and light, double stainless steel sink, sink top with bread board, 40-gallon water tank, fiberglass sink with cabinet and medicine chest and mirror in the "powder room," outside porch light, screen doors, safety glass windows, water repellent curtains, 250-foot extension cord for outside hookup to 110-volt electric, air conditioning, automatic furnace-heater, spun glass insulation, onward and upward!

Storage while at home may present a problem, although the various camping clubs and the enthusiast magazines are constantly working to prevent or correct restrictive legislation which would prevent a man from parking his slide-on unit in his own backyard, for example.

Woodall's Trailer Travel magazine reports this ruling by the New York State Comptroller, November 20, 1969:

"A town may not, by ordinance, regulate the location of unused or unoccupied trailers which are parked or stored on the private property of the trailer owners. A town may not accomplish such regulation or restriction by means of zoning."

So check out your own community regulations.

Chassis Mounted Campers

The largest, most comfortable and most expensive of the truck mounted campers (as differentiated from motor homes) are the chassis mounts.

Actually, not too much more expensive than a slide-on with the proper size pickup, perhaps $1000 more costly, all items being equal.

As the name explains, these units are permanently mounted on the truck frame after removal of the standard truck bed, providing a lowered center of gravity and a much larger floor area.

Designers have made good use of these factors, providing more headroom, greatly increased storage area and a wider choice of roomy, inviting interior arrangements.

Chassis mount campers are usually sold complete with the truck especially prepared for the "house car" it is to carry. This is important and buyers are well advised to follow manufacturers' recommendations regarding tires, springs, shock absorbers, engines, transmissions, axle ratios and cooling systems.

These can have much effect on the safety, handling, comfort and longevity of a truck/camper operation. Selection of a properly equipped truck is well worth the novice buyer's full attention.

Because many chassis mount campers, fully loaded with passengers and gear, weigh about three tons, dual wheels are most often used on the rear to provide safe support for the massive gross vehicle weight (GVW).

The chassis mounts provide better highway stability and more interior spaciousness because truck and camper are engineered as a unit.

The big three of the auto/truck industry work closely with the camper manufacturers, the truck makers determining the campers' needs, and engineering to accommodate them.

At the same time, the truck makers provide the camper makers with engineering information, in advance of the new model introduction, so the camper can be designed and built and ready for sale at the same time.

Chassis mount construction and materials are often excellent, with insulated floors, header and stud walls, formica kitchen surfaces, foam cushions and mattresses, top quality hardware, baked enamel exterior finish and plastic coated interior panels.

This all adds to the initial cost, of course, but also sustains the retail value when the time comes for resale or trade in.

The trucks are equipped with power steering, power brakes and automatic transmission, as well as the dual wheels, heavy duty suspension and bucket seats.

Some trucks, called crew cab, provide four doors into the cab, along with a bench seat behind the two front buckets, seating five people in the cab.

Inside, some units have a wide bed in the cab over section, a dining area which converts into either twin beds or a double bed, double wardrobe, bathroom with automatic toilet, shower, sink, hot water heater, thermostat oven/broiler range, combination gas/electric refrigerator which uses electric power in camp, and bottled gas on the highway, safety-vented wall furnace and air conditioning, television antenna, on and on.

A walk-through passage between the camper and the truck cab is more easily accommodated in the chassis mount, making the entire truck/camper more of an integral unit.

First time drivers of large campers are paralyzed by a fear of crunching the new machine or sweeping everyone else off into the ditches.

The first few miles down the road will cure this as the powerful, strongly sprung truck will handle not too much differently from a large family auto, with the added advantage of improved visibility, because you are looking over the traffic ahead, not through it.

You will need a little more brake stopping distance, wider turning radius and some adjustments while changing lanes, passing, backing and parking.

You can return to the camper lot or showroom better prepared, now, to appraise the situation and make judgments. Manufacturers will supply detailed brochures and information by mail, if the dealer doesn't have them, and most will be glad to have you visit the factory and watch the campers being built.

Remember, the camper factories are in your area because of the old shipping problem which keeps the manufacturers small and independent, rather than being dominated by a few big fellows.

If you are still undecided, you might try a trip or two in rental units.

Our Chapter 1 has already given you complete information about rentals available from the auto renters, as well as the airlines' fly in/camp out programs.

The phone book yellow pages list many local camper renters under the camping and renting listings.

Rentals may go from $50 for slide-on without truck up to $250 for a chassis mount or motor home.

When you have made the decision, placed the order and taken delivery, check all the appliances, be sure you have the directions to each and the guarantees and warranties and directory of service centers coast to coast. Store these items safely in the camper.

Before leaving the dealer, be sure you understand everything about everything, including the truck. Don't hesitate to ask questions.

Learning can be fun, but trying to figure out a gas oven an hour before dinner time, under the baleful glare of a famished family, does little for a fellow's ulcers.

Also, remember, the truck manufacturer does not warranty the camper nor the interior equipment. In case of major service requirements, you may have to seek out any number of repair centers, although one attempt is being made to set up a string of camper/motor home land-based marinas to provide complete service.

That plan is detailed in Chapter 12, herein.

But back to that original visit to the camper sales lot–there are several ways to overcome that hesitation, and perhaps the foregoing has been helpful.

The most important item, though, is to first determine your family needs in a camper, your camping plans and your budget.

The Pickup Truck

Whether you are buying a simple camper cap, a slide-on or a small chassis mount camper, you do need–an obvious if not astute observation–a pickup truck.

If you already own a pickup truck, the big questions are:

Is it big enough? Does it have the proper equipment?

"Our biggest concern," said one truck firm executive, "is the guy who bought the pickup without the idea of putting a camper on it, and later puts a fairly heavy rig on top of it and wonders why he's having problems."

Most important to consider–type of springs, shocks, steering, load carrying capacity, transmission, axles, brakes and tires.

Too often the customer may be inclined to underspecify his truck need, and later becomes unhappy when things break and the maintenance cost rises.

Don't let that happen to you.

The manufacturers of trucks supply "campers special" equipment packages and "trailer towing" packages–heavy duty springs, axles, alternator, battery, camper wiring harness for easy connection of special use equipment and larger wheel rim size and heavy duty tires.

While talk of "gross vehicle weight," "optimum gear ratio," "axle load capacity," "torque curve peak," "maximum tire load rating factor" and other equally technical sounding terms might stump the average passenger car customer, the experienced camper pickup truck owner is usually right at home with them.

He not only knows their meaning, he also understands how to apply them to get the highest possible satisfaction and service from the vehicle he buys.

This was pointed out to us by Bert Bouwkamp, Director of Product and Market Planning for Chrysler and Dodge Truck Division.

The sudden rise in popularity of the camper pickup has caused truck makers to completely revise their design and marketing concepts.

Until recently, buying a pickup truck was a relatively simple matter. The customer had a choice of color, trim, one or two engine specs, stick shift or automatic, but little else.

A pickup was a pickup, to handle light loads, such as hay bales, bags of cement, odds and ends. It was quite satisfactory for this use.

Then pickup owners started to install camper units for the weekend and vacation fun.

"Suddenly there were dozens of camper unit manufacturers," Bouwkamp said, "all offering units which varied in size and weight. Our existing wheels, tires, power and drive train components, front and rear axles, suspension systems were not able to cope with these wide variances in camper unit weights.

"Dodge, along with its competitors, initiated accelerated development programs to solve the problems. Where we used to get by with one front axle, we now offer three, all designed to handle different load capacities. The same is true of rear axles, wheels, suspension systems, all the various components."

Today's experienced buyer has a pretty good idea of his particular needs. He knows the camper he has in mind is so many feet long, so many high and weighs a certain amount.

He has a good idea how much extra equipment he'll be carrying and how many people. What he wants to know from the truck specialists is if they have the choice of equipment to do the job for him.

Unfortunately the first-time truck buyer doesn't have this equipment know-how and background, so the truck makers and dealers are there to guide him.

One buyer, because of cost limitations, might have wanted a six-cylinder engine to haul around his 10½-foot cab over unit, Bouwkamp explained.

"On the highway, the engine would be constantly operating at wide-open throttle to maintain any semblance of cruising speed. It would be straining and would result in a short, unreliable engine life as well as an unhappy owner.

"What he needs is a larger V8. With a V8 and a rear axle ratio that's matched to the engine torque curve and gross vehicle weight, he can cruise comfortably at part throttle and no strain. In the long run, it will be more economical, more trouble free."

Tires—some buyers have a tendency to skimp here. They are just asking for trouble. The tire's load rating factor has to be high enough to handle gross vehicle weight with a little left over for safety factor.

Camper pickup suspensions are designed from a handling standpoint. The added weight of a camper unit isn't as important as where the weight is. It's up high and as a result raises the center of gravity of the entire vehicle.

If the springs aren't matched to gross vehicle weight you end up with a unit that wallows down the highway like a drunken elephant.

If there happens to be a side wind blowing, it gets even worse. With the wide selection of springs available, there's no reason why a buyer should end up with this particular problem.

Fortunately some camper pickup customers understand these technical aspects and it is to be hoped that the newcomers will also be pointed in the right direction.

Tires

You've heard the call of adventure. The open road stretches before you.

For the camping enthusiast, there are few greater thrills than a family outing in one of America's hundreds of vacation lands.

Careful, thorough planning of the trip is essential to avoid disappointment, long delays on the road or even more serious consequences.

The maps, sporting equipment, hundreds of pounds of supplies, of people—these are all part of your trip and the tires on your RV are also part of the adventure.

With hundreds of different types and brands available, again the customer is confused. So, some basic questions—and answers.

Will the vehicle be driven mainly on highways and paved roads, or will it be taken over rough terrain, through deep sand at the beach?

Once the camping enthusiast is sure of the demands to be made of his vehicle, he's off to a good start in planning the trip.

First, the RV must have adequate size tires to bear up under the load. The tire's load carrying capacity is clearly marked on each sidewall.

It used to be the ply rating that described the tire, but that is changing to "load range" and the ply description is being phased out. Tire dealers will supply the load range chart so you can select the correct tire for your total vehicle weight.

"Camping vehicles should be weighed at truck weight scales," said Goodyear's Robert L. French. "The RV should be fully loaded or an estimate of the weight it will carry should be made.

"If more weight is to be carried than the original equipment tires are rated to support, then replace the tires with some that will do the job." It's that simple.

Also, "nothing is more harmful than underinflation, which increases the possibility of rapid tread wear and premature tire failure."

Check your tire pressure during the trip, but always when the tire is cold, early in the day, not after a high speed run. To be accurate, pressure reading should be made after the RV has been parked at least three hours, French added, or driven not over a mile (to a service station) at moderate speed.

"Highway speeds cause a normal increase in pressure, but do not bleed air from them. If the tires are bled when hot, they will be underinflated when cool."

French also warns there is a wide gap in the accuracy of some inexpensive tire gauges. Get a good one.

The raised center of gravity when a slide-on is added to a pickup truck results in a swaying effect on the tires, so the use of a lower profile, squatty tire reduces the sway and offers greater stability on the highway, according to French.

"The configuration of the tires is such they won't fit conventional pickup, panel, van or camper wheels," he explained. "However, the tires' improved performance more than compensates for the cost of switching to the proper wheels."

Towing a travel trailer behind a pickup or wagon or sedan requires the same careful attention to correct tire inflation and load capacity, the tire expert said.

"Since the travel trailer's wheels turn freely on the trailer's axle, there is little torque. This usually means long life for the tires if they are not underinflated or overloaded. Weather deterioration frequently affects the tires before actual wear becomes evident."

4. Self-Contained Motor Campers

□ Not very long ago, camping was a matter of roughing it while enjoying the great outdoors. Campers didn't ask for it, but that was how it was.

There were a few sophisticated camping outfits in use, tiny trailers, home built vans, trucks and buses and other towed and driven outfits, but the majority of campers relied on the tent and related gear.

Those outfits didn't make for great comfort or convenience, but then the idea was to get out, away from home, by the best means available.

History doesn't record it, but quite likely a few wives of confirmed campers finally banded together and demanded some changes.

Washing pots and pans in stream water heated over a campfire just wasn't their idea of fun. Nor was cooking for a family over the same campfire. Nor was sleeping on the ground in an unheated tent. Still, they didn't ask for much . . . to begin with.

If only they could have a simple bed upon which to rest their aching bodies, and perhaps an ice box into which they could store some better foods, and maybe a bit of storage space inside, away from the bugs.

"Blasphemous!" shouted the men.

"Or else!" answered the women.

So, mild self-containment began.

And how it began! The end result today is astounding, and it is difficult to imagine how self-containment can go any further, but it probably will.

About the only way, it seems, to improve would be to motorize the whole house and take it along to the mountains or seashore or desert. Wouldn't that jam up the rush hour traffic on the freeways!

In a family van converted for camping, you can cook, you can eat, you can sleep, you can even enjoy a Scotch-on-the-rocks with the rocks being manufactured right in the van.

Suggested to the manufacturer is the only item of importance left out—an auto pilot so the driver can enjoy the television with the rest of the family, enroute.

But that is getting ahead of the story of self-containment, because things didn't just jump from the one to the other—and even today, the camper has a wide choice of luxuries.

There are still a few rugged outdoorsmen among us who might prefer to skip the air conditioning and the stereo and many will want, urgently, to escape from the endless television repeats.

Camping out moved uptown. It modernized, became attractive to the gentler people while still remaining a sport for hunters and fishermen.

Tent trailers, simple van type units and an occasional pickup truck camper, usually built at home, began to replace tents in certain families.

Some men rebuilt old hearses, or school buses.

Each unit contained at least one bed of foam rubber, extra storage space and usually a small ice box for cold storage of food and the fish they hoped to catch.

You spread a sleeping bag on the bed and every day or so tossed a chunk of ice in the ice box. Toilet facilities were either provided by the campground or you carried one of the ungainly little portable units which folded for storage.

For cooking purposes and other hot water needs, the then new two- and three-burner portable stoves did the job nicely.

Still, why cook on a tiny little stove and haul fuel around when mobile home dwellers had long since proven the worth of bottled LP (liquid propane) gas systems?

It wasn't long before gas ranges nearly equaling those at home began appearing in the camping outfits. On the powered RVs, the LP bottle could easily fit into one of the storage spaces, and on the towed units, a bottle or two nestled into the A-frame hitch.

And now LP gas is being used to power automobiles and has captured the world land speed record at 622.407 mph. How far we have come!

Campers became the most popular of all the camping vehicles. Set on a pickup truck, the camper unit came equipped with beds, an ice box, a cooking stove with an LP gas system and ample space for storing other needed items, as we have already discussed in this book.

So did camping trailers, more and more of which were being seen on the highways and in campgrounds.

Auto manufacturers, notably the Dodge Division, plunged headlong into the vacation vehicle market. Designers and engineers came up with heavy duty pickup trucks to haul the heavier and more elaborate campers and then came vans of beauty and efficiency, made for conversion.

Finally, the first true motor homes began to appear.

Since these outfits had nearly everything but the kitchen sink, the kitchen sink was added. Self-containment was becoming a reality. With the kitchen sink was added a fresh water holding system with a pump. The later addition of a water heater paved the way for easier dish washing, shaving and showers.

The pump systems narrowed down to three most popular, depending upon the type of vehicle desired by the camper. Most popular was a simple hand pump lever which brought the water from the tank to the sink, similar to marine type hand pumps aboard most smaller cabin cruisers. Mounted alongside the faucet, it was convenient, quick and easy and almost trouble-free.

Two other systems soon became even more popular since the truck mounted campers and motor homes had batteries aboard, and since the trailers were always reasonably near the battery of the towing vehicle.

Some vacation vehicle makers used a pressure system for water supply, adding a small compressor between the fresh water tank and sink.

Driven by the battery, the water system worked just as the one at home. As the water flowed from the faucet, the pressure dropped and with the drop in pressure the compressor turned itself on to rebuild. A flow of water was assured until the tank ran dry, and with no hand pumping.

The third method of water supply used a small pump to force the water from the tank to the faucet. The pump was activated when the faucet handle was turned on and stopped when the water flow was shut off.

Both methods are still in everyday use in hundreds of RVs, with the compressor system more popular.

About the same time, builders were also realizing that with LP gas available and with plug-in 110 volts at most campsites, there was no reason why the ice box couldn't be replaced with a real, if somewhat compact, refrigerator.

Other makers chose to go the way of the 12V/110V units, but the result was the same. Campers could keep the food cold and they could make ice, rather than buy it.

With refrigerators working on either gas or electricity, and with the changeover easy and simple, the box could stay in operation under any camping circumstance.

Selling prices of motor homes range:

Compact conversions	\$4,500 to \$ 7,500
Motor homes	\$5,000 to \$20,000 and up
four-wheel drive extra	

Van Conversions

Typical of vacation vehicles with all these conveniences is the compact van or wagon conversion.

The basic box shape of the Maxi Wagon is an ideal foundation for a camper conversion.

The raised roof section, usually of fiberglass, provides good standing room inside.

Double doors on side open wide for easy access to interior.

Total space utilization includes bed over front seats (left) and flat-top engine cover.

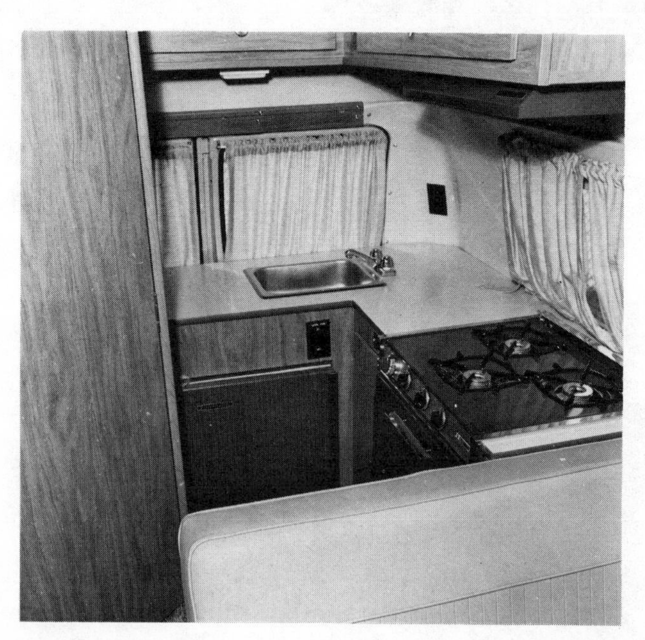

Pump systems provide water under pressure, just turn the faucet on.

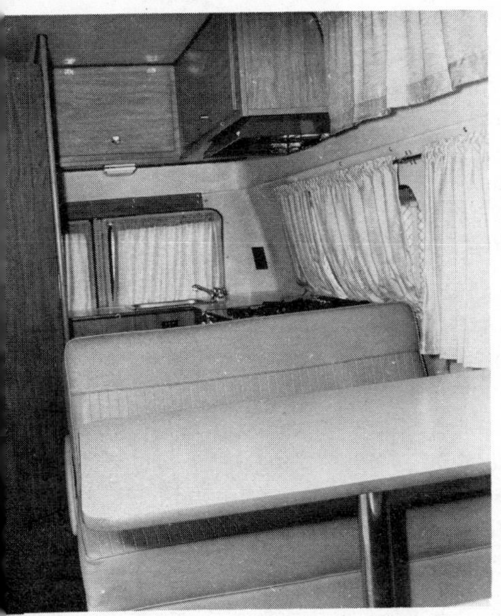

Home-style van accessories include a sink, a stove and even a complete flush toilet.

Family Wagon is a good description of this "useful-year-round" van.

Several manufacturers turn them out.

Slab sided, flat topped, squared off fore and aft, the compact van at first resembled nothing so much as a box on four wheels.

The homely little wagon never won any beauty contests, but if awards were handed out for versatility and functionalism it would win them hands down.

Today, they are sculptured–well, if not beauties, at least close to it–functional and attractive in this new age.

When it comes to holding or carrying things, the basic box shape is hard to beat. It has been around since before the dawn of recorded time and for all his technological progress man hasn't been able to improve it. The compact van was originally conceived as a lower cost, lighter weight, easier to maneuver supplement to the existing panel truck lines.

However, instead of merely supplementing, the compact van has virtually wiped out panel truck sales and they are fast becoming a thing of the past.

All the former users and buyers of panel trucks, such as plumbers, electricians, carpet layers, florists and photographers, were quick to realize that not only did the compact van do everything a panel would, it did it at a lower basic cost and at a lower overall operating cost.

While the compact van may be smaller on the outside, it is actually larger on the inside–mission impossible.

No one knows when it happened or who did it, but shortly after the introduction of the compact van some enterprising soul decided this would make an excellent camping vehicle.

In a short time, dozens of manufacturers were offering custom interiors which converted the vans into miniature homes on wheels.

These conversions found immediate acceptance with a large segment of the camping fraternity who found them much more practical than the camper pickup units to which they had been accustomed.

Now, the camper van conversions are making ever-increasing inroads on camper pickup sales just as the basic vans did on panel truck sales.

The compact van's shorter wheelbase, 109 or 127 inches, makes it easier than a pickup to maneuver in traffic and its lighter, more evenly distributed weight makes it easier to handle and more economical to operate on the road.

It's hard to believe until you see them parked side by side, but even the largest compact van is shorter overall than either a more standard passenger car or station wagon. In some cases it weighs less too, even with full camper equipment.

On the inside the vans have absolutely no waste space. A pickup has the engine mounted in front of the driver and requires a long hood to cover it.

In a van, the engine is located between the driver and front passenger seats. It takes up almost no usable space since the engine cover does double duty as a spare seat.

The Dodge Sportsman Wagon is typical of what is available today. It is offered on either 109- or 127-inch wheelbase and comes with six-cylinder and V8 engines, stick shift or automatic transmission and a variety of suspension options and rated to carry up to 3750 pounds.

Camper conversion units are manufactured by private independent companies and are sold through Dodge dealers, independent camper dealers or direct from the camper makers, in some cases.

The fiberglass top section provides standing height. Inside is all the usual equipment found in a camper pickup unit: stove, oven, refrigerator, table seating, sleeping area, storage space. Some include toilet and shower.

Interiors are custom made of materials chosen for long life and ease of maintenance. All are color coordinated.

While lacking some of the room of the larger chassis mounts, the compact van conversion can comfortably accommodate families of four and six.

Many owners find the compact camper vans also come in handy for everyday use, for shopping, driving to and from work, hauling light objects, things that would be difficult with a pickup because of its greater bulk.

The van conversion will even seat six people after conversion and can be operated as a passenger car, a really good twelve-month machine.

Brand new for the 1971 season was the Maxi Wagon which is 18 inches longer than the usual body on the Dodge Sportsman Wagon B300.

Utilizing the 127-inch wheelbase Sportsman chassis, the Maxi offers roomier interior for a camper conversion or a fifteen-passenger wagon—take your choice.

Without seats, you have a load space of a full eleven feet behind the driver. With seats, even set up for twelve-passenger configuration, you have twenty-two inches of luggage space behind the rear seat.

Maxi dresses turn us off, but the Maxi Wagon turns us on.

Starting with a compact van, either 109- or 127-inch wheelbase, whichever the customer prefers, the camper manufacturer buys a stripped van, with the front seats only.

First, he cuts off the top and completely rebuilds the interior, with a bubble roof permanently attached, or a top with flexible sides which is hydraulically lifted at the campsite, and lowered for highway travel.

Either way, the floor to ceiling height is increased a little more than two feet.

Some builders buy the chassis from several dealers, manufacture the conversions and sell the RV back to the dealers and to independent dealers.

In other cases, the franchised auto/truck dealer will buy his chassis from the factory as usual, then order the conversion from the camper maker, then sell the finished product.

The only thing that is certain is that the big three auto/truck makers do not build campers, conversions or motor homes, but they do work closely together in engineering and design.

Dodge's new dual rear wheel front section compact is specially designed for compact camper conversion manufacturers. They like this model because it facilitates their conversion process by eliminating the need to cut off and scrap large portions of sheet metal. Offered as an option on both the high line and new low line MB300s, the dual rear wheel front section package boasts an 8300 GVW which fills a void in the market and is certain to prove successful.

This Chinook Western van conversion features seats that can open into full-sized beds.

When you think of the camper manufacturer cutting off the top of the van or wagon and throwing it away, or in the case of the chassis mount, cutting off the entire truck body and throwing it away, the obvious thought is what a waste of time and material. The truck factory builds it and the camper factory junks it.

The truck manufacturers are exploring the economics involved in the "we build it, you throw it away" syndrome, and while it is engineeringly feasible to provide the converter with only that which he needs, it could be more costly.

"We talked with several converters," Dodge's Roland Swain told us, "about van conversions and chassis mount cutaways, where most of the body is cut off to be replaced by a camper body, and the strange thing is their biggest problem is getting rid of the scrap.

"It only takes from one and a half to two hours to cut away the body.

"It's a big hunk of steel. It used to be the scrap people would pick it up, but when the price of scrap got so low, they said, 'We'll pick it up if you pay us.'

"Now, they tell the converters, 'We'll pick it up only if you'll cut it up into two-foot squares and bundle it.' "

The problems of making special changes on an auto factory production line are well known. Shipping is also a problem. If you don't have a complete body, it must be braced to keep it from getting out of shape.

Then, if you don't have a complete body which you can lock up, there will be added pilferage along the way.

"Believe me," Swain said, "there is somebody between here and Los Angeles who is building a motor home a piece at a time.

"No kidding. In one shipment we will lose a carburetor, the next one we will lose a power steering chuck, the next one a wheel.

"He steals a different piece each time. I know it's not that simple, but it sure seems that way.

"We do lose a lot of batteries and alternators."

The converted van can be, literally, a home on wheels.

With a full size foam rubber bed, which folds under an ample rear seat, with other unfolding cots, a four burner gas range, including oven and broiler, with two-way refrigerator, 12 and 110 volts, or gas and electricity, with sink and fresh water holding tank, a table dropped from the wall for dining and with ample storage space, including a near full length wardrobe, what more could you ask?

Lunch can be prepared easily, even while the unit is in motion, and eaten in comfort. Roadside rest stops become full-fledged living areas.

After dinner, a nap in complete comfort is ready and waiting, since most of these vehicles are air-conditioned and ride well.

While the law takes a dim view of passengers riding in the trailers, in a van it makes little difference whether you are all sitting up front as in a conventional station wagon, or relaxed on a couch. Fasten your safety belts, please.

An after dinner drink? Sure, but not for the driver, obviously.

No problem with the petite ice cubes from the refrigerator. Dishwashing and cleanup? There's a sink aboard for that.

You know, that after dinner drink item raises a couple of interesting questions. First, an open bottle of booze in an automobile might get you into trouble, but in the van camper, that's your home, as long as it's stored properly in a cabinet.

Second, it's a violation of state laws in many locales to transport an "X" amount of liquor across state lines without paying the state tax.

If you bought several bottles of booze in a state with low taxes, and put it in the trunk of your auto, you can be arrested, fined, the liquor confiscated and the automobile also confiscated.

That's a fact, it has happened, more than once. So what is the situation with the family which has a half-dozen bottles of various brands in the liquor cabinet of their rolling home, primarily for their own use? It could be sticky, hence this word of caution.

Self-containment in these vehicles and in similarly equipped trailers and motor homes is almost complete. Almost? Some campers are still carrying around the portable toilets. Heating on cold winter nights is also a problem.

With LP gas available, wall type thermostatically controlled heaters are easy to install; so the RV becomes air conditioned, heated and with small electric pumps and sanitary holding tanks, completely self-contained with flush toilet and shower.

The RV traveler can plug into the campsite 110 volts, or use his own 12-volt system. To save batteries, some men use portable electric generators to convert to 110 volt.

The majority install twin battery systems, one in the car and one for the camper, with the car battery always in reserve. Just crank up the car and both batteries get a full charge.

In the mountains or the desert, the average camper can eat and live almost as well as at home, and some insist it is better.

The two-battery system is not a new idea. Twenty years ago, before the day of heavy duty 12-volt batteries and alternators, and before the transistorized mobile telephones and two-way radios, a fellow in Daytona Beach, Florida came up with a twin battery installation which was widely used by police departments and early mobile telephone users, long plagued by dead batteries and stalled autos.

He mounted a spare battery between the grille and the radiator of the auto, installed a second generator alongside the normal one and had no more problems. No drain on the car battery and both batteries were being charged whenever the engine was running.

Toilet systems. A less than delicate subject, but important to the camper. At first, regular mobile home toilets were installed, in place of the fold-up portables, but these proved less than adequate, because they required sewage connections at the campgrounds, a limiting factor.

The first solution to this problem was the installation of a regular marine-type toilet, which dumps its contents into a sanitary holding tank, which the camper later dumps into one of the many service station and campgrounds receiving systems.

Meanwhile, the water from the sink and shower was considered as sanitary, so it was just dumped on the ground underneath the RV.

In this day of ecology consciousness, that is now a "no no."

A more expensive toilet has come into use, called the Monomatic type, into which the camper puts a specified amount of water and pre-measured packet of chemicals at the start of the trip.

Through up to eighty or so flushings, the system reuses the water, filters keeping everything clean and fresh, and periodically, the system is dumped at a holding tank service station, through a handy valve underneath the vehicle, and fresh water and chemicals are again added.

There's another system on the market, the Destroilet, in which the waste is piped, burned by the engine exhaust and pumped into the atmosphere through the regular engine exhaust pipe, the makers claiming no additional air pollution beyond the normal auto exhaust.

The Monomatic system makers have since added a holding tank, so even these will last a full season before dumping.

Complete self-containment? Almost. To get around the ban on dumping the sink and shower drain on the ground, campers now place buckets or containers under the drain, and dump the buckets into the assigned receptacle, but that's a light chore.

Motor Homes

When motor homes were a novelty, it was not unusual for the curious campers to come visiting, to look over the new plush style of living.

"Doggone," one veteran said. "They had no compunction about waking you up at two o'clock in the morning.

"You had no real choice–show it to them or ask them to come back in the morning.

"You might as well invite them in, like in the old joke about the wrong number phone call in the middle of the night and the caller apologizes. 'That's okay,' said the sleepy fellow, 'I had to get up anyway to answer the phone.'

"I finally solved my problem by posting a sign: 'This vehicle will be shown tomorrow afternoon from two until five. Please come then.' "

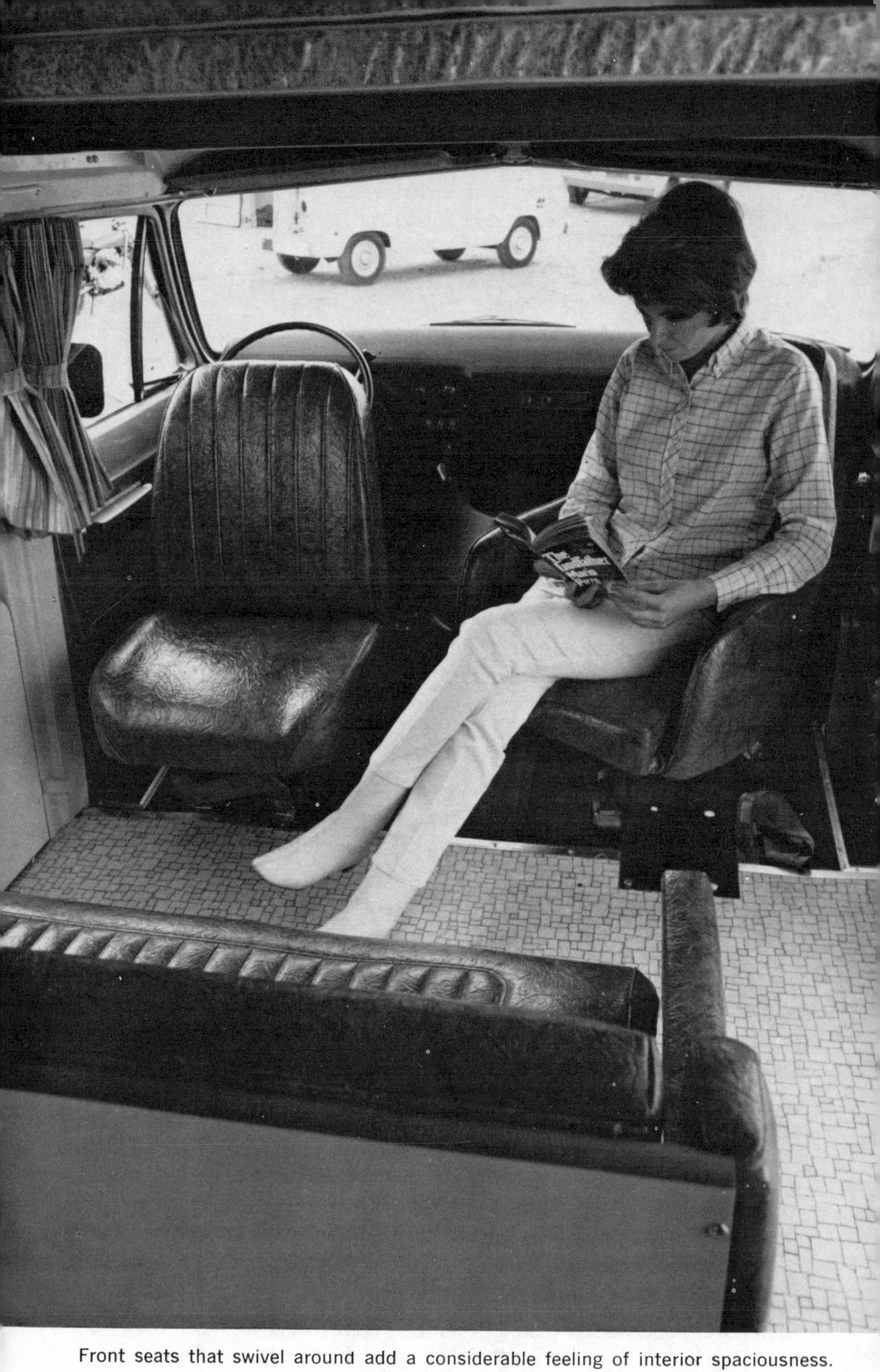

Front seats that swivel around add a considerable feeling of interior spaciousness.

Today, when you pull into a trailer park with a sophisticated unit–something they haven't seen–you'll find the interest of the campers is phenomenal.

It's like being a member of a small city. Spend a few days there and you know everybody in the camp. For the kids, it's just as if they've lived there all their lives.

The people who have been at this camping business eight or ten years have finally settled on the equipment which is perfect for them.

They are interested in your rig, not for themselves, but only to compare notes. The RV market is as individual as the thousands upon thousands of people in it, everyone to his own taste.

The true motor home is a single purpose vehicle and appeals to those with relatively fat check books. Some deluxe models can cost as high as $100,000 or $150,000, certainly out of range of even the moderately affluent guy.

Dodge was probably the first supplier of truck chassis to the motor home field, and certainly the major supplier to the industry as it has mushroomed over the past decade.

Quite accidentally, an innovator named Ray Frank in Brown City, Michigan became the first production builder of motor homes, the first with a moving assembly line, and we cover that interesting story a little later in this book

"We try to work closely with all camper manufacturers," explained Dodge truck operations boss Joe James, in an exclusive interview, "from the standpoint of technical know-how and direction.

"We attempt to provide the right kind of chassis for their needs."

Prior to the introduction of new models, the company produces a Body Builders' Book with technical specifications of all pertinent truck chassis and bodies.

"Each camper builder is quite individualistic. That's what makes this market so interesting, and they make their designs from our specifications and build a single prototype, and go from there.

"We try to direct them as to the cooling implications and the load implications."

The manufacturer tries to release the secret advance new model body specifications to the motor home makers "in the market at the same time as we are making public introductions."

It is estimated that some 70 per cent of motor homes are built on Dodge chassis. United Press International quoted an 80 per cent figure not too long ago.

"If we don't give the motor home manufacturers the technical information and do it fast, they will use somebody else's chassis.

"We built the first chassis that was designed for motor home application exclusively. It did get us a pretty good jump on the market for a few years," James continued.

Motor home chassis are estimated to account for about 10 per cent of the industry's truck production, about 20 to 25 per cent for Dodge. That is reason enough to continue cultivating the market.

The East North Central area (Midwestern states) produces about 42 per cent of the RVs in this country's million dollar business, according to Mobile Home RV Dealer Magazine, while the Pacific Coast states take care of 30 per cent of production.

Indiana, California and Michigan are the big producers of RVs, Michigan probably as a sort of spillover from Indiana, which has long been the nation's leader in construction of large mobile homes.

Another Michigan factor is the availability of workers trained to handle large sheet material, as well as the availability of engineering and production facilities.

Two factors influence California as a center. The state is a major market in the sale of campers. Second, like Michigan, is the availability of aircraft-skilled tradesmen, trained to work with large sheet material.

Such units as the Dodge Motor Home, which is produced by Travco, now contain just about everything to make vacation outfits totally self-contained–pioneering in comfort!

Before leaving home, the camper fills LP bottles with gas, he fills fresh water holding tanks, puts the needed chemicals in the sanitary system, stores food and other staples in the cupboards, and has the vehicle lubed, safety-checked and filled with petrol; you know, "go juice"–gasoline.

From that moment on, the Travco-built motor homes and the other fancy trailers, vans, pickups, chassis mounts so equipped, make the tourist fully self-contained and self-sustaining in every sense of the words.

He can cook, eat, sleep, keep warm or cool, shower, use the on-board toilet facilities any place, any time, without leaving behind a single trace when he moves on.

Are you listening, ecologists, no air or ground pollution!

He can live in comfort. Many have radio, television, stereo, yet he can live in the beautiful outdoors, alongside a sparkling mountain stream, or deep in the desert, or up in the mountains, with a blanket of stars for a cover until he retreats inside.

If he selects an organized campgrounds, he plugs in the 110 volts, attaches to the fresh water system and the sewage disposal and adds a hose for the sink and shower drain disposal.

When these facilities are not immediately available, he reverts to self-containment for whatever features he needs.

Completely versatile, most of these modern camping vehicles will accept what is there and work on their own built-ins for whatever is not there.

Yes, it's a far, far cry from the tent, to be sure, and even a far, far cry from the caveman's abode, but just as close to nature as you wish it to be.

Learning to Drive a Motor Home

Driving a motor home is not a nerve racking experience as some people might surmise.

Rollie Swain, an auto/truck industrialist and an experienced camper on a personal hobby basis, described it best:

"Ten years ago I purchased my first motor home and took delivery in Detroit. I was as nervous as a new bride.

"After getting gas and checking it over in a service station, we moseyed off and got down on the expressway. Even ten years ago, the Detroit freeways were crowded, fast and frightening.

"Once we were rolling, however, I began to get a little confidence. After little more than an hour or so, we were past Toledo, so I pulled into the Holiday Inn near the Ohio Turnpike.

"As we parked, my wife Dorothy said, 'I think I can drive it.' From then on, she wheels that thing like a truck driver. There is no effort.

"If you can drive a passenger car, you can drive a motor home–or a pickup camper.

"One advantage is that you see over the traffic, not through it. One tip for beginners. When Dorothy started driving, I took a piece of tape, then from the driver's seat, 'eyeballed' the edge of the road–and stuck the tape on the dashboard.

"With that, you can learn to gauge the vehicle until you get acquainted with how wide it is, how much clearance you need.

"One other advantage, especially in a city, people get out of your way.

"Nevertheless, at first sight, it is an awesome thing."

Special Custom Vehicles

ROSSETT DODGE CLUB CAR

Back in the days before strips of concrete replaced ribbons of steel, people like the Vanderbilts, the Rockefellers and Diamond Jim Brady used plush and private railroad cars to get around to various and sundry places of business and enjoyment.

Barney Rossett, president of Grove Press in New York City, found himself in somewhat similar need by modern standards and commissioned a "club car" to be built.

His needs were much like those of businessmen of the earlier era. He needed a vehicle which had all the comforts and necessities of his office, with none of the time-wasting difficulties associated with travel.

His commission for the club car went to the brothers Cumberford, Bob and Jim, of Cumberford Design International, Inc., Tuxedo Park, New York.

Most motor homes are built on Dodge chassis with wheelbases from 104 to 178 inches. Usually the 318-cubic-inch engine is standard. These motor homes by Superior, Champion and Travco (top to bottom) accommodate up to eight people.

Pictured here (top to bottom) are Winnebago, Chinook and all-new Sightseer built on Dodge chassis with three-speed automatic transmission, vacuum hydraulic power brakes, integral power steering and heavy duty shocks front and rear.

Price was not an object, but design, esthetics, utility and comfort were. The total tab was in the area of $20,000.

The Cumberfords started with a Dodge 108 wagon powered with a 318-cubic-inch V8 engine, automatic transmission and limited slip rear end.

They took everything out of it and started to rebuild. Passenger car chrome wheels were installed, with Goodyear radial ply tires. All chrome trim was removed and Mercedes silver laquer finish sprayed over the body, with a bold navy blue stripe added around the belt line.

Front and rear bumpers were each extended six inches for greater parking protection. Marine rubber bumpers were fixed to the front and rear bumpers and side areas between the wheel wells to protect the silver finish.

Rolls Royce headlamps were mounted as fog lamps and truck headlights were mounted in the grille for regular driving lights.

Lucas spotlights were added to the front and rear of the roof. A tropical sunroof provides a thermal barrier for added interior cooling and heating, while a station wagon luggage rack was placed on top of the sunroof to provide additional cargo space, or permit its use as an observation deck.

The finishing touch was provided, outside, by tune control Italian air horn trumpets.

Inside, all seat cushions and backrests are of hand-rubbed old English leather. Carpeting throughout, a top layer of all wool pile over an insulating foam and sound dampening foam carpet.

Headlining and interior paneling is a psychedelic multicolored striped pattern of Herman Miller fine woven wool, called Jacob's Coat.

In the driving area–the cockpit–the front seats are contour fitted with built-in headrests, separated by a cloth and leather center console between the driver and passenger seats.

The console houses an AM-FM-SW stereo radio and stereo tape player and mobile telephone unit, with which you can call any place in the world, by direct dial.

Encased in the womb of psychedelic cloth and brown hand-rubbed leather of the rear compartment is a desk, book shelf, bar, refrigerator with six ice cube trays and a capacity for continuous production of more cubes, a sink with hot and cold running water, a hot plate for coffee or light meals and a television set.

In addition to the hot plate, there is a thermos bottle which, when powered from any one of five cigarette lighting units, permits coffee to be made while underway.

Hidden beneath the bar is a 110-volt outlet for powering video recorders, electric typewriters, dictaphones, electric shaver, outdoor lights or the after-the-ball vacuum cleaner to spruce up the place.

In this literal lap of luxury there is seating capacity for five people, not counting the driver and one more up front.

There is a form-fitting bench type rear seat and dual see-through plastic swivel chairs at $495 a copy in the approximate center of the main compartment.

Just to make sure nothing gets lost and nobody gets confused, the Rossett special is equipped with a burglar alarm system, "door ajar" warning lights and pilot lights for each individual piece of equipment to alert the driver to which items are in use, or which might have been left on inadvertently.

A rear storage compartment, accessible from the outside, holds a heavy duty jack, two space saver tires, fire extinguisher, constant charge flashlight, two cables (the car is equipped with permanent tow hooks front and aft), a fuse panel for the 12-volt system and circuit breaker for the 110-volt system, automatic relay switch for household current which cuts out the auxiliary generator, heater for rear compartment, water and air, back up and loading light switches and things like that.

Just in case you think they forgot something, the Cumberfords pointed out Mr. Rossett did not want a trailer hitch.

Other items include separate front and rear air conditioners and heaters, with individual front and rear controls, added brake lights, directional signals, flasher warning systems and race driver-type seat belts, an auxiliary fuel tank bringing the capacity to 35 gallons, plus two electric fuel pumps.

However, don't believe the rumor going around that the club car is fueled with champagne. They keep that in the bar. It was Andy Granatelli's Indianapolis turbine "whooshmobile" which was fueled with champagne . . . or was that Chanel number five?

The Cumberfords are race car builders as well as designers and innovators in luxury, and in this area they could not resist the temptation to romance the 318 truck engine a bit, installing dual exhausts before making delivery to Mr. Rossett.

The end result is a neat little race car rumble from the outside, but not heard inside because of the heavy insulation.

The racing influence carries over to the special steering wheel, a leather-covered black anodized aluminum spider with flexible rim made by Moretti, who also makes them for Ferrari's race cars. Personally, we'll go the Dan Gurney-styled Olsonite route, keep it on the all-American path.

The Cumberfords, incidentally, contend the club car will outdrag and outcorner a good many domestic and foreign passenger cars. The only addition to the stock suspension system is a set of Koni shock absorbers from Peter Pizey.

Other items of minor interest are: humidity gauge, 24-hour clock to let you know when the party's over and complete dashboard instrumentation so you are not bothered by idiot light flashers.

So, if you really don't have anything planned for that twenty grand that makes your mattress so lumpy, give it to the brothers Cumberford and they'll figure something out, real racy.

AS IT WAS IN THE BEGINNING

The motor home business all began because aviation weather was not reliable.

Michigan novelty manufacturer Ray Frank and his son, Ronald, are licensed pilots who became discouraged when their travel plans were too often thwarted by bad weather.

That was back in 1958.

"I bought a Ford truck chassis," Ray Frank recalled, "and we built our motor home and went on a Florida trip."

Within a year, Ray Frank motor homes were being sold on a custom-built schedule.

People showed so much interest in his personal family motor home, Ray Frank recognized a market existed, so started to accept the proffered customized orders.

In 1961, Ray Frank switched to the Dodge chassis.

"There were other motor home builders, on a custom order basis," he told us, "but we were the first to operate on a production basis and the first to have a moving assembly line."

Dodge public relations chief Frank Wylie heard about Ray Frank's new idea for production line use of his company's chassis, so he put together a news story with photos and mailed it out to the newspapers around the country.

Joe James continues the story. Joe is the assistant general manager at Dodge, the man in charge of all truck operations.

"At the time, I was regional manager out in Portland, Oregon, which is a great camper area.

"The story Frank Wylie put out was a P.R. type thing. 'Here is something somebody has done with a Dodge chassis!'

"The story was printed all over the country, but we had missed it in our office. We had received the press kit okay, but like most press kits, you figure you already know what's in it, so you toss it in the trash can.

"But Frank Wylie had really slugged one past us that time. We were getting lots of phone calls: 'Where can I buy one?'

"At first, my reaction was, 'What are you talking about? We don't build a motor home!'

" 'Oh, I saw it in the paper,' they said, so we tried to check it out, and finally found the article and then traced the source, back to Frank Wylie.

"As far as I know, Frank Wylie had as much to do with getting the motor home concept rolling as anybody.

"Of course, Ray Frank was the original innovator, but Frank Wylie was the guy who put it on the map, and it was done in a rather innocent casual way, really."

Incidentally, Ray Frank happily confirms that story of Frank Wylie introducing his motor home idea to the public.

Later, Ray Frank left that original company which became Travco Corporation, now headed by Peter R. Fink as president, while Ray Frank and his son build the Xplorer van conversion at Brown City, Michigan.

Still innovating, Ray Frank's conversion goes beyond some other designs, because he cuts away the entire van body, all the way down to the floor pan, just after the B post, then completely rebuilds from there.

The finished product has a fiberglass body, completely reinforced.

It is, in actuality, a chassis mount motor home/camper, but on the lighter van chassis, more maneuverable.

It's quite sophisticated, selling in the $7500 range.

5. Trailer Towing

☐ A chapter on towing vehicles takes on two phases:

1. Towing an automobile behind your pickup, van conversion or motor home.
2. The vehicle you use to tow a trailer.

Let's take problem number one first.

Towing an Auto Behind the Motor Camper

There is one inconvenience which might become a major inconvenience to motor home camping, and that is the lack of available convenient transportation once you are set up in the campground.

This same situation applies, perhaps in a lesser degree, to those owners of van conversions.

When you want to go in town or take a side trip, you have to take your house with you.

Three alternatives:

1. Carry a motorcycle, mini bike or bicycle (or plural) with you;
2. Rent an auto while there;
3. Tow a small automobile behind your camper.

In addition to the inconvenience of towing, today's automatic transmission cars cannot be towed as is, without expensive noises being heard.

Problem is, when you drive the transmission from the rear end, the oil pump is not activated. Without oil, you get burned bearings and gears. The oil pump is activated only when the engine is running.

The only practical solution is to disconnect the drive shaft.

One veteran camper advised, "It's not too difficult. There are four bolts on the upper end and four on the lower end of the drive shaft.

"I only loosen the lower end, shove the shaft forward–it has a telescoping joint–and strap it into place under the car. Be sure you fasten it securely."

Towing Vehicles for Trailers

Now, more complex is the problem of towing a camper trailer, large or small.

It has been mentioned in this book that tent or pop-up trailers are easy to tow and they can be handled by intermediate and standard size autos, with relative ease.

However, all towing autos should be equipped with the manufacturers' "trailer towing package" of heavy duty scope.

For the larger camper trailers, the biggest problem seems to be to convince the buyer he needs a vehicle that is big enough.

It is not that the dealer is just trying to sell you an extra dollar's worth, but he is trying to sell you your requirement. People seem to think, when they have a three-quarter ton truck, that anything they can pile onto it is fair game. That's not true.

"There is nothing for free in a truck," a favorite comment of Dodge's Roland Swain. "If you need a bigger wheel or a bigger tire, it will cost a little more money.

"If you get a transmission that will handle 1300 pounds torque, it costs more than a transmission to handle 900 pounds torque.

"Trucks are built from the frame up with the ability to carry a specific load."

This also applies, in a sense, to your automobile if it is to be used to tow a trailer. The factory towing package makes the car more suitable for the extraordinary heavy duty use.

Trailer Towing Packages

All auto/truck manufacturers offer a complete line of vehicles capable of towing a wide variety of utility, boat and travel trailers with ease, comfort and safety.

The popularity of Dodge vehicles for this purpose reflects the attention given to the design of the major components, so we will use them as the examples.

The factory-installed components included in the trailer towing packages are listed for quick and easy identification. Also, the specific provisions for continued warranty protection are defined more clearly.

The newest idea in trailers is the fifth wheeler, a trailer that has been cut out in front to fit over the tow vehicle instead of tagging along behind it. The hitch can be mounted over the rear axle in the bed of a pickup or, on some models, even on the roof of a car. This better distribution of weight on the tow vehicle allows much heavier hitch weights and improves handling at highway speeds.

Monitor

Continued growth of recreational vehicle use has prompted changes in trailer towing equipment made available as options on 1973 models.

Dodge makes three separate trailer towing equipment packages available for order by the new car purchaser so that the items can be factory installed. These are the heavy duty package, the trailer wiring package and the trailer towing package.

The packages are available only by ordering certain optional minimum required equipment such as automatic transmission, power disc brakes and larger tire sizes. Specific minimum engine sizes are required for respective cars and trailer towing package combinations.

For example the Dart would have to be ordered with at least a 225-cubic-inch engine, Charger or Coronet with the 318 and the Polara or Monaco with 360 engine.

What's in the Packages

The three trailer packages, which include separate equipment for different uses, may be ordered separately or in combination depending upon the intended usage.

For instance, the wiring package is available for vehicles intended to pull light or medium weight trailers or boats, which do not require the complete trailer towing package.

The heavy duty package is available for more rugged towing needs, and the wiring and heavy duty packages may be ordered together.

The trailer towing package contains all the items of the heavy duty and the wiring packages, plus an externally-mounted transmission oil cooler (for intermediate and standard size cars) and a 3.23 to 1 ratio rear axle.

The heavy duty package consists of maximum cooling equipment (high capacity radiator, fan shroud and coolant reserve system), heavy duty suspension (larger front sway bar, larger torsion bars, higher rear leaf spring rate) and extra-wide wheel rims.

The trailer wiring package consists of a Chrysler 60-ampere heavy duty alternator, a heavy duty stop lamp switch, a variable load turn signal flasher and a trailer wiring harness. The harness has seven wires to connect into the trailer outlet to operate trailer lighting equipment. The wires are for: ground; right stop and turn signal; left stop and turn signal; tail, license and side marker lights; back-up lamp; electric trailer brake; and auxiliary.

Hitches

A full line of Mopar Class I and Class II hitches for towing of light and medium weight travel and camping trailers, boats and snowmobiles is available for all Dodge vehicles.

In addition, a bolt-on, load equalizer hitch platform will be available for the Coronet, Charger, Polara and Monaco models.

All hitches are extra cost and dealer-installed items.

Minimum Size Engine Requirements for Full Frontal Area Trailer
(55 Square Feet, except where noted)

	Minimum Size Engine Required	Maximum Recom-mended Weight	No Trailer Towing Package Required up to:
COMPACT			
Dart*	225ci—Max. 20 sq. ft. frontal area trailers up to 2000 pounds.	2000 lbs.	1000 lbs.
Dart*	318ci	2500 lbs.	1000 lbs.
INTERMEDIATE			
Charger / Coronet Sedans & Hardtops**	318ci	4000 lbs.	1500 lbs.
	400ci	5000 lbs.	1500 lbs.
Coronet Station Wagons	318ci—Max. 20 sq. ft. frontal area trailers up to 3000 pounds.	3000 lbs.	1500 lbs.
Coronet Station Wagons	400ci 2-bbl.	6000 lbs.	1500 lbs.
STANDARD			
Polara / Monaco Sedans & Hardtops	360ci	5000 lbs.	2000 lbs.
	440ci 4-bbl.	7000 lbs.	2000 lbs.
Polara / Monaco 2 & 3 Seat Wagons	360ci	4000 lbs.	2000 lbs
	440ci 4-bbl.	7000 lbs.	2000 lbs.

NOTE
*D78 x 14 Minimum size tires recommended for 1000- to 2500-pound trailers.
**Trailer towing package (Sales Code A35) not available on cars equipped with rear sway bar: Charger with Sales Code A57; all models with 440 ci engines.

Sportsman wagons can be used to pull trailers of up to 2000 pounds gross loaded weight without an equalizer hitch, provided that the tongue load does not exceed 200 pounds.

Sportsman Wagons

Equipped with the trailer towing package and other required items, Sportsman wagons are able to pull trailers with maximum gross loaded weight ranging from 2000 to 6000 pounds.

Trailer Towing Package — Code YC4 (Items Included in the Package Price)

Increased cooling capacity, heavy duty shock absorbers (front and rear), 50-amp. alternator, 70-amp./hour battery, heavy duty variable-load flasher and wiring harness.

Minimum Required Items (Extra Cost—Coded Separately)

MODEL	B100	B200	B300
Maximum Trailer Weight (with equalizer hitch)	4000 lbs.	5500 lbs.	6000 lbs.
Maximum Tongue Load	400 lbs.	650 lbs.	750 lbs.
Maximum GCW (gross combined weight of loaded trailer and van)	8500 lbs.	9500 lbs.	10,500 lbs.
Required Minimum Equipment (not included in package)			
Engine*	225 Six	318 V8	318 V8
Transmission	Automatic	Automatic	Automatic
Rear Springs	1420 lbs.	1555 lbs.	2570 lbs.
Rear Axle*	3.9 w/225	3.2 w/318	4.1 w/318
Tires	F78-14-B (4PR) Pass. Car	H78-15-B (4PR) Pass. Car	8.00-16.5-E (10PR) Truck Type

*These engine/rear axle ratio combinations are minimums for less than maximum hauling. They are recommended for up to 6000 GCW on the B100 and B200, and up to 9000 GCW on the B300. For maximum GCW the B100 and B200 require a 360 V8 with 3.55 rear axle, the B300 requires the 360 with a 4.1 axle. In-between combinations are available on the B100 and B200, check with your dealer.

Requirements for Warranty Protection

The manufacturer's passenger car warranty will apply to cars used to haul trailers for noncommercial use, but if the loaded trailer weight exceeds the allowable pounds, the following conditions must be met:

1. Equip the vehicle with a factory-installed trailer towing package.
2. If the loaded tongue weight exceeds the allowable limits, equip the vehicle with a properly installed frame-type, load equalizer hitch.
3. Loaded trailer weight must not exceed the allowable limits.
4. The vehicle must be serviced as outlined under "Service Requirements" (see page 85).

Other Recommendations

If the engine temperature indicates an overheating condition, particularly on very hot days, the following action is recommended:

On the highways	– Reduce the road speed.
Up steep hills	– Select a lower transmission gear.
In city traffic	– While stopped, put transmission in neutral and idle engine at higher speed.
Air conditioning on	– Turn the air-conditioning system off.

Equalizer Hitch Attachments

The information contained in the following sections is aimed at providing an approved method for attaching a frame-type load equalizer hitch onto the underbody structure of various Dodge-built cars. The hitch may be one of several excellent types produced by independent hitch manufacturers and sold through their respective outlets.

It is of prime importance that the hitch be attached to the tow vehicle in such a way as to minimize any adverse effects upon the automobile's structure or its basic ride and handling characteristics.

To help achieve this objective, engineers have established certain recommendations to serve as a guide for experienced hitch installers and show novices how the hitch should be attached to the car.

The drawings are purposely kept simple and show only minimum construction requirements. The hitch installer may either bolt or weld the hitch assembly onto the body rails, depending upon the owner's preference.

It is worth repeating here that engineers endorse the use of the frame-type hitch and use of the axle-type hitch is not recommended because of the possible risk resulting from seriously overloading the rear axle shafts, bearings, wheels and tires.

The advantage of the frame-type hitch lies in its ability to disperse the towing loads into the vehicle's underbody structure, without overloading or overworking any single chassis component.

BASIC HITCH SUPPLIED IN KIT FORM

Frame-type hitches are usually sold through franchised trailer dealers, many of whom maintain their own welding shops to fabricate and install the completed hitch onto the automobile.

Typical frame-type, load-equalizer hitch components, major parts included by most manufacturers in the trailer hitch kit are:

(1) The frame-type tow bar or draw bar
(2) Ball mount with trunnion
(3) Spring bars—with chains and saddles

HITCH ATTACHMENT RECOMMENDATION

The following drawings show the completed hitch assemblies, fitted with front and rear cross members, straps, and gussets. The welded-on parts are made from ordinary low-carbon steel and may be welded by either acetylene torch or electric arc. The assembly details include only minimum dimensions because the car, itself, will dictate over-all size.

Prior to installing the completed hitch onto the car, it is mandatory that all undercoating material be removed from the contact areas. This is necessary to maintain the specified 40 to 50 pound feet torque on the attaching bolts that secure the hitch to the body rails.

FRAME-TYPE, LOAD EQUALIZER HITCH INSTALLATION

Dart: The equalizer hitch for Dart requires that the front cross member be bolted onto the body floor pan, in addition to being attached to the body rails. This provides for better load distribution on these compact-size models.

Coronet (All Models, Except Station Wagons): The front cross member of the equalizer hitch recommended for Dodge Coronet is attached to the body rails;

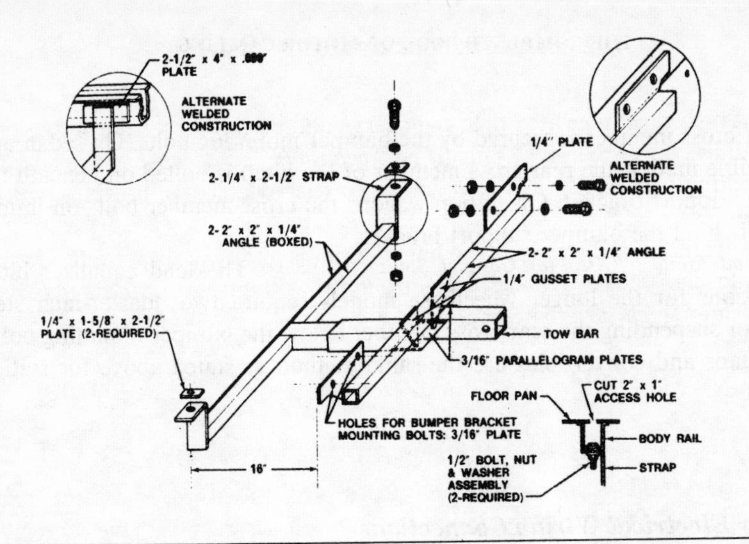

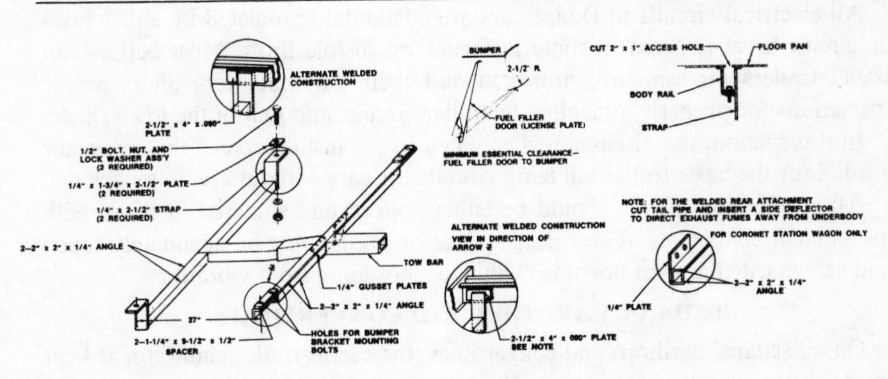

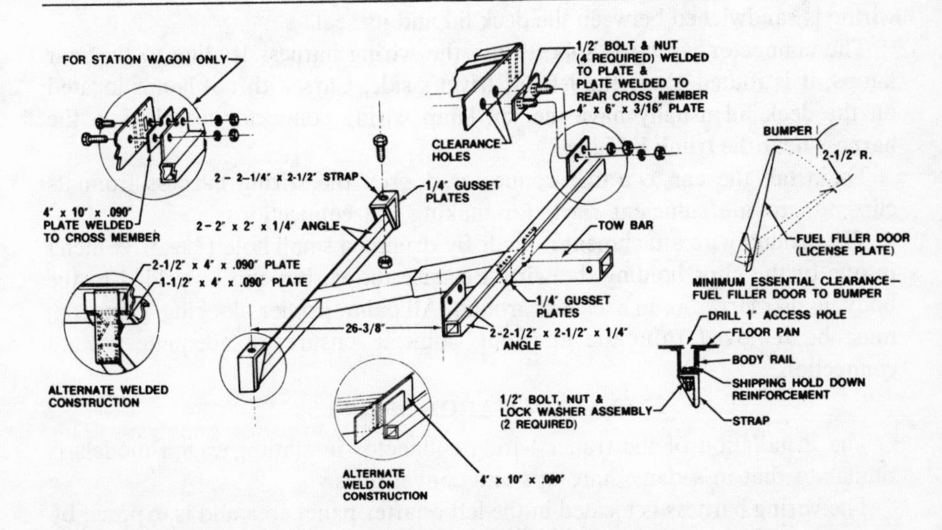

Basic frame-type hitches for Darts (top) Coronets (center) and Polaras (bottom).

the rear cross member is secured by the bumper mounting bolts. On sedan and convertible models the rear cross member of the hitch is bolted on beneath the bumper support bracket. On station wagons the cross member bolts on immediately behind the bumper support bracket.

Polara and Monaco (Also for Coronet Station Wagons): The load equalizer hitch installations for the longer wheelbase models require two quarter-inch steel plates for suspending the rear cross member below the bumper mounting bolts. The sedans and convertibles use the same method as stated above for station wagons.

Trailer Electrical Wiring Connections

All electrical circuits in Dodge cars are adequately protected by either fuses or circuit breakers, and in some instances by fusible links. Most better-built travel trailers are similarly protected and their manufacturers offer specific instuctions for properly attaching the trailer circuit onto that of the tow vehicle.

In this section, the discussion is confined to the installation of the connector needed for the basic trailer tail lamp circuits for cars without a wiring package.

All wiring connections should be either spliced and soldered or made with mechanical connectors. The wiring splices or joints must be adequately taped and safeguarded against possible chafing or loosening from vibration.

SEDANS, HARDTOPS AND CONVERTIBLES

On all sedans, hardtops and convertibles, the car-to-trailer connector is kept inside the trunk when not in use. When connected to the trailer, the connector wiring is sandwiched between the deck lid and its seal.

The connector wiring is spliced into the wiring harness leading to the rear lamps; it is routed along the left or driver's side. Cars with tail lamps located on the deck lid usually have the tail lamp wiring connector attached to the harness near the trunk lid hinge.

To install the car-to-trailer connector, loosen the wiring harness from its clips to provide sufficient slack for making the connections.

The ground wire attachment is made by drilling a small hole (3/32 or 1/8 inch) in one of the clips holding the wire. Because the wiring clip is welded to the body, it also serves as an excellent ground. All paint, primer, flocking, gum, etc., must be removed from the attaching point to ensure an adequate ground connection.

STATION WAGON MODELS

The installation of the trailer wiring connector in station wagon models is similar to that in sedans, hardtops and convertibles.

The wiring harness is located in the left quarter panel area and is exposed by removing the left tail lamp housing completely. By following the tail lamp wiring forward, the tape-wrapped junction is easily located.

Service Requirements

Towing trailers is considered heavy duty service. However, when cars are equipped with trailer towing packages and are used for towing, they need very little special attention beyond that normally required for everyday driving.

SPECIAL REQUIREMENTS

In addition to the normal service requirements outlined in the owner's manual:

1. The transmission oil and transmission oil filter must be changed, and the transmission bands adjusted, every 24,000 miles.
2. The rear axle lubricant must be changed every 36,000 miles or three years, whichever occurs first.

HELPFUL REMINDERS

The rear axle lubricant must be kept free of water to avoid axle failure. Water can enter the vent hole in the axle housing if it is submerged in water, for example, during boat launching. If this occurs, the axle lubricant must be changed immediately.

The larger-than-standard capacity of the cooling system requires slightly more antifreeze for adequate winter protection.

Air Stream Trailer Towing

More than 3200 Air Stream trailer owners were gathered for their annual convention at Hershey, Pennsylvania.

"For five years you have been telling me," said Dodge's Roland Swain, "what you need in a tow vehicle. This year I've brought it to you, our new B2 and B3.

"It's a truck with a 5500 pound rear axle which will stand the load of a heavy pin weight, which these things (Air Stream) have.

"You want a seat for more than two people. We can give it to you in five-passenger, eight-passenger, even twelve-passenger. What's your pleasure?

"Last year, you said it was too long, so this year I've brought it to you in two wheelbases, 109 and 127 inches.

"It's deluxed up to where it costs as much as a car and rides equally well."

That's what he told the Air Stream conventioneers, then added to us, "Only time will tell if we are right on that or not."

That is the story of engineering, designing and building–only time will tell, in the market place, if the concept is acceptable to you, the customer.

6. Trailers

☐ Little more than a dozen years ago, the market for the small travel trailer was in California where the weather made it possible for almost year round use of the RVs.

At first the buyers were primarily the rugged outdoorsmen who were looking for something better than a pup tent for their hunting, fishing and camping forays.

The trailer world starts with what might be described as a utility trailer loaded with camping gear, then to the pop-up or tent trailers, mentioned elsewhere in this book, to the travel trailers, some fully self-contained except for the motive power.

Travel trailers are built by several hundred manufacturers spread coast to coast, and there are literally hundreds of available floor plans to suit every family need.

Retail prices range from $700 to $10,000 each, the most expensive generally the aircraft type, stressed and stretched aluminum skin over a light framework, monocoque construction.

The riveted aircraft type, such as the monocoque Avion trailer, is an expensive form of construction, but there are advantages–the areodynamic design, the curved end section and curved sides.

Aerodynamic streamlining offers advantages even at 50 miles an hour, so we are assured by Avion's Robert Cayo; more so at 60 and 65 mph on the interstate throughways.

"The decided advantage comes," Cayo said, "where there is a cross wind, or a passing truck, especially going in the opposite direction.

"A flat-sided trailer might be swayed by the blast of air from the truck, but the curved sides minimize this potential hazard."

A travel trailer is an alternate solution for those who don't want a van conversion.

Towing's not hard to learn despite width. Screen door gives insect-free ventilation.

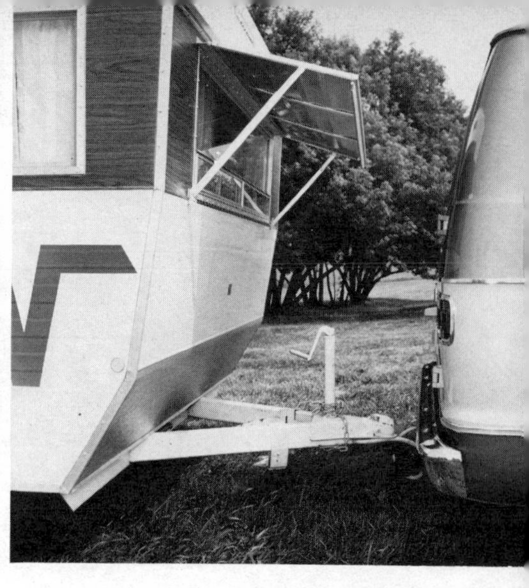

Air conditioning and window canopies make trailer living a comfortable experience.

Wood paneled interiors look smart and add a feeling of comfort to functional designs.

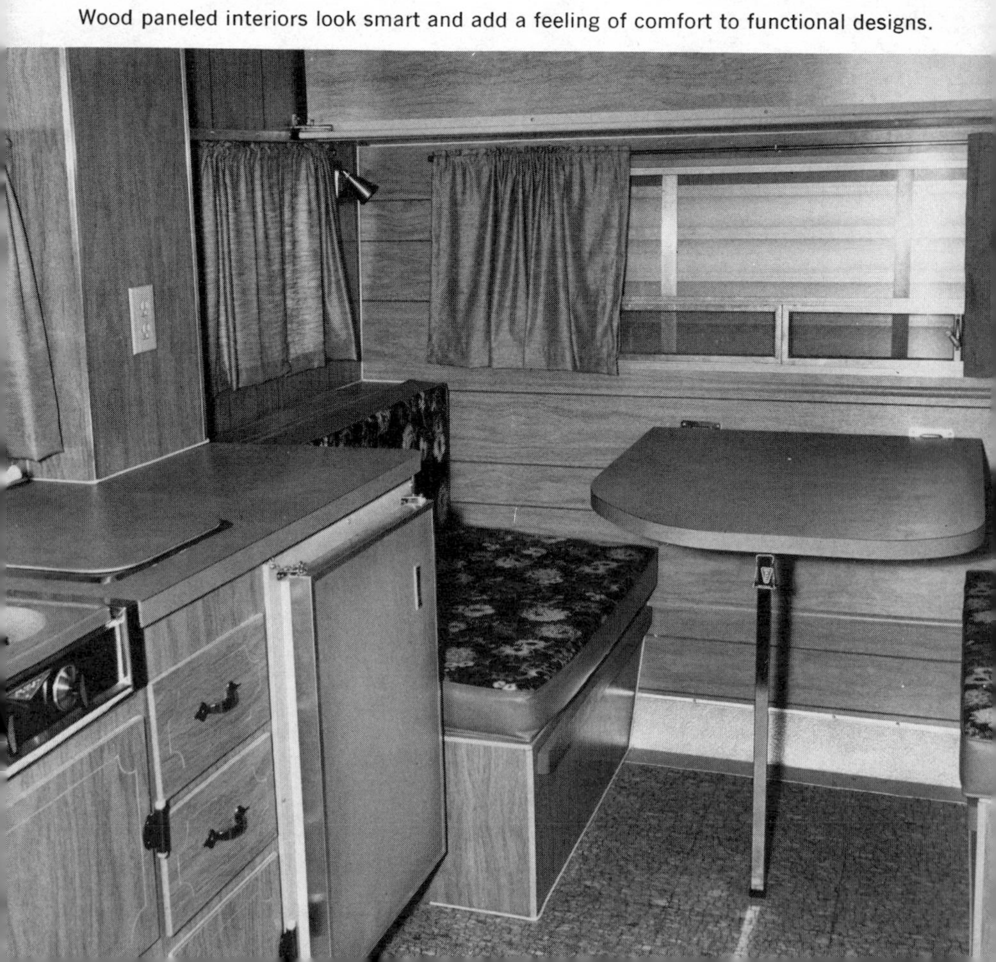

In addition to such basic items as beds, sinks, stoves and refrigerators, trailers can even be had with such luxury items as washers and dryers.

Some trailers come with complete bathrooms that have showers in addition to a sink and a toilet.

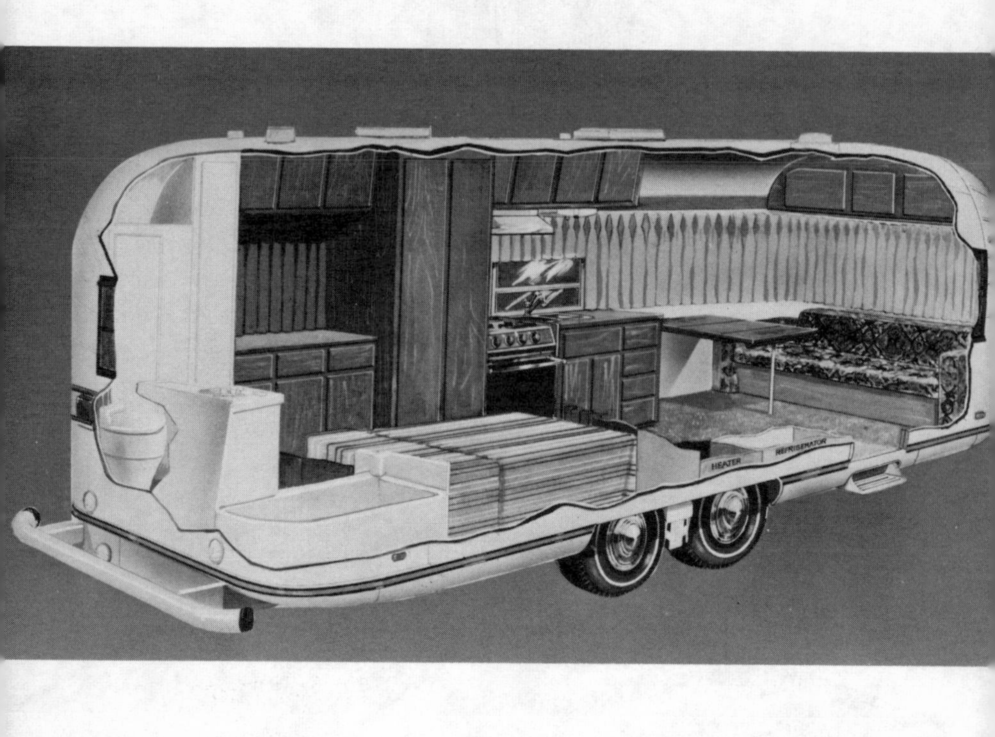
HEATER
REFRIGERATOR

Ultra
AVION

Larger trailers can be complete homes-away-from-home whether you set them up at a campsite like the dune buggy enthusiasts above or whether you just move around the country stopping only to look at the sights or catch a few fish for dinner like the family on the opposite page.

Also, the Avion style travel trailer is lighter, about two-thirds the weight of the more conventional box-shaped trailers of equivalent size.

The 31-foot Avion, for example, weighs in at about 5200 pounds compared with 8000 pounds for the conventional design.

Some of the weight savings is achieved by the use of vinyl laminated aluminum for the interior skin instead of conventional plywood.

Within the travel trailer industry, the sizes of the various factories vary from those which produce two or three units a week to thirty-five a day.

"The main problem of a new company is being able to build enough units. We have always been able to sell more than we can build. In 1970 we were building six a day. Now it is ten a day, year round."

Speaking was Ken Parker of Kon Tiki, one of the newer outfits in the business, and the "always" he mentioned is the short period from 1968 to now.

"We feel very firm about maintaining a consistent rate of production year round, so we can keep our crew together, all thirty-three of them."

Kon Tiki builds travel trailers from fifteen feet to twenty-three feet, about the middle range of the market.

Some firms build units as small as twelve or thirteen feet and a few go as large as thirty-five feet.

Some thirty-five-foot trailer owners–the trailer is thirty-five feet, not the owner–use them as less expensive mobile homes. In the trade they are called "park" models.

Some travel trailers can be fitted like a home on wheels, with dishwashers, sink disposals, even washers and dryers, believe it or not. That, however, sounds like gilding the lily.

"Once in a while," Parker said, "we have requests for custom-built trailers, but we don't do it.

"We are strictly a production line, just like an automobile factory. It's just a matter of assembling parts.

"We have an assembly line. We cut the wood to the proper sizes, then install it."

About thirty man-hours are needed to build a trailer.

If you wonder about the reluctance to fill custom orders, Parker explains it simply.

"In this business, you have to turn over your money fast, because seventy per cent of our cost is in the material. We work with about a ten or twelve per cent labor figure."

If your tastes, or your pocketbook, lead you more in the direction of the smaller, less costly camping trailers, you are in good company, because campers now represent some twenty per cent of the unit volume. More correctly, they did in 1968, when the industry produced more than 96,000 camper trailers.

That was a gain of twenty-one per cent over 1967 and it is certain the percentage has climbed even higher in the ensuing two years or so.

Of course, the advantage of a trailer, whether it be a low camper or a larger travel trailer, is that you can tow it with a conventional family auto.

One warning, which is repeated in more detail in the chapter about towing vehicles, is to be sure your auto is equipped with the factory recommended heavy duty towing package.

Don't take chances of a breakdown which will spoil the vacation.

7. Tenting

☐ Self-containment. Shower and toilet. Innerspring beds for six or eight. Hot and cold running whatever-you-want. Pure luxury as you rough it? Dollars, dollars . . . and dollars!

With their motorized palaces on wheels, equipped with champagne in the refrigerator, or Scotch on the rocks, TV dinners for the oven and air conditioning and thermostatically controlled heating in case the temperature should vary from a perfect 72 degrees, they call it camping out.

Don't knock it. It's darned nice if you go for that type of outdoorsmanship. It's comfortable, convenient, clean and neat.

Ask any wife. Some of these new units even come equipped with an automatic dishwasher–and they'll accept a mess kit if you still cling to the old ways.

There remains, however, an element which feels camping out should be just that. They don't necessarily feel this way for economy reasons, although this is certainly a darn good reason, but because they enjoy getting a bit closer to nature than the modern units provide.

Yet they don't "rough it" as the term has come to be known. Without all the expensive luxuries, but with some skill and knowledge, they still enjoy comfort, convenience, cleanliness and neatness–more, perhaps, than some of the less knowledgeable of the gentlemen campers.

These are the tent campers and there are far more of them than you might imagine. In the face of rocketing sales of wheeled and motored vacation units, tent sales have continued a steady climb.

Not the little vehicles with wheels which open up into a luxury canvas unit, also rising in sales, but the honest-to-goodness pitch and strike, stake-in-the-ground tent, with the single concession to luxury being a heavy duty canvas floor, in some cases.

Why a tent? Reasons are varied. Economy is certainly one. Convenience in the form of a small, packaged, easy to carry shelter is another. The ability to build this shelter anywhere cannot be ignored. The desire to be only a canvas thickness away from the outdoors is an important reason to campers who prefer tents.

Let's break the breed down a bit. The professional camper, the trail guide, the deep woods hunter or fisherman, the Boy Scout, the men we have come to know as backwoodsmen, they all need tents.

Everything they bring with them, food, shelter, clothing and whatever luxury they allow themselves, must be packed in on their backs.

Their tent shelters may run from a simple eight-by-eight tarpaulin, which they can pitch over a ridgepole lashed to a tree trunk, to a fully floored pup tent.

These shelters can be erected anywhere and even a ridgepole tarp will shelter a man from the heaviest storm if it is pegged solidly at the corners and ditched around the edges.

Come on now. There is something to be said for snuggling down into a warm sleeping bag beneath a tarp or in a pup tent, far back in the wilds and with a steady rain drumming on the canvas roof.

Outside, hanging from a tree limb, or inside if the storm is all that bad, will be the rucksack containing all the other basic necessities for preserving life and limb in relative comfort.

The food will probably be freeze dried, for this is the lightest, easiest to pack and prepare food known. Where these men travel, this somewhat tasty food can be supplemented with fish and game.

There will be a convenient flashlight or lantern, a change of socks, perhaps a shaving kit (hold the lotion) and probably a weapon of some sort. There will be a canteen and water purification tablets.

There will be matches, a map and a compass. Depending upon the reason for the outing, there will be hunting gear or fishing gear or perhaps a camera outfit. You'll probably find a length of rope somewhere in the pack.

That's about it, depending upon the individual camper. Everything he carries can be folded, rolled, packed and carried on the back.

He is his own man, he is self-sustaining, he could live no matter what happened back in the city–or even if the city simply disappeared. He has no ties to civilization and needs none. He is the true, old-fashioned, honest-to-goodness camper.

He is in the minority today, even though he has available to him the vast majority of camping areas, including everywhere nobody else is.

Though he lives in relative comfort in the wilds, he has always been known as a rugged outdoorsman and he is fading from the scene in our mad rush for more and more comfort and convenience.

Still, you might want to try his method at least once, if only for the sake of comparison. Leave the luxury gear at home, put on your heavy shoes, don your spartan pack and try the woods.

Do it in the city park, then if worse comes to worst this first time you can always hail a passing policeman for help, or to bum a ride home.

Most tenters are in the other group, that great majority known as amateur campers. We do it for pure fun, trying to make it as comfortable as possible at the same time.

We have a nice home with hot showers and television, yet we prefer to get out away from all this from time to time, especially from the boob tube.

So, we pack our gear, and this becomes quite a bit more involved than with the back pack, and we head for–where?

For us, the state has provided. National parks abound, State parks dot the areas in between and private campgrounds fill the remaining points of interest.

The wonderful part of all of this is that, barring the real wilderness areas of our country, these parks and campgrounds are situated in America's loveliest spots. Where else but Yosemite, for example, could you live and eat and sleep in your own "home" at the base of some of the world's largest and oldest trees, or beneath granite crags of breathtaking beauty, or beside crystal clear tumbling mountain streams–all for the modest price of a tent and a couple of bucks a day to the Rangers?

The instant you tire of this rugged living, you have, only a stone's throw away, a modern hotel complex with stores, restaurants and other conveniences. A modern hotel? We didn't think you would chicken out, but so be it.

Generally speaking, the same is true with State parks and private campgrounds, all of which abound. Most of these areas are at or near recreation areas with all the conveniences.

The hot shower and flush toilet that didn't come as a built-in will be nearby and the short walk may figure to a dollar a step in savings. We'll agree to that concession to modern living.

A Detroit, Michigan judge, who started camping with his father and brothers in 1933, rates the Greenbelt, Maryland National Park near the nation's capital as the best within commuting distance of any large city.

Judge Gillis and his sons still use the umbrella tent his father bought for use at the 1933 Century of Progress. Mrs. Gillis gets her vacation by getting rid of the three males, the judge said.

Of course you might decide to go even farther from civilization with your gear, gaining in natural beauty and solitude and sacrificing only a few of the conveniences. Bring these along with you, as we'll explain shortly, and you've lost nothing. Meanwhile, you have camped where your gentlemen camper brothers with their self-contained wonders are unable or unwilling to go.

It is also a good way to get away from the cares of the world, the constant bad news we read and hear daily, politics, deadlines, budgets, profit and loss, the stock market. Sounds great, doesn't it!

The amount of baggage you haul will be in direct relation to the amount of comfort you seek, the number of people who will be seeking it and the depth into the woods you plan to penetrate.

First, there will be the tent itself. Just the two of you? There's nothing really wrong with a pup tent, if all you plan to do is sleep in it. These little units are terrible if you plan to invite the campers at the next site over for a game of bridge, but otherwise they'll do the job nicely.

They are light, easy to pitch and strike (no friend, this is not the picket line kind of strike, this is the take-it-down-and-pack-it to leave kind, getaway day), easy to carry and sell in the neighborhood of only ten or twenty dollars.

Fully zippered models with an outside framework to hold them steady, fewer stakes to pound and a heavy duty canvas floor are only about thirty dollars.

But this usually isn't the cup of tea of the average family tent camper. There are the children to consider and Mother wants at least a bit of space in the habitat. So your choice of tents is restricted.

Restricted? Yes, to literally hundreds of larger models encompassing size and feature choices enough to drive a sober man to drink.

Do you want picture windows in your tent? You can have them—and don't laugh. This feature makes for cross-ventilation that is a pleasure on warm summer nights at the site.

A floor is almost a basic necessity. Most modern tents include this feature automatically, a few of solid materials, but most of heavy duty canvas.

A hint here. Make it a rule to remove your shoes upon entering and make everybody live by it. The tent will remain spotless inside and much more pleasant to live in and store away. You'll find that kicking off shoes at the door is no problem. The Japanese have been doing it for centuries and they haven't found it to be a great chore.

A friend recalled the time they had just put down a beautiful new white wall-to-wall carpet in the apartment.

Friend and wife came home to be greeted by some out of town guests, all sitting in the living room in their stocking feet.

It was the first day for the new white carpet and, by golly, their son wasn't taking any chances when he welcomed the guests at the door.

Floored tents come in all sizes, either outside framed or staked over poles. Here, the choice is a personal one. The frames, even though they fold down, are extra items to carry and store, but the tent will stay neater and perhaps a bit more solid at the site. Then, too, you must also carry poles for this type of a unit.

The trend is without question to the outside frame tents, if trends mean anything to you. Manufacturers claim they are easier to set up and take down. Many campers insist, however, that their main advantage lies in the fact that they keep the tent neat and solid and square looking.

Also, if the tent is umbrella style, there is no space stealing center pole with the outside frame model.

Modern tents come in square, round and rectangular sizes, with and without screened front porches or patios. Bear in mind that the more elaborate the fixtures, the more difficult the unit will be to pitch and strike, but the more comfortable and convenient it will be to live in. Obviously, the larger the tent, the heavier the folded up unit is to carry.

You will see what has become a typical unit at campgrounds across the country and this might be a tent to consider.

It will be about nine by twelve feet in size, with an outside frame. It will have an umbrella style center area with a single side room. It will come equipped with nylon or fiberglass mesh-covered windows and zippered storm enclosures. The door will be mesh covered and flap covered, both with easy operating zippers.

The tent will weigh in the neighborhood of sixty pounds. The floor will be of heavy canvas. The colors will vary, according to the tastes of mother-camper.

The price. Less than $100 unless you desire gold-plated hardware. Properly cared for, this tent will last for many, many years and is as comfortable and convenient as any tent could be. In a pinch, six adults can spend a night of relative comfort inside, in a rainstorm.

You need more space? If you don't mind spending about $150 and lugging eighty pounds or so of canvas, you can buy a similar unit with side rooms on both sides of the main umbrella. These will run about nine by eighteen feet inside, and otherwise will have the same features.

This latter unit will put you in the luxury class of tenters.

Unfortunately, the tent is not the only item you must consider when a camping trip of this sort is planned. Whether or not you decide to eat at the local restaurant, there are other things you will need.

This, in fact, is the reason for the startling increase in sales of the tent trailer unit, for many families found that a small utility trailer became a standard part of their equipment anyhow.

Into the trailer, hooked to the family auto, went first the basic tent and poles and frames and other accessories. Then, since there are no light switches in a tent, went lanterns and flashlights.

Some campers pack folding cots, others prefer sleeping bags on the floor of the tent, but one way or the other you'll probably use sleeping bags. Sheets and blankets are a nuisance in a tent. The trailer, you can see, is already beginning to fill up.

If you plan to take the children along–and this is a wonderful way for a family to vacation together–the load is even greater. If you plan to cook, and most families do, you'll pack the butane or alcohol two- or three-burner stove.

Don't forget food for the family for the length of the trip. Into the most necessary cooler box or refrigerator operated by the car battery, you'll pack food which must remain cold–luncheon meats, steaks, eggs, bacon and the like.

Into other corrugated cartons or sacks you can pack canned goods, bread and other cupboard or pantry stored foods.

Another hint. You can eat almost as well as you do at home if you will include the convenience foods available today. These powdered, flaked, dry foods need only water to bring them back to full life and there's nothing like flapjacks for breakfast at the campsite, a batch of hot chile-con-carne for lunch and mashed potatoes for dinner with your steak.

Powdered eggs aren't bad either, if you can forget that men in combat are often forced to eat them or starve.

In any case, the food you take along will depend upon your experience as a tent camper and your particular needs.

By all means look over the shoulders of your neighbors in the next site. Tent campers are great ones to share experiences, good and bad, so you can pick up many tips this way.

Camp clothing will also be packed into the trailer. Here you must bear down hard on the wives. Clothing for such a trip is necessarily spartan. Jeans, T-shirts, heavy shoes, a warm sweater or jacket and customary underwear changes should do it unless you plan to stay for an extended time near a swanky resort.

The disadvantages, if you consider them so, of tent camping are apparent. In a wheeled and powered unit, for example, many of the above mentioned chores would be unnecessary due to built-ins, or handled by having permanent gear aboard. Other problems in a tent can be wind and water.

Although normally quite secure, high winds can whip and flap the tents and even blow them down. Not often, it is true, but it can happen. The only recourse of the camper in this situation is to strike the tent and sleep in the car.

If nature doesn't often show herself in this way, she does very often appear as a cold night.

A tent is difficult to heat in spite of the tent heaters presently on the market, another piece of equipment to haul. As a matter of fact, a butane or other Coleman-type lantern does the job just about as well if you can sleep with all the glare. Snuggled down inside a warm sleeping bag, you probably won't even notice the cold anyhow.

Then you have the problem, if it is that, of pitching and striking a tent–even though most manufacturers of tents have this chore planned down to a simple science that any wife can handle, but won't!

Tent camping is obviously not as comfortable and convenient as camping in the modern motored units–but then is this latter really camping? Many

For people who plan to do a lot of tent camping and who don't really care to rough it all that much, the compact, complete tent trailer is a logical compromise. Only 39 inches high when closed, this Sherwood Regent model opens to 20 feet with a 54-inch bed at either end and has a three-burner stove, icebox and sink.

campers feel it is not. They feel that to really enjoy the outing, you must get a bit closer to nature than these units allow.

How much does it all cost? Effectively, this is impossible to say, for campers' tastes vary so widely.

It will probably fall somewhere between $250 and $500 for a modern, comfortable tent and all new accessory equipment, including a small trailer to haul with. The simplest tent trailers start at around $350 and go on up to about $1300, so you can see that it is again a matter of taste as well as economy.

Be that as it may, simple tent camping has been around longer than any of them—and will without a doubt be around for as long as man enjoys real 100 per cent camping.

Likely, families will still be tenting on that day when we can plug our fancy motorized vacation units into a computerized highway and sleep all the way to the campgrounds, for there is something pleasant and serene about a tent—the smell, the feel, the harkening back to our ancestors—which cannot be equaled by any other shelter.

8. *Off-Road Camping*

☐ Family camping is one of the most satisfying and economical forms of outdoor recreation. The growth of special vehicle production and the availability of options designed for trailer towing for passenger cars is proof of the popularity of this form of recreation.

In addition to thousands of camping areas with paved parking and complete sanitary facilities, there are millions of acres of limited access land to attract the hunter, fisherman and outdoor enthusiast who wants to get away from it all.

Unless one lives in the heart of such an area, transportation is essential and this must be good transport, capable of negotiating dirt roads and rutted trails safely and without a costly breakdown, bodily injury or a rescue operation which could run a modest vacation budget into financial disaster.

The most popular vehicle for the occasional off-road camper is the family car. This might be supplemented by a light tent trailer or a heavier camper-trailer.

For more frequent forays into the great outdoors, the slide-on or chassis mounted camper is desirable, as are the compact sportsman wagons or van conversions.

The ultimate in luxury and comfort afield are the motor home, self-contained vehicles. All are ideally suited to paved road travel when properly loaded, but limited in varying degrees for off-road use.

The passenger car, whether it is sedan or station wagon, has a design load limit geared to normal use. Recognizing the fact that it might be more heavily loaded, either with passenger or camping gear, or be towing a trailer, factory-designed options to increase the load limit are available, often called trailer towing packages.

Heavy duty springs and shocks, load-rated for a wide range of trailer weights, extra capacity radiators, transmission coolers and heavy duty tires can be ordered to make the family car safe for the job of transporting passengers and giving creature comforts over some pretty rough going.

Even with the heavy duty suspension options, careful leading of passenger car or wagon is a must for all kind of highway or off-road travel. Tail-heavy cars are not only hazardous on the highway, but virtually impossible to navigate on any but the best back country roads.

While rear luggage compartment capacity is generous in its cubic footage, it is rather limited in weight capacity, especially when carrying rear seat passengers.

Off-road camping with just a passenger car necessitates carrying tent, sleeping bags, groceries, stove, water supply and clothing.

Always load the heavier items as far forward in the rear compartment as possible or ahead of the rear axle inside the car, reserving the rearmost section for lighter goods.

Water cans, for example the flat five-gallon kind of either plastic or metal, can add a lot of rear end weight if placed in the trunk but will store nicely on the floor of the rear passenger compartment, restricting leg room for adults, but furnishing ideal foot rests for the kids. Either one is better than bottoming-out damage or getting the rear overhang stuck on the edge of a dry creek bed.

Roof racks are handy cargo carriers and safe if properly used. Only lightweight cargo should be carried here and load height should never exceed 18 inches from the roof line.

Covering and lashing down are very important to prevent weather damage, loss of cargo and hazard to following cars.

A properly mounted tarpaulin should lap under the load at the forward end and then be lashed securely all around to prevent wind pocketing underneath and lifting the cover.

The only thing worse than a flapping tarp is a wet sleeping bag.

Heavy duty, oversize tires, four-ply nylon or better are recommended for all types of off-road use whether or not a trailer is towed. Negotiating rocks and ruts requires a tire of much higher impact resistance than needed for paved highway use. A cut tire miles from nowhere is a serious problem.

Be sure that the spare is also capable of good rough service. A baldy is not even reliable as an emergency replacement in areas that could damage a good heavy duty tire. A good tire pump or emergency air tank is nice to have along on an off-road tour.

Often, cars can be extricated from soft sand or gravel by deflating the tires a bit to increase traction area. It's nice to be able to pump them back up to normal operating pressures again.

Getting unstuck and the ability to pull out of poor traction areas can be more easily done with a car equipped with limited slip or sure-grip differential. Such an option is definitely recommended for off-road travel.

Be sure to include some emergency tools in the camping equipment gear. A good working bumper jack, plus a small screw jack, an axe, some 12-inch squares of thick lumber for basing up the jack and a long-handled shovel will prove invaluable for freeing a bogged down car.

Some off-road enthusiasts carry several rolls of old carpeting or heavy canvas about 18 inches wide, cut into 10-foot lengths. Spread out under the rear wheels they can provide better footing for the tires in soft dirt, sand or gravel and also work well on icy surfaces.

On any back country trip by motor vehicle of any kind, a set of skid chains can prove invaluable in an emergency. If there is a possibility of snow or ice conditions, they are a must as some tests rate them superior to the best snow tires on icy surfaces.

Even with a properly equipped vehicle, safe back country travel requires excellent judgment and skill on the part of the driver.

Passenger cars, with their relatively low ground clearance and long front and rear overhang, are limited to the degree of abrupt banking or grade they can negotiate without hanging up.

Deeply rutted roads with rocky centers can knock a hole in the crankcase, tear off the exhaust system and damage the differential if the driver is not careful in judging his clearance and speed.

Trailer towing, except with the very small tent trailers, is also hazardous, with the extra danger of wiping off roof vents and side protrusions on overhanging branches or heavy brush.

Many back country enthusiasts prefer a pickup truck, either single or crew cab, with four-wheel-drive option for the real rough country.

These vehicles are capable of carrying a lot of bulky cargo on the bed with no noticeable lowering of body ground clearance.

Bigger wheels and tires, plus higher overall body height despite long rear overhang, allows travel over much rougher country than with passenger cars.

However, load heavy cargo well forward with the lighter stuff reserved for extreme tail end. Again, tires are very important and must be of premium heavy duty quality to withstand the high impact of rock-rutted back country roads. Much the same emergency equipment is recommended for trucks, camper trucks, vans and motor homes as for passenger cars.

When a slide-on camper body is added to a pickup truck, the center of gravity is raised considerably, limiting the degree of side tilt before roll over. Great care must be taken when angling up or down trails to avoid such danger.

Stowing everything from dishes to supplies must be carefully done to avoid scattering them all over the interior as the rig sways a great deal more on off-road travel than it does on the pavement.

Tires are even more important because of the additional overall weight of camper body and its cargo. The same is true of chassis mounted campers, although the manufacturers are generally careful to supply adequate tires and chassis for their units.

Off-road or wilderness camping can be done with almost any kind of vehicle but you must be fully prepared with more equipment, including emergency items, than you would normally take on an outing to a populated area.

The bulk of both cab-over slide-ons and chassis mounts limits their ability to follow the trail of a smaller or four-wheel-drive vehicle, but with good driver judgment and skill, they can negotiate some fairly rough terrain.

The sportsman van type vehicle is as good an all purpose combination in-town highway and back country transportation package as one could desire.

Whether used to carry a lot of tent camping cargo or equipped with all of the creature comforts including either a bubble or pop-up top, their low center of gravity, excellent roadability, adequate horsepower, and forward control driving position, give them passenger car comfort and driving ease and nearly the same rough country off-road agility of a pickup truck.

The rather short front and rear overhang is high enough to allow passage over some fairly steep drop-offs that one finds when fording stream beds or dry gullies.

They are available in a choice of front and rear axle load ratings to suit about any gross weight or trailer towing requirement, along with optional V8 engines, automatic transmissions and anti-spin differentials.

The large motor homes which are virtual Pullman cars on rubber tires are not exactly designed for extremely rough off-road travel.

Their overall dimensions rather limit them to fairly wide roadways with good side and top clearance. Maneuverability on sharp switchbacks is difficult if not impossible.

With gross vehicle weights of 10,000 pounds and up, the makers are very careful to select the proper chassis, springs, axles and tire loadings for the design use, i.e., paved or improved roads.

Even with the dual tires supplied with most vehicles of this type, they will bog down in soft surfaces and it is just not practical to venture too deeply into primitive areas unless the road surface is good.

As camping areas become more and more civilized and crowded, there is an increasing desire for the real outdoor enthusiast to penetrate deeper into virgin territory.

Hunters and fishermen especially will stop at nothing to find that unfished lake or unhunted stretch of forest or mountain. Very often their enthusiasm overshadows their motorized equipment, skill in its use and personal judgment.

The old cliché of "follow a few simple rules" does not hold true for off-road camping with large motor vehicles.

While most of the rules are simple, there are more than a few that should be followed for an enjoyable off-road camping trip. Follow these and the chances of success can be 100 per cent.

Be sure that your vehicle is properly equipped for the trip with preventive maintenance and checks on battery, alternator, cooling system, transmission fluid, power steering pump, fan belts, brakes and fluid and tires.

Assuming the car is properly equipped for trailer towing with chassis mounted hitch and equalizer coupling rated for the tongue and trailer weight, remember that the total length of car and trailer might be as long as 50 feet, limiting back country travel somewhat.

Automatic transmissions are great for trailering, but long pulls in lower gears with heavy rigs will raise hydraulic fluid temperatures to the breaking point. Investigate the need for an additional transmission cooler before such a trip.

Take along spares, including the proper tools to handle the replacement. Fan belts are especially vulnerable to the hard use and dust and dirt one encounters in back country travel.

A spare tire for both vehicle and trailer should not be overlooked, as well as properly working jacks and lug wrenches to do the job.

Oil bath air cleaners will prolong engine life in the dust of off-road travel, but the dry element type does a good job if maintained. These should be serviced once the campsite is reached to insure efficient operation and adequate protection on the way back out.

Trail dust seeping into even the best sealed car trunk or camper door can spoil the anticipated relaxation when one reaches the campsite if a thorough housecleaning of cargo or interior is necessary.

Keep camper and trailer windows and doors closed on dusty stretches. Sealing rear doors and trunks with air conditioner duct tape is worth the time and effort in protecting interiors from a layer of the gritty stuff. Do not seal vents to appliances with pilot lights such as water heaters, gas refrigerators or space heaters.

Check LP gas tanks and plumbing before starting out and after arrival at location. Loose tank hold downs can fracture the copper lines used on most systems and back country is no place for an explosion or fire.

Tanks should be free of any movement that can be aggravated by the extra vibration and bumping of rutted and pot holed roads.

Make sure slide-on camper bodies are securely tied down to the truck bed. Turnbuckles should be safety wired or locked tightly with an extra wing nut and checked periodically enroute.

Any added appendages such as exterior spare tire mount, trail bike carrier or luggage rack should also be checked for loose mounts, cracked brackets or missing nuts and bolts; and the addition of lock washers or safety wire is recommended.

As one is apt to be squeezing through brush lined trails and under low branches, be sure the roof vents are closed and utility connections and water fill pipes are not wiped off in the process. Carry a wrench of the proper size on the seat to loosen mounting nuts on extension side mirrors so they can be folded back to prevent damage from brush or branches.

Many back country campers tow small boats behind both passenger cars and camper rigs. The boat hull is a handy and easy to load cargo carrier but, remember, most boat trailers, especially the tires, are designed for the boat and trailer only.

Any heavy cargo dictates the need for extra capacity tires, either for highway or off-road travel. Don't forget a spare.

Be sure there is enough fuel for the round trip. Remote back country is not noted for its gas stations or passing motorists.

Carry extra fuel only in approved containers, stored away from exhaust heat, electrical connections or sharp tools that might puncture the container. Include a pouring spout in the emergency kit.

Extra water for the cooling system is a good idea, but never add water to a boiling radiator unless the engine is running. For mountain camping where sub-freezing temperatures may be the rule at night, antifreeze of the permanent type is necessary.

Select the campsite carefully. It is always a good idea to turn the rig around, heading back out so there is no last minute problem of maneuvering when it's time to break camp.

Vehicles should be parked on firm level ground with good clearance all around. Avoid a campsite close to steep banks that show signs of landslide or tinder-dry brush in high fire hazard areas.

Know something about the climate of the area and if occasional thunderstorms or cloudbursts are the rule, give dry washes or wide creek banks plenty of room to fill with water without washing out the campsite.

Respect all fire closure areas and secure the proper fire permit if required. Fire permits are usually necessary for camp stoves also if they are used outside a camper or trailer.

Campsites under shade trees are always desirable, but be sure to avoid those with heavy dead branches that might come crashing down at the slightest breeze.

Avoid excessive use of the vehicle battery. Lighting poses a steady drain that might not leave enough reserve power for starting the engine, so run it occasionally to recharge the battery.

Remember, it takes about fifteen minutes of fast engine idle to restore the current used in starting, more if the battery is nearly exhausted. The heavy duty 70 amp/hour optional batteries are a good investment for off-road camping trips.

The prime necessity to successful off-road camping is good judgment and skill in the proper use of the proper vehicle for the existing trail.

When in doubt about the road ahead, explore on foot for soft surfaces, water too deep for the vehicle or banks too steep for the front or rear overhang.

Be prepared for emergencies with the proper tools and spares, and don't feel it's chicken to pass up a route you are not sure you can make.

While getting there is great fun and adventure, getting back without incident never spoiled an off-road camping trip.

9. Cooking—Menus

☐ Much of the advice you read or hear about camper cooking usually centers around jiffy this and jiffy that and how to prepare an eight-course meal for sixteen people in ten minutes, using only a can opener.

All you hear about are canned foods or dehydrated foods or the newer freeze-dried items.

These are fine, in their place. For example, if you spend all your time backpacking and are limited in how much you can carry.

However, if you own a modern camper, trailer, camper van or motor home, you could be doing your stomach a disservice if you limit yourself to just those items.

Many campers don't like to eat that way and they don't.

This does not mean they prepare great time-consuming menus, but they are willing to spend more than ten minutes getting ready for what they consider the most relaxing and therefore most important part of the camping day.

They don't want to eat too differently from the way they do at home. After a week in the wilds, they want to return home still on speaking terms with their stomachs. They do it with frozen foods.

This means most meals are built around fresh meats, vegetables and fruits. This also gives them a supply of ready-to-bake pies, pastries and dinner rolls or bread.

They rely little on canned or dried fruits, using them only sparingly to supplement the frozen foods.

So, who's got a portable freezer or frozen food locker? Chances are everyone has—they just haven't thought of them that way.

If you are an average camper, you probably started out with a standard passenger car or station wagon and carried a tent, sleeping bags, portable stove and an ice chest.

When you bought your camper, you figured you didn't need these items any more, so stored them.

Dust off that old ice chest. It's your new frozen food locker in disguise. All you do is add dry ice, your frozen foods and you are in business. If you don't have an ice chest, they are readily available in most sporting goods stores, many hardware stores, discount stores and even super drug stores.

The medium to large size ice chest can easily accommodate about 20 pounds of dry ice, plus a good variety of packaged frozen foods and meats. If the ice chest is well insulated, and most modern ones are, and if the lid fits tightly, your dry ice should last five days before it needs replenishing.

Where do you buy dry ice? It is listed in the yellow pages, about a dime a pound.

With proper planning you can get by with opening it twice a day, either the night before, or the early morning, take out the frozen meat and put that in your camper ice box. Later in the day, take out the vegetables and desserts.

Most dry ice comes wrapped in heavy brown paper, about two pounds per package. Leave it in the paper as this wrapping acts an insulator to make it last longer. Place the food packages toward the bottom of the chest, with the dry ice on top.

Warning–do not touch the dry ice with your hands. You will suffer bad "burns," actually frostbite. Also, do not leave that ice chest in the closed up living quarters, otherwise that carbon dioxide will eat up the oxygen.

The menus you can prepare using frozen foods are limitless. Using pre-prepared sauces will enable you to duplicate anything you usually fix in your kitchen.

And it won't take much more time than if you were preparing canned, dried or dehydrated foods. The family will love you for it.

Old-fashioned bear-size appetites go with the wide open spaces and fresh air. This calls for good 'n hearty cooking. A bit of planning ahead will assure meal time success in camp.

Keep the meals simple, hearty and easy to fix. Even the cook needs a vacation, so use the convenience foods, in addition to the frozen items mentioned earlier, such as canned condensed soups.

Plan your food supply according to the area in which you will be camping, but be flexible. If you pass a fresh fruit and vegetable stand, or find one nearby the camp, incorporate the fresh foods into the menu, especially those which need little cooking or preparation.

Plan bigger helpings than you do at home. The fresh air, plus climbing, swimming and running creates big appetites.

Switch duties among the family members so the chores do not become boring. Let each take his or her turn at cooking, dishwashing, house cleaning and grounds keeping.

For outdoor campfire cooking, wrap foods which might scorch in heavy duty aluminum foil. All-in-one meat and vegetable meals are favored by experienced campers, since it is likely the stove will accommodate only one or two pots.

You can save space, avoid breakage and reduce dishwashing by using paper or plastic coated plates, cups, even spoons and forks.

A delicious dish you cook in one pan, and quickly, who could ask for more?

The basics of skillet cooking are simple. Have a heavy-bottom pan that heats evenly, is roomy enough to hold all the ingredients without crowding.

Combine foods. As in casseroles, many recipes call for meat or fish or cheese, plus a pasta or potatoes, plus sauce.

Condensed soups used as sauces give luscious flavor, mingling through all the ingredients and resulting in irresistible eating.

Serve your quick supper dish piping hot, with a salad and warm rolls, then collect the compliments!

The Menus

SKILLET CHICKEN DELIGHT

- 2 pounds chicken parts
- ¼ cup flour
- ¼ cup butter or margarine
- 1 can (10½ ounces) condensed chicken gumbo soup
- ½ soup can water
- 2 tablespoons ketchup

Dust chicken with flour, brown in butter. Stir in soup, water and ketchup. Cover; simmer 45 minutes or until chicken is tender. Stir often. Makes 4 to 6 servings.

CHICKEN CROQUETTES WITH SAUCE

- 1 can (10½ ounces) condensed cream of chicken soup
- 1½ cups minced cooked chicken
- ¼ cup fine dry bread crumbs
- 2 tablespoons minced parsley
- 1 tablespoon finely minced onion
- Bread crumbs
- Shortening
- ¼ cup milk

Combine ⅓ cup soup with chicken, ¼ cup crumbs, parsley and onion. Form into 6 croquettes; roll in bread crumbs. Chill. Fry croquettes in shortening until thoroughly heated and lightly browned. Blend remaining soup with milk; heat; serve over croquettes. Makes 3 servings.

One-burner cooking can be more appetizing than you might have though

Add a can of soup and a few herbs to chicken and you have a simple, delicious meal.

CREAMED CHICKEN

½ cup chopped celery
2 tablespoons butter or margarine
1 can (10½ ounces) condensed cream of chicken soup
⅓ to ½ cup milk
1 can (5 ounces) boned chicken or turkey, or 1 cup diced cooked chicken or turkey

Cook celery in butter until tender. Blend in other ingredients. Heat; stir often. Serve over split corn bread squares, biscuits or toast. Makes 3 servings.

CHUNKY CHICKEN HASH

1 can (10½ ounces) condensed cream of mushroom soup
⅓ to ½ cup milk
1 can (5 ounces) boned chicken or turkey, or 1 cup diced cooked chicken or turkey
1 can (8 ounces) cut green beans, drained
2 tablespoons diced pimiento
Dash nutmeg
Dash pepper
3 cups hot cooked rice

Blend soup and milk; add chicken, beans, pimiento, nutmeg and pepper. Heat slowly; stir often. Serve over cooked rice. Makes 4 servings.

SEAFOOD MARYLAND

- 1 can (10 ounces) frozen condensed cream of shrimp soup
- ½ cup light cream
- 2 cups cut-up cooked seafood (lobster, shrimp, white fish)
- 1 tablespoon chopped parsley
- 1 teaspoon lemon juice
- Toast

Heat soup and cream together slowly until soup is thawed; stir often. Add seafood, parsley and lemon juice. Heat. Serve over toast. Makes 3 to 4 servings.

STROGANOFF SAUCE

- ¼ cup chopped onion
- ½ teaspoon paprika
- 2 tablespoons butter or margarine
- 1 can (10½ ounces) condensed golden mushroom soup
- ¼ cup sour cream

In saucepan, cook onion with paprika in butter until tender. Stir in soup and sour cream. Heat; stir now and then. Makes 1½ cups sauce. Serve with beef patties or sliced cooked beef or veal.

SOUPER STROGANOFF

- 1½ pounds round steak, cut in thin strips
- ¼ cup flour
- Dash pepper
- ¼ cup butter or margarine
- 1 can (4 ounces) sliced mushrooms, drained
- ½ cup chopped onion
- 1 small clove garlic, minced
- 1 can (10½ ounces) condensed beef broth or consommé
- 1 cup sour cream
- 3 cups cooked noodles

Dust meat with flour and pepper. In skillet, brown meat in butter. Add mushrooms, onion and garlic; brown lightly. Stir in soup. Cover; cook 1 hour or until meat is tender; stir often. Gradually blend in sour cream; cook over low heat for 5 minutes. Serve over noodles. Makes 4 generous servings.

CHILI LIVER

- 4 slices bacon
- 1 pound liver, sliced
- 2 tablespoons flour
- 1 can (10½ ounces) condensed onion soup
- ¼ cup chili sauce or ketchup

Cook bacon until crisp; remove from pan; drain and crumble. Dust liver with flour; brown in bacon drippings. Add bacon and remaining ingredients. Cover; simmer 30 minutes or until tender. Uncover; cook for a few minutes to thicken sauce. Makes 4 servings.

CREAMY HAM AND PEAS WITH NOODLES

- 1½ cups diced cooked ham
- ¼ cup chopped onion
- 2 tablespoons butter or margarine
- 1 can (10½ ounces) condensed cream of celery soup
- ½ cup milk
- 1 can (8 ounces) peas, drained
- Cooked noodles
- Toasted slivered almonds

In saucepan, brown ham and cook onion in butter until tender. Stir in soup, milk and peas. Heat; stir now and then. Serve on noodles; sprinkle with almonds. Makes 4 servings.

BARBECUED BOLOGNA ROAST

- 1 can (10¾ ounces) condensed tomato soup
- 2 to 4 tablespoons sweet pickle relish
- ¼ cup chopped onion
- 1 tablespoon brown sugar
- 1 tablespoon vinegar or lemon juice
- 1 tablespoon Worcestershire
- 1 to 1½ pounds bologna, in one piece

Combine all ingredients for sauce. Cover; simmer for 10 minutes. Slash bologna in 2 or 3 places, about ½-inch deep. Place on grill over glowing coals. Cook, brushing with sauce and turning every few minutes until nicely browned. Slice and serve. Spoon on remaining hot sauce. Makes 4 to 6 servings.

FRISKY SOUR

- 2 cans (10½ ounces each) condensed beef broth
- ½ soup can water
- 2 ice cubes
- ¼ to ⅓ cup lemon juice

Put all ingredients in a shaker or jar with tight fitting cover. Cover and shake well. Serve in cold drink cups. Makes 4 to 6 servings.

SPANISH RICE WITH TUNA

- ½ cup chopped onion
- ¼ cup chopped green pepper
- 2 tablespoons butter or margarine
- 1 can (10¾ ounces) condensed tomato soup
- 1 soup can water
- ½ cup rice
- 1 teaspoon salt
- 1 teaspoon Worcestershire
- ½ small clove garlic, minced
- 1 can (7 ounces) tuna, drained and flaked

In saucepan, cook onion and green pepper in butter until tender. Stir in soup, water, rice and seasonings. Cover; cook over low heat 20 minutes; stir now and then. Add tuna. Cook 10 minutes longer or until rice is tender. Makes 4 servings.

CELERY STICKS WITH PEANUT BUTTER ORANGE FILLING

½ cup plain or crunchy peanut butter
¼ cup orange juice
⅛ teaspoon salt
8 stalks celery

Blend peanut butter, orange juice and salt. Fill celery stalks. Makes 4 servings.

SKILLET HERBED CHICKEN

2 pounds chicken parts
2 tablespoons butter or margarine
1 can (10½ ounces) condensed cream of chicken soup
½ cup sour cream
¼ teaspoon each: marjoram, paprika and thyme
Dash of cloves

In skillet, brown chicken in butter; add remaining ingredients. Cover; cook over low heat 45 minutes, or until tender. Stir now and then. Uncover the last 5 minutes to thicken. Makes 4 servings.

TOMATO BLOSSOM SOUP

1 can (10½ ounces) condensed cream of celery soup
1 can (10¾ ounces) condensed tomato soup
1 cup milk
1 cup water
½ cup shredded process cheese

In saucepan, combine soups, milk, water and cloves. Gradually blend in water. Add cheese and oregano. Heat; stir now and then. Garnish with chopped parsley, chopped green onion or thinly sliced onion. Makes 5 or 6 servings.

LONDON BROIL

1 cup salad oil
½ cup wine vinegar
¼ cup chopped onion
1 teaspoon salt
Dash pepper
Dash garlic powder
1 teaspoon oregano
1 flank steak, about 3 pounds
1 can (4 ounces) sliced mushrooms

Combine first seven ingredients in jar with cover. Shake well. Marinate flank steak in mixture for about 2 hours, turning meat occasionally. Broil the meat about 3 inches from heat about 5 minutes on each side for medium rare. Cut, on the diagonal, into thick slices. Heat mushrooms with pan juices. Pour over meat. Makes 6 servings.

RED EYE

1 can (10¾ ounces) condensed tomato soup
½ soup can water
1 tablespoon lemon juice
1 bottle (7 ounces) chilled club soda
Lemon peel

Combine soup, water and lemon juice. Stir to blend. Add soda just before serving. Pour over cracked ice in glasses. Garnish with lemon peel. Makes 3 to 4 servings.

GREEN DE MENTHE

- 1 can (10½ ounces) condensed cream of celery soup
- 1 soup can milk
- 2 tablespoons chopped parsley
- Sprigs of mint

In blender; combine all ingredients. Cover, blend until smooth. Place in refrigerator for at least 4 hours. Serve in chilled glasses. Garnish with mint. Makes 2 to 3 servings.

SOUP ON THE ROCKS

- 3 cans (10½ ounces each) condensed beef broth
- Ice cubes

Pour beef broth right from the can over ice cubes or cracked ice, allowing ½ can per serving. Garnish each serving with a slice of lime or lemon if desired. Makes 6 servings.

RANCHERO SOPA

- 1 can (10½ ounces) condensed cream of chicken soup
- 1 can (10½ ounces) condensed cream of mushroom soup
- 1 soup can milk
- 1 soup can water
- ¼ cup chopped peanuts
- ¼ cup chopped pimiento
- 1 tablespoon chopped parsley

In saucepan, blend soups; gradually stir in milk and water. Add remaining ingredients. Heat; stir now and then. Makes 4 to 6 servings.

WATUSI SIP

- 2 cans (10½ ounces each) condensed beef broth
- ½ soup can water
- 8 ice cubes
- ¼ cup lime juice

Put all ingredients in a shaker. Cover and shake well. Serve in chilled glasses; garnish with lime slice if desired. Makes 4 to 6 servings.

FRANKS CON CHILI

- 1 can (11 ounces) condensed chili beef soup
- ⅓ cup water
- 2 teaspoons prepared mustard
- 1 pound frankfurters, cooked
- Frankfurter buns, split and toasted

Combine soup, water and mustard. Heat. Place hot frankfurters on buns, spoon on soup mixture. Garnish with onion rings or shredded cheese. Makes 8 to 10 servings.

POTATO CELERY SALAD

Make potato salad with cooked–diced or sliced–new potatoes. Add chopped green pepper, shredded carrots, snipped chives and mayonnaise diluted with a bit of vinegar. Garnish platter of chilled salad with one-inch lengths of green celery stalks filled with two or three different cheese spreads.

MINTED LIMEADE ON GREEN ROCKS

Prepare limeade with frozen concentrate. Allow one can diluted as directed, to be poured into ice trays for lime flavored cubes. Add a few drops green food coloring for bright green cubes. Garnish glasses with sprigs of mint.

After a day of climbing the well-worn trails, the "cowboys" will return to camp exhausted and hungry. Welcome them back with the pleasing aroma of a robust western bean 'n bacon vegetable chowder with franks. It's so easy to fix when you use a can each of condensed bean 'n bacon and vegetable soups. You'll be prepared for big appetities, 'cause this makes plenty.

Spread out a bandana cloth, put out the sesame seed bread sticks and ring the dinner bell. You can serve the chowder right from the pot. For dessert–a mixed fresh fruit medley.

And, for the brisk mornings, before the sun warms the ground, start them off with a chill-chasing cup of hot soup. When you pack several kinds and mix them, you'll add variety which your campers will find mighty pleasin'.

For a quick skillet supper, try luncheon meat with peaches and peas in a cream of chicken sauce.

BEAN 'n BACON VEGETABLE CHOWDER

- ¼ cup chopped green pepper
- ¼ cup chopped onion
- 2 frankfurters, cut in ½-inch slices
- 2 tablespoons butter or margarine
- 1 can (11½ ounces) condensed bean with bacon soup
- 1 can (10¾ ounces) condensed vegetable soup
- 1½ soup cans water

In saucepan, cook green pepper and onion and brown frankfurters in butter until vegetables are tender. Blend in soups and water. Heat; simmer a few minutes to blend flavors. Makes 4 to 5 servings.

WESTERN SKILLET SUPPER

- 1 can (12 ounces) luncheon meat, cut into 8 slices
- 1 tablespoon butter or margarine
- 1 can (8¾ ounces) sliced cling peaches, drained
- 1 can (10½ ounces) condensed cream of chicken soup
- ¼ cup milk
- 1 can (8½ ounces) peas, drained

Lightly brown luncheon meat in butter; spoon peach slices over meat. Blend soup and milk; pour over peaches. Top with peas. Simmer 15 minutes; stir now and then. Makes 4 servings.

CAMPER BONANZA

- 1 pound ground beef
- 1 small onion, chopped
- 1 tablespoon shortening
- 1 can (10½ ounces) condensed cream of mushroom soup
- ⅓ cup water
- 2 tablespoons ketchup
- 1 teaspoon Worcestershire
- Dash salt and pepper
- 1 can (8 ounces) whole white potatoes, drained and quartered
- 1 can (8 ounces) peas, drained

Brown beef with onion in shortening; stir to separate meat particles. Add soup, water and seasonings. Stir in vegetables. Heat; stir now and then. Makes 4 servings.

TUNA OMELET

Sauce:

- 1 can (10¾ ounces) condensed cream of vegetable soup
- ½ cup milk
- 1 can (7 ounces) tuna, drained and flaked

Omelet:

- 8 eggs
- ½ cup milk
- ¼ teaspoon salt
- Dash pepper
- 4 tablespoons butter or margarine

For *sauce*, combine soup, milk and tuna. Heat; stir now and then. For *omelet,* beat eggs, milk and seasonings together. Heat butter in skillet; pour in egg mixture. Cook slowly. As undersurface becomes set, start lifting it slightly with spatula to let uncooked portion flow underneath and cook. When omelet is cooked but still moist, loosen edges and bottom. Pour half of sauce in center; fold one half over and roll omelet onto warm platter. Pour over remaining sauce. Makes 4 servings.

Campsite meals should, of course, be kept as uncomplicated as possible so that the vacation is enjoyed to the fullest. Baking is liable to present a problem, but skillet dishes which cook directly over the grill or stove are very popular. Many of them depend on canned condensed soups for seasoning, flavor and saucy goodness. The wise camper therefore will become a collector of quick and easy supper-in-a-skillet recipes before vacation time. Here is a trio of all-in-one dishes that have been tested and found tried and true.

SKILLET CHICKEN SUPPER

2 pounds chicken parts
2 tablespoons butter or margarine
1 can (11 ounces) condensed bisque of tomato soup
1 can (3 ounces) sliced mushrooms
Dash pepper
1 can (8 ounces) cut green beans, drained
1 can (8 ounces) whole onions, drained

Brown chicken in butter in skillet. Pour off drippings. Add soup, mushrooms and pepper. Cover; cook over low heat 45 minutes. Stir often. Add green beans and onions; cook 5 minutes longer. Makes 4 to 6 servings.

FIVE-IN-ONE SUPPER

½ pound frankfurters, sliced
1 can (1 pound) whole white potatoes, drained and diced
½ small onion, sliced
2 tablespoons butter or margarine
1 can (10½ ounces) condensed cream of mushroom soup
¼ can water
1 can (8 ounces) cut green beans, drained

Brown frankfurters and potatoes and cook onion in butter until tender. Add soup, water and green beans. Simmer 10 minutes; stir now and then. Makes 4 servings.

CAMPFIRE ASPARAGUS AND EGG HASH

1 can (10½ ounces) condensed cream of potato soup
½ to ¾ cup milk
4 hard-cooked eggs, sliced
1 can (8 ounces) asparagus cuts, drained
Dash pepper
4 slices toast
Paprika

Blend soup and milk; gently stir in eggs, asparagus and pepper. Heat; stir now and then. Serve over toast. Garnish with paprika, if desired. Makes 4 servings.

There's no reason for mealtime monotony to stray into camp–especially if you practice the art of "souper" skillet cookery.

The simplest foods and preparations are best. A skillet supper of cabbage and sausages with sauce of canned condensed cream of potato soup can be pure delight and, best of all, it's so easy to prepare.

CHOW'S ON – CABBAGE AND SAUSAGE SUPPER

- 4 cups shredded cabbage
- ½ cup water
- 1 can (10½ ounces) condensed cream of potato soup
- 2 cans (4 ounces each) Vienna sausage, cut in 1-inch slices
- ⅛ teaspoon pepper

Steam cabbage and water in covered skillet until tender, about 10 minutes. Stir in soup, sausage and pepper. Cover and heat; stir now and then. Makes 4 servings.

Or, here's a "souper" skillet combo that is sure to please woodsmen, large and small–ground beef, green pepper, condensed onion soup and barbecue beans on toasted buns. It's a hot and handsome "scramble" that will bring cheers from the whole family on wheels.

BEEF 'n BEANS ON BUNS

- 1 pound ground beef
- 1 small green pepper, slivered
- 1 tablespoon shortening
- 1 can (10½ ounces) condensed onion soup
- 2 tablespoons water
- 1 can (1 pound) barbecue beans
- 2 tablespoons chili sauce
- 6 buns, toasted and buttered

Brown beef and green pepper in shortening; stir to separate meat particles. Pour off drippings. Add soup, water, beans and chili sauce. Simmer 10 to 15 minutes or until slightly thickened. Stir now and then. Serve on buns. Makes 6 servings.

10. Check List for Camper Clothing

□ A camper trip for a get-away-from-it-all outing to mountains, beach or state park is planned for only one reason, fun.

To make the vacation a relaxed and happy time for every member of the family, Mother included, easy care clothing is the first basic requirement.

This takes careful and organized planning and the careful answers to two simple questions: "Where will we be going?" and "What will be needed?"

This is not the time for fancy luggage and lots of clothing. It's the time for the canvas bag and basic clothing essentials. Gear should be packed into medium sized bags.

Several medium sized bags pack more flexibly than one large one and adapt more easily to camper closets and storage areas.

Pack overnight items separately, so they can be found easily without searching and fumbling.

Jackets, raincoats and dress or suit, if a night in town is on the agenda, can be hung on hangers, the wire type is best for accommodating as many items as possible in limited closet space.

Camp clothing should be functional, made of serviceable fabrics which can be easily washed, and there are many to choose from in this age of miracle fabric blends.

Materials should be rugged, resistant to dirt, snagging and tearing. The experienced camper always keeps his needs simple, with every article of wearing apparel calculated to best serve for chosen locale, activities and length of camping stay.

Shirts

There's a variety of shirts which are practical and inexpensive for the camper wardrobe, but before making a definite decision you must know what your plan of action is going to be.

Cotton T-shirts, sweat shirts and man-tailored cotton or nylon or dacron shirts are ideal for men, women and children.

Sleeveless blouses are cool for a sunny beach area, desert retreat or summertime campsite, but long-sleeved tops offer more protection against insect bites, scratches and sunburn. This is the time for the children and Dad to wear out and toss out T-shirts which have seen better days.

Wool shirts are the best solution for cold weather outings, northern regions or mountains where altitude makes days and nights cool. In all shirts, shoulders should be roomy and pockets ample.

A simplified item of casual clothing, preferred by men and children, is the one-piece jump suit of cotton seersucker or corduroy. It's easy to keep together in confined camper quarters.

Jackets

Windbreaker, cotton, canvas or army field jackets are all good choices for average camping conditions, however the lightweight nylon hooded parka is the acknowledged favorite among many sports-minded men and women, because of the active life it can lead.

When the weather gets rough, a thick wool jacket is warm and sturdy and holds in body heat. Other types are the quilted and pile or fleece lined jackets which are insulated to give excellent protection against extreme cold.

No coat for active sportswear should be longer than fingertip length. A longer coat drags on the ground when climbing or bending. Fit should be easy so as not to hamper freedom of movement.

Sweaters

A sweater is the best traveling companion a camper can have. A cardigan can be tossed on over a sleeveless blouse or worn over a slip-on or turtleneck sweater, in the layer-on-layer type of outdoor dressing that adapts to every temperature change.

Inexpensive, hard-wearing synthetic blends, such as orlon or nylon and soft wools, on up to heavy sweater jackets of raw wool, have their place, depending on the weather conditions.

Pants

Durable cotton slacks or levis are standard equipment for both men and women. These should be without cuffs and loose in fit. The waist band should be easy enough to allow room for heavy underwear, if needed, or a heavy shirt.

Slacks with elasticized waistbands are a natural when you can find them. Pockets are handy for carrying change, comb, matches or lipstick. Unfortunately, the no-belt slacks pose a problem for men who wear sunglasses and normally use a glasses case which slides on the belt.

Shorts are cool and practical for beach or well traveled trails, but offer no protection against poison ivy or scratches when hiking through rough brush covered hills.

For the lady who doesn't like to wear shorts, culottes or divided skirt can be a smart substitute.

Shoes

Every knowledgeable camper understands the importance of correct foot gear in making the difference between a happy vacation and a disaster.

Loafers are a good choice for strolling about the campsite or mountain paths, but they don't offer enough protection for long, rugged hikes.

Canvas sneakers are inexpensive and also serve a useful purpose for the average camper. It is a good idea to take along an old pair for every member of the family. They come in handy for fording pebble strewn mountain streams.

Another shoe which can be packed into your bag is the sandal, or rubber zori. They give relaxed comfort for beach or in-camper loafing.

The leather boot, six to eight inches high, is the correct hiking shoe. It should be soft and pliant enough to mold to the foot. Feet change size on long hikes, due to increased circulation, becoming both longer and wider.

Cleated rubber or composition soles are best for two reasons: They are sturdy enough to withstand the rigors and abuse of rocky trails. Hiking boots should never have all leather soles and heels, they slip easily on pine needles and smooth slopes.

Old shoes are the most dependable and all new shoes and boots should be broken in before initiating them on a camping trip.

Socks

Wool, blended with nylon or dacron, makes the most satisfactory and inexpensive socks for all around camp wear.

The percentage of synthetic fibers should not be more than 40 per cent, in order to maintain the best qualities of both: the warmth and softness of wool, the strength of dacron and nylon. Too high a percentage of synthetic yarn content tends to make socks harsh on sensitive feet.

If 100 per cent wool socks are selected, be sure to buy top grade wool. Although more expensive, they are economical in the long run, giving better wear than cheaper wools.

An innovation for the anti-cold-feet campaign is the battery powered sock. Each sock has its own battery, which is carried in a small plastic pouch, supported by an elastic strap at the top of each sock. When turned on, the extra-strength alkaline batteries which are suggested for use in the socks, give five hours of constant heat. The wiring and heating element is sewn inside side and toe. These must be worn with loose pants or tuck-ins.

Whatever the sock selection, correctness of fit is a prime consideration, if walking hours are to be happy hours. Socks should not be so short they slip under the heels, nor so long they wrinkle under the toe, and they should always reach above shoe or boot top.

A good idea is to take along extra pairs for every member of the family, in case of emergency.

Rainwear

Fair weather or foul, it's important to have proper gear which is designed to give ultimate protection.

The old-fashioned rainslicker and hat, plastic raincoat or poncho of water-proof fabrics are all satisfactory, with the lightweight water-repellent nylon hooded parka at the top of many clothes-for-camping lists.

The reason: It is light in weight, comfortable and serves many purposes, from walking in the rain, to giving added warmth on clear crisp days or night around the campfire.

The poncho, too, serves a dual purpose of rain cover-up or ground cloth. Some active sportsmen prefer a rain hat to hood because it gives more air ventilation.

For foot covering there are two choices: first, the rubber boot which is the most durable and gives the best protection; secondly, the stretchy rubber rain boot that goes on over shoes or sport boots. They fold small to fit into pocket, tackle box or auto glove compartment.

Swimsuits

For the swimmer, sailor and waterskier, it is always a good idea to tuck trunks or swimsuits into the tote, so you will be ready to take advantage of ocean or lake if the occasion arises.

For the children who play all day there should be an extra suit for each so one can be drying while the other takes to the water.

Accessories

The visored cap is an outdoor favorite; made of cotton it protects the eyes from the sun and rain if worn under a hooded parka. Choose it in heavy wool with ear muffs for zero temperatures.

Cotton gloves save tender hands from scratches and scrapes when gathering wood for the campfire, or from blisters when cooking outdoors.

Wool lined leather gloves, thick wool gloves or mittens, warm the hands from winter winds.

Take several cotton bandanas. They serve many needs, from neck scarf to head covering, add protection when tied under a hat, can be used as a pot holder, bandage or for carrying nature's treasures gathered from beach or desert.

Fabrics which drip and dry and require no ironing are the answers in the in-camp laundry problem. Laundry does not become too much of a chore if dirty clothing is washed when taken off.

There are individually wrapped packages of soap powder, enough for one washing, which are easy to use and take up no room in limited storage space. Laundry equipment should not be bulky. A covered plastic bucket and a plastic clothesline (fiber absorbs water and can be messy to pack).

For a family on an extended camper trip, clothes can be washed in a launderette when driving through a town. They can be washed and dried almost by the time you stop and stock up at the local vegetable stand.

If any member of the family is exposed to poison ivy, be sure to wash the clothes immediately, using a household disinfectant in the water.

It is a good idea, also, to pack the sun tan lotion, insect repellent and first aid kit.

Purses

An easy to carry type is a small purse secured around the waist on a leather belt. Another idea is the miniature over-the-shoulder bag, with a strap long enough to reach from right shoulder to left hip. This prevents it from slipping off the shoulder.

Conclusion

Check your list, gather up your clothing gear, round up the family and be on your way to a relaxed and pleasurable camping vacation.

II. Camping Tips

☐ There you are in a donut shop at 4 A.M and the wife has her hair up in curlers and the kids are limp flip-flops sprawled in semi-comatose positions throughout the camper.

It's late or it's early, depending on your point of view, and you're getting a jump on the traffic to the mountains or the sea or the desert.

It's your first vacation with the RV. You'll be driving that ungainly thing some 1500 miles (maybe more) and the thought of it hits you where the glazed dough sits like a leaden sponge in the pit of your belly.

Heck of a responsibility, isn't it? You're combining traffic and highways with Mother Nature and the implied mastery of the elements, and you're about to chew off a bigger chunk of the outdoors than was ever dreamed of by Dan'l Boone or Davey Crockett.

What the heck are you doing here, anyway? You're no Leather Stocking, no trail blazer, just an average guy. Maybe a little smarter (or you couldn't afford the travel rig), maybe a little more concerned with your family (or you wouldn't be here to begin with), maybe a bit more adventurous (or you wouldn't have had the courage to start out).

In these days there is no freedom so complete as getting away from it all in a recreation vehicle. Doing so is a return to basic frontier values. Male and female roles become more clearly defined. Children are a part of each adventure. In every way it's the best, most wholesome sort of shared family experience.

You and your family are about to become free. You'll be happy wanderers with seven league boots and a mobile knapsack large enough to hold a small country general store.

You look out the window of the shop at the RV. It may be a self-contained unit, a pickup camper combo, a personally outfitted panel truck or a spartan four-wheel-drive rig for the back country.

There are as many RV trips to choose from as there are State parks, stretches of beach, chunks of mountain, skinny dippin' holes and fresh water fishing spots.

You'll have your own slice of the sun and you'll be driving on superhighways, dusty country roads and, perhaps, going over the top, into the out-back.

You're smart enough to realize disaster is just as much around the next corner on a vacation as it is in everyday life, maybe closer. And as you pay the bill and walk out of the shop toward the vehicle, the early morning air hits you like the caress of a cold hearted woman and you ponder the situation. They didn't tell you adventure was like this, did they?

We're not going to tell you not to worry about it. Worrying's natural at a time like this. You wouldn't be human or a breadwinner or a father if you didn't worry at times like this.

The odds are pretty good that it'll be worth it. The odds are you'll be doing it again and again; that each time you strike out into the wilderness and come back, you'll be a better person for it and the family will be closer.

It isn't the only way to be free but a better one hasn't been invented.

There is one common denominator which applies to every trip, every vacation, every tour. It's the same one you apply to each act of your life. A thing termed "common sense." Avail yourself of a fresh supply. After that, sit back behind the wheel and let it happen, go with your natural instincts.

You'll be surprised how much you know that you were never taught. Providing you planned well, a thing called "sense of self-preservation" will take over.

That's fine, you say, but how do you go about planning?

Simple. Break it down into categories, recheck the list, give yourself short lectures, recheck the list and let it all hang out.

It's a toss-up as to the single most important thing you can do to prepare for a camper vacation or weekend. It's entirely possible that the most important thing hasn't occurred to you. Driving. You know you're a great driver. But does the other guy?

Somewhere in the consideration of each trip should be a time for evaluation of your driving habits. Aren't there some aspects of safe driving in which you might improve? Perhaps in patience? Perhaps in how to handle a top heavy rig in soft sand? Perhaps in ways to use a gearbox on a mountain trail?

Slaughter is an unpleasant word. But more people are butchered on the highways each year than in wars. You know that already, but think about it for awhile. If you think about it hard enough, chances are you'll be all right.

Then there's a thing about your attitude. Is the trip you're about to take close to everyone's heart, or did you just ram it down their throats? After all, it's everyone's trip. It belongs to the entire family and to the people who may be going along with you.

Plan ahead to allow time for stops in Indian curio stores, be prepared to deviate from your course so that you can seek out side roads to towns with likely sounding names.

You might even stop by the side of the road for awhile to read those bronze plaques set into boulders near state historical landmarks. You might learn something and, besides, you helped pay for them, didn't you?

There's nothing so futile as trying to make passenger car speeds along a highway or off the road in a recreation vehicle. Not only that, but hurrying sort of defeats the purpose of a vacation.

Plan your route well in advance. There are few service stations in the mountains or desert for advice on directions. In many cases, there are no roads.

If there aren't any service stations for directions, there are also no stations for gasoline, oil and water.

You'd better know how much of each you're going to need. Figuring gas and oil is simple. You've taken a shakedown cruise to determine your RV's mileage and oil consumption. But water is something else.

You'll need water more than anything. You drink it, cook with it, wash with it, bathe in it and the machine consumes it. How much should you take? Some foolhardy writers attempt to come up with formulas. Don't pay any attention to those. It depends on the writer who wrote the book. Chances are he's some sort of hardened outdoorsman who takes pride in existing on a gallon of water a day.

Take along more water than you'll ever need. If you have to have a rule of thumb, plan on 40 to 50 gallons for four on a weekend trip into the desert. Go from there and add or subtract. But take more water than you expect to need.

There are many ways to store water. Perhaps your camper has built in tanks. Find out the capacity and divide by the number of persons going along on the trip and the number of days you'll be gone. If the average number of gallons per day is marginal in terms of survival, buy some extra 10-gallon cans.

All sorts of cans are available at all sorts of prices. Buy some. They'll clutter up your "House Beautiful" of a camper and your wife will mutter about it. But at least she'll be around to mutter about it.

That brings up another thing about trips. You'll be confined with people in the small area of a moving or stationary vehicle for days. A pre-trip peace pact isn't a bad idea.

Basically this is just an agreement on everyone's part that they'll do nothing to ruin the vacation. Beyond appendicitis, you'd be surprised how easy such pacts are to keep. Call it what you will, a planning session, a fireside chat or a summit conference, it's worth the time and effort.

But peace pacts aren't the end of preparation. Along with spending time with others in a vehicle, you'll need sustenance, shelter and situational savvy. The shelter is, of course, implied. But shelter bogs down after awhile into confinement unless comfort and recreation are provided for.

If your camper has built-ins, the chances are that comfort has been provided for. But you'll still need blankets, changes of clothes, utensils, accessories, camping gear and equipment.

A trip to the nearest sporting goods store will blow your mind, boggle your breathing and bust your checking account. Simply walking up and down the aisles, you'll be able to see things you never thought of and never could have gotten through a trip without.

Recreational needs are different. If you're going fishing, obviously you have taken along fishing gear. This holds true for specific trips of other natures. But there are handy, inexpensive items which go well with simply exploring.

History books about certain areas are readily available for each section of the country. It's fun to pause near Custer's last stand and peruse the pages for added information. Or which way did the Nez Perce go when they reached Grant's Pass?

For children, there are books of games to play while traveling. You might even test your skill. A couple of ball gloves are things every family has on hand. Take them along. A game of catch is fun after a day behind the wheel and it's a good way to stretch those travel constricted muscles.

Firearms are generally out. Guns are illegal in most State parks and plinking, except for the desert under carefully controlled situations, can really be a disaster. Besides, the gun laws are currently in such a state of flux you could be arrested for simply having them along. Best leave the firearms at home. Save them for hunting.

Situational savvy is a thing which comes from experience. There's no sense in planning a week's stay in the desert if you've never been there before. One rock will look like another after four or five hours and the days will stretch ahead of you like a prison sentence.

Take your out of doors easy in the beginning. Try out the spots nearest home, the spots nearest civilization before you get in over your head.

If you're determined to rough it, learn all you can about the area before you get there. Five years in the Boy Scouts—twenty years ago—does not prepare you for the present.

There is one cop out, if you're going to go heavy the first trip. Buy yourself a library. There's a spot somewhere in any camper where a stack of books can be placed without taking up needed room for water, food and supplies and equipment. Stock the library with camping manuals, Forest Service maps and a first aid handbook.

The most common vacation and camping malady is sunburn. Blisters, cuts and abrasions come next. The serious problems, sun stroke and heat exhaustion, have similar symptoms, but treatment differs. Pick up a good first aid book. Read it. Carry it in the vehicle.

Along the human line, what about food? Well, you'll need it and you'll consume it, in many cases whether you need it or not. You'll put away a seemingly unending series of candy bars, packages of peanuts, boxes of dried fruit and salt water taffy.

Better yet, a little planning and you'll actually eat better on a trip than you do at home. Don't let the wife know it, though.

Fruits and fruit juices are high on the list of what to take. Ease of storage, if the fruits and juices are in cans, make them ideal for vehicle usage. You can carry goodies to your heart's content and your budget's misery. Also fruits and fruit juices are high in sugar content, hence high in energy value.

Frozen foods are good, also, stored in a portable camping ice box with inexpensive dry ice.

All sorts of things come in cans. Use new eyes on your next visit to a supermarket. You can find filet mignon in cans if you look for it. Packaged and dehydrated foods are also available in just about every shape and size.

Of course, this goes back to the water question. Did you bring more than enough? Nothing is more frustrating than to awaken and yearn for some flapjacks and learn you don't have enough water to mix them.

Taking along food presupposes some method of making flame to cook on. Most campers have some sort of built-in burners. Generally butane is the fuel. In self-contained units, the butane storage tanks are big enough to last a week in the out-back. But top off the butane tanks anyway.

Some refrigeration units also work with butane. Ice, however, is your best bet for refrigeration. It's inexpensive and even the stores in the desert have ice available.

Many sizes of self-contained cooking burners are available at camping goods stores. From back-packing midgets to ovens, everything is available. What you buy will depend on where you're going and how long you expect to stay. If you don't trust your judgment, inform the salesman of your needs, solicit his advice and then check out what he says at the next store down the block.

Planning for the ultimate emergency is something most camping tip chapters gloss over. Everything is kept to a hearty ho-ho-ho. That's nice, but what if you have an extreme mechanical malfunction in the desert? What if you're forty miles from nowhere and can't move that truck an inch?

Assuming your vehicle is in good shape and assuming it has received regular maintenance, chances are your extreme mechanical breakdown will be a flat tire. Naturally, you've got a mounted spare. Suppose it happens again?

Two handy items to have on every trip, in every car, are tire patching kits (good ones) and one of those air pumps which works off engine compression after being screwed into a spark plug hole.

What else can happen? Well, fan belts can break, radiator hoses can burst, fuel pumps can stop. A complete set of spares would include replacement fan belts, radiator hoses and clamps and tools to work with. A fuel pump is not that hard to replace.

Surprisingly, two items you should take along must be taken on faith. Two large vise grips and a whole bunch of heavy mechanic's wire are almost indispensable. You'll use them more than anything else, including Junior's Cub Scout handaxe.

A chapter could be written on the use of vise grips and mechanic's wire. Just take some along. And, yes, by all means, purchase a multi-purpose pocket knife. You always wanted one anyway. Very handy item, that.

But suppose you can't fix the breakdown? The first rule is: stay with the vehicle. You've got shelter, food, water and the group stays together. Besides, an air search can spot a vehicle in the desert or mountains or along the shore much more easily than it can an individual. This presupposes, of course, that this breakdown occurs in the wilderness, miles from civilization.

But, how does the air search know to search for you?

It doesn't. Unless you gave word before you left. A good method is to check out with a friend or neighbor before leaving on an extended trip. Tell them where you'll be going, exactly how long you'll be gone, what routes you'll be taking and when you expect to be back. Ask them to notify the authorities if you haven't returned by a certain time on a certain date. Air search wheels will be set in motion.

Obviously, if the neighbor knows where you're at, it'll be easier to find you. Providing you stayed with the vehicle and providing you didn't stay an extra week at your Aunt Cloris' in Keokuk and forgot to notify your neighbor of the change in plans.

There is never an excuse for having to walk out of the desert or mountains. The odds are simply too great against success. Take the extra fifteen minutes to notify people and stay with the vehicle in case of emergency.

Next to tires, the most common occurrence is running out of gas or ripping the oil pan off on rocks. Gas consumption goes way up in low gear travels through rough country. Watch the gas gauge on the first couple of short trips. The one redeeming factor is that in low gear trips through rough country you won't be covering a whole lot of miles. It balances out.

It's a good idea to have a spare 10-gallon can of gas. As for the oil pan, careful driving will save a lot of dollars.

If you wish, you can take along an extra pan and a set of gaskets. But if you get into that, you might as well take along an extra engine and tow a hoist. What about an extra transmission and rear end? No, the answer is careful driving. The state of the mechanical art is such these days that you can rely on the equipment if you can rely on your common sense.

That's it, then. It isn't all you need to know. You'll never reach the stage where you'll know it all about survival on a swing through the wilderness.

12. Boats, Boat Trailers and Cycles

□ Years ago it was written that "a vagabond, when rich, is called a tourist."

Today's growing mass of American vagabonds at heart say it isn't so—even though more and more of them are showing signs of affluence. They just don't want to spoil their image. Or motives.

Of course, these weekend and week-long nomads—recreation-bound families—long since have abandoned their spartan companions, the knapsack, bed roll and pup tent in favor of motor campers.

Greater numbers of them are burdening their modern-day pack mule, the recreation vehicle, with boats and motorcycles as well. Certainly that's a sign of better times.

Nevertheless, these embellishments of prosperity haven't changed the basic attraction to the outdoors—a call to the bucolic. Today's vagabond just wants to see and enjoy more of the untouched wilderness with his boat or trail penetrator, the motorbike.

That hardly reclassifies him as a tourist.

Desire for expanded horizons, though, doesn't classify him as a seasoned pioneer either. Many seemingly intrepid travelers towing boat or bike for the first time are not always prepared for such adventures.

Undeniably, a boat or motorcycle adds new dimensions to any lake, sea, stream or trail excursion. But they pose some special problems, too.

A few fundamental precautions and preparations taken at the outset can avert the otherwise inevitable disasters that turn many camping, riding and boating expeditions into best-forgotten, but unforgettable memories.

Foremost, of course, is selecting the proper boat, motorbike and trailer for the application. It's not a decision for the uninitiated. But, as a word of warning, select your counsel carefully.

It is just as possible to be sold inadequate equipment by a salesman who fears losing a sale as it is to be oversold. The purchase should be tailored to the buyer and his needs.

Neither boating nor cycling, however, are confined to the wealthy. The choices run from the modest pocketbook to the most well padded.

The properly prepared boatsman doesn't fall into that category which describes the two happiest days of a boat owner's life as the day he buys his boat and the day he sells it.

Most of today's boat buyers–87 per cent, in fact–intend to haul them by trailer. In general, the sizes for such use range from 12 to 26 footers. Anything bigger is larger than the average outdoorsman should try to haul himself.

The assortment is varied, starting with car-toppers which are best defined as something not so big that it can't be handled by two people (roughly up to 300 pounds). The cost of these aluminum or fiberglass boats ranges from $200 to $300, plus the price of a 6 to 10 horsepower engine. A car-topper usually is a fisherman's choice.

First-time buyers usually start with 15- or 16-foot runabouts, which cost about $1500, plus another $1000 for a suitable powerplant, generally in the range of 60 to 90 horsepower, depending on the use–water skiing, fishing or pleasure boating.

Boat buying is a lot like car buying. The sticker price is only the beginning. Accessories run the gamut and many of them must be considered as part of the initial cost, e.g., life jackets and anchors. Many of these items, incidentally, are mandatory under safety regulations. It's best to check which ones are.

A major consideration for the new boat buyer is the trailer. The cheapest is not necessarily the least expensive. They'll run upward from slightly under $200. Many new boaters face problems immediately, simply because they bought the wrong kind of trailer. Modern hull shapes often require special supports. In mismatches, it is possible to warp the bottom of a boat's hull.

A boat makes a too handy cargo carrier but most boat trailers are not designed to carry added weight–so watch it.

And a trailer means special accessories, too. Winches, for example, run from $15 to more than $100 for power systems which work off the car's electrical output to handle hefty boats.

Adding a trailer to a car also means buying adequate rearview mirrors. Also, lighting regulations must be observed–tail lights, brake lights, license plate illumination and turn signals.

It is wise to carry spare bulbs, fuses and wiring for trailer lights which are repeatedly doused into water. Since brakes are often applied while launching a boat, a hot bulb is often dipped into the water.

It is not uncommon for a camping trip to be spoiled by seizure of a trailer wheel bearing. Due to repeated dunkings, it is wise to check them often to see if they need to be repacked with grease. There are protective devices, costing around $12, to cover wheel hubs and eliminate a constant vigil.

Also, it might be wise to consider bigger wheels for your trailer. " 'Bitty' wheels," pointed out one expert, "must turn faster, creating friction and building up heat." Heat, of course, is a tire's worst enemy.

What about a spare trailer tire? A trailer jack? A lug-nut wrench? None of these items from the automobile will fit the trailer, unless you have changed to automotive type wheels and tires. Even then, you'll need a special jack.

Then, there's the matter of the automobile. Is your car or recreation vehicle outfitted for a trailer?

There's perhaps a $35 investment due for welding a good, frame-type, load-distributing trailer hitch.

How does the car ride, once it is hitched to a trailer? Most manufacturers provide towing packages, such as heavy duty shock absorbers and springs, designed to restore the level of the auto's ride.

If weight is badly distributed, controlability of the car is affected, headlights are aimed too high and trailers themselves become more vulnerable to cross winds.

As a rule of thumb, if the total poundage of trailer, trailer load, car and car load does not exceed twice the car's empty weight, a compatible towing combination has been achieved.

While most trailers are built with a margin of safety for their listed load capacities, it is easy to abuse this factor by overloading the boat itself. It is best to stow only the light objects in the boat, placing the heavy objects in the automobile trunk.

Will you be crossing state borders with your trailered boat? If so, you'll find laws of the road differ somewhat from state to state. Generally, speed limits are reduced and it is necessary to keep in the right-hand lane. The Outboard Boating Club of America (333 North Michigan Avenue, Chicago, Illinois) has published a digest of state boat trailer laws.

Hint department: When buying that trailer, think about the problem which might occur while trying to back it up when it isn't loaded. It could become invisible. Why not then add pipe racks as reference points?

Another hint: When launching a boat from a ramp (fees, incidentally, run about $1.50), why not learn to take advantage of the boat's own power for getting it off the trailer and into the water. And vice versa when returning it to the trailer–drive it onto the trailer.

Some boat owners, in fact, assist the car in pulling the trailer out of the water by applying power when the boat is in the trailer and still in the water. This careful nudge is a handy trick where a concrete ramp is not available, keeping the car's rear wheels from spinning helplessly at the water's edge. Hand winching is work.

Taut lines, extended too far out into the water, are dangerous if they should snap. Also, why get wet, trying to guide a boat back onto the trailer? A lousy way to start a boat trip is in wet clothes. And it's even worse to head home that way.

When Alexander Woolcott said, "I must get out of these wet clothes and into a dry martini" he wasn't launching a boat. Besides, dry martinis aren't always available.

Surprisingly, many boaters forget to take along at least a small tool kit or a spare propeller for that possible encounter with a sand bar. They find themselves stranded for lack of a simple tool like a screwdriver or a spare sparkplug. Maybe it is because they were too concerned with remembering to pack the beer or booze. Walking for help from a boat is difficult, even if you know where the rocks are.

Even the astronauts on the moon wished for a screwdriver to fix the TV!

Hauling a motorcycle, even two of them, obviously is far less complicated than a boat. There are rare cases, in fact, where a trailer is no longer necessary. Simple racks have been designed that allow mounting motorcycles easily on the back of cars, campers or trucks.

Double-loop carriers, which attach to bumpers, in some cases don't even require tools to mount. Those currently on the market range in price from $16.95 to $24.95. In most cases, one person can mount a trail motorcycle on them, lifting one end of the bike into place at a time.

Which bike is most suited to off-the-road use? For example, Yamaha International, which claims to be the largest manufacturer of off-road trail bikes in the U.S. market, offers seven such models ranging in size from 80cc up to 350cc engines.

However, a spokesman with the company recommends that for camping the most practical sizes are the small to medium vehicles, about 80cc to 180cc.

"They're easy to put in or take out of a pickup truck, or fit onto a front or rear bumper carrier on a passenger car or pickup," he said. Most of them weigh little more than 200 pounds.

He suggests avoiding transporting bikes by trailer if possible since it is necessary to comply with special highway trailer laws, such as restricted speed, if they are used.

Small trail bikes are recommended for family campers for many reasons. Mainly, they can be used by most members of the family, including older children.

Most of these vehicles also can carry two riders without strain although this application isn't recommended if the terrain is steep or excessively rugged. Also, lighter machines are easier for the non-expert to handle off the road, particularly

Don't get the trailer's wheels into the water when you are launching your boat.

Small motorcycles can provide excellent transportation around a campsite.

under rutted and rocky conditions.

Economics is another major factor. The small and medium size classes of trail bikes scale in price from $300 to $600. Fuel and maintenance also are low-cost items. Off-the-road vehicles don't require many of the features or accessories of street bikes or face the multitude of licensing regulations that confront owners of highway motorcycles.

Less emphasis for trail riding has been put on the small 50cc size motorcycle which triggered a market boom in this country because, as one motorcycle official said, "after a week people found they were ready for something bigger."

Trail bikes have gained increasing popularity with many new riders and families due to simplifications that have come along in recent years–automatic mixing of gas and oil for two-cycle engines, electric starters and changeover sprockets which permit changing gears for open road or trail applications easily without taking off the rear wheel.

Another fast growing two-wheel market is the small, mini-bike field which is exclusively an off-the-road mode of transportation that is easily carried in the trunk of a car. They are light, less than 100 pounds, and are less expensive than motorcycles, ranging from $130 to slightly more than $200.

Parents have found mini-bikes, built lower to the ground with small tires, acceptable from a safety standpoint for bicycle age children.

While most small motorcycles of the trail variety are not difficult for even the novice to operate, manufacturers suggest a reasonable period of instruction before embarking on a trail blazing trip.

No one should ride without a helmet.

Motorbikes, of course, have added to the mobility of the camper who can easily spread himself beyond the congested areas. But they also add hazards if the simple precautions aren't taken.

Boats and bikes give the adventuresome outdoorsman the opportunity to get away from it all–including assistance.

Albeit, the vagabond at heart is still a carefree spirit.

Please don't call him a tourist.

13. *Maintenance Tips*

□ Nothing can ruin a vacation trip or even a simple weekend outing quicker than a breakdown or equipment failure.

If there's a more pathetic sight than a camper or trailer unit sitting alongside the road with the hood up or a wheel off, we haven't seen it.

Trip time is supposed to be the happy time, no cares, no worries, just "get away from it all" time. The only problem should be how to see everything you want to see in the time you have available and how to do it within your budget. Throw in the added burden of an unscheduled interruption and that's usually the end of both timing and budget.

But these interruptions do happen, and usually to the same people. Most of us, within our circle of friends, can probably count at least one to whom traveling is not so much a series of different places as a series of different misfortunes.

"Yellowstone? Yeah, had a wheel fall off the trailer there once."

Or:

"Yosemite? Nope, boiled the radiator dry going in, busted the block and never did get to see the place."

And then there are others who travel tens of thousands of trouble-free miles and would be hard pressed to remember when they ever had trouble. They are the people who know what the term "Preventive Maintenance" means and how to apply it to get the best results.

The term is self-explanatory. It means knowing your equipment well enough to know what is likely to give you trouble and to attend to it before the trouble has a chance to start. Preventive maintenance is a never ending job and one you'll have to do yourself if you want it done right.

Also under the heading of preventive maintenance is the storing and securing of all household items before hitting the road.

Dishes should be securely stored in closets and drawers and cushioned to prevent breakage. The same goes for breakable containers in the refrigerator, Cokes, glass jars and opened cartons of milk.

As careful as your driver might be, there just might be reason for a panic stop.

Also, if you have any vents open for fresh air in the trailer or camper, put away loose paper, newspapers, letters, memos–or you may have to play that kids' game, "pick up."

As *Detroit Free Press* columnist Bob Talbert said: "The worst thing about living in a trailer is there is no place to put anything except where it belongs!"

Every rig is set up differently and develops its own peculiarities. Outside of standard servicing, you can't expect either a dealership or a service station to handle all the servicing your equipment needs or demands.

If you are a serious traveler your library will include an owner's manual and/or service manual on every piece of equipment you own. They are indispensable but at the same time are little more than a guide to some of the parts and pieces that need servicing.

Your particular equipment, depending on the usage, will require servicing much more often than recommended in the manuals. Also, we have yet to see a manual tell you that after 28.7 miles of back country usage the grapple bolt securing the frammis latch has a tendency to vibrate loose and must be tightened. Information like that can only come through experience.

In the following paragraphs we've listed what years of experience have taught are the common and uncommon maintenance tips necessary to assure trouble-free traveling. At best they are only a guide–until you add to your own experience.

The Vehicle (Tow Cars, Trucks, Vans and Motor Homes)

ENGINE

Carburetor: Vacuum leaks in the intake system not only cause poor performance, they also can burn spark plugs, intake or exhaust valves and pistons.

Periodically tighten carburetor-to-manifold and manifold-to-head stud nuts to prevent air leaks. Keep the exterior of the carburetor clean and have it overhauled at regular intervals. Carburetor linkage pivot points should be kept clean and lubicated with engine oil.

Fuel Filters: Most carburetors have a wire mesh strainer located in the fuel inlet connector. These should be checked periodically and replaced as required. If the carburetor floods, check here first. In-line filters will usually last to the recommended service interval.

Fuel Pump and Lines: The fuel pump should be checked regularly to make sure the mounting bolts, cover-to-body bolts, diaphragm cover screws and inlet and outlet connections are tight.

Air Cleaners: Several types of air cleaners are now in use: oil bath; paper element; polyurethane and paper element with polyurethane wrap. They have to be kept clean for best engine performance.

If most of your traveling is done on paved roads, the recommended service interval will suffice. If you get off the road, out in the dust, you may have to check and clean them as often as several times a day.

Oil bath types are cleaned by replacing the oil. Use the recommended oil and observe fill marks to prevent overfilling. The paper element type cleaner should also be inspected for dust leaks, holes or other damage. Sometimes the paper element can be tapped lightly to remove excess loose dirt. Never use an air hose to remove dirt as this will damage the element. This is a good spare to carry.

The polyurethane element can be cleaned by washing it in solvent to remove oil and dirt. Squeeze, don't wring or shake it dry, dip in engine oil and squeeze lightly again to remove excess oil.

Positive Crankcase Ventilation System: Regularly check the P.C.V. valve for a clogged condition. This is most easily done by removing the crankcase breather cap and covering the opening with the palm of the hand. If a vacuum can be felt the valve is okay. If a buildup of pressure results, the valve needs cleaning or replacing. Check all hoses and fittings and tighten or replace if necessary.

A clogged P.C.V. system results in a loss of crankcase ventilation which will cause an increased formation of acids, sludge buildup and oil dilution.

Crankcase Breather: At each oil change, or sooner if vehicle is driven off-road, the crankcase breather should be removed and washed in solvent. Do not oil element.

Manifold Heat Control Valve: Check this valve regularly for freedom of movement. If shaft is sticking, free it up with a suitable solvent.

Drive Belts: Check all drive belts, fan, generator, air conditioning and power steering periodically for proper tension. Replace any belt that is worn or frayed. These are good spares to carry.

Oil System: Carry several extra cans of oil with your spare equipment. Check engine oil level every morning when on the road, before you start the engine. Also check it at each fuel stop. When adding oil do not overfill.

Change oil and filter at recommended intervals or sooner if you do much off-road driving. Always use a good quality oil. Periodically check for leaks around filter, oil pan, rocker arm covers and any external lines.

Cooling System: Coolant level in radiator should be checked every morning when traveling, before engine is started. Do not check coolant level when engine is at operating temperature as the sudden release of pressure may cause coolant loss. If an overheat condition exists, let engine cool down before removing cap or adding coolant.

It is a good idea to use a glycol base year-around type coolant. The concentration should be enough to give freezing protection to at least minus 20°F. Completely drain and flush system every two years. Quality glycol-base coolants contain an inhibitor to keep rust and scale from building up in the system.

When adding coolant, do not overfill. With engine cold, level should be approximately three inches below filler neck. When engine is warm, keep level half inch to an inch below filler neck.

Periodically check radiator, radiator hoses and water pump for leaks. Check all fittings and mounting bolts for tightness. For emergencies carry extra water, several hose clamps and a good brand of radiator stop leak.

Engine Electrical: Check liquid level in battery frequently, especially in hot weather. If level is down to the level, or below the level of the plates, add water to each cell to the recommended level. If level is continually low, check condition of generator or alternator regulator. Distilled water should be used to prevent the possibility of impurities being added to the electrolyte.

Battery terminals should be checked periodically for both tightness and cleanliness. When corrosion appears on the terminals, they should be cleaned in a solution of baking soda and water or ammonia and water. After cleaning, the top of the battery should be flushed off with clean water. A light film of grease spread evenly over the terminals and connections will help keep corrosion to a minimum.

Generator or alternator connections must be kept tight and free from corrosion or anything that will cause high resistance in the circuit.

Check starting motor attaching bolts and solenoid mounting bolts and connections periodically.

The distributor should be checked periodically for cleanliness. Dust can short it out. Point gap and condition should also be checked. Make sure distributor cam is getting lubrication. Have distributor overhauled at recommended intervals.

Spark plugs should be checked and cleaned at regular intervals. The recommended spark plug heat range may not be the one that'll give you the best performance for the type of driving you do. Have somebody who knows how "read" them to make sure.

All engine wiring and connections should be checked regularly for tightness and integrity of insulation. Make sure they aren't in a position where road vibrations or engine movement can cause chafing. Also make sure that wiring isn't in a position where engine heat can melt or burn through insulation.

Engine Tune-up: For best service tune-ups should be performed at factory recommended intervals–providing nothing happens to warrant them being checked sooner.

DRIVE TRAIN

Clutch and Manual Transmission: Clutch pedal free travel should be checked periodically and adjusted to specified distance as required. Lubricate cross shaft or linkage with recommended water resistant chassis grease as required.

Lubricant level in manual transmissions should be checked at specified intervals or as required when vehicle is driven off-road. Use recommended lubricant and don't overfill.

Automatic Transmission: Fluid level in automatic transmissions should be checked regularly. Condition of fluid should also be checked. ATF is red in color and if it appears brown it should be changed. This is a sign it is either dirty or it has been overheated.

Change fluid at specified intervals and clean dirt screen located in transmission oil pan. If engine has reached overheat condition, check condition of transmission fluid–you may have overheated that too. Add several quarts of automatic transmission fluid to your list of spares.

Shift linkage for both manual and automatic transmissions should be checked periodically for security and lubrication.

Rear axle: Lubricant level should be checked at the recommended interval. Use only recommended lubricant. Drain and change as specified or sooner if vehicle is used off-road.

Some drive shaft universal joints are sealed while others have grease fittings. Off-road use of vehicle dictates more frequent service than specified interval.

CHASSIS

Suspension: Check shock absorbers regularly for both condition and security. You'll be surprised how fast even heavy duty shocks can wear out.

Check spring bushings for wear regularly. Check and tighten attaching bolts as required.

If lubrication points are provided in ball joints and steering or tie rod ends, they should be attended to as specified, or sooner if vehicle is used off-road. Check all attaching bolts regularly.

Steering: Proper wheel alignment is necessary for good handling and long tire life. It should be checked at specified intervals or sooner if you've been out bashing around in the rocks. Check for bent tie rod and drag link.

Check steering gearbox attaching bolts frequently. Also lubricant level. Use only specified grease.

Fluid level in power steering pump reservoirs should be checked when it is hot. Use only specified fluid and don't overfill.

Wheel Bearings: Specified wheel bearing checking and re-packing intervals are good only in normal use. If vehicle is operated off-road or if wheels have been submerged in water, they will have to be checked as required.

When re-packing front wheel bearings, be sure to clean them thoroughly first in a suitable solvent. Do not use an air hose to spin them dry. When re-packing use only a high melting point wheel bearing lubricant that meets the manufacturer's specifications.

Check oil seals and replace if necessary. When tightening wheel bearings observe manufacturer's pre-load specification. Use new cotter keys and make sure wheel bearing grease cap is properly installed.

Rear wheel bearings receive lubrication from the rear axle. However, off-road use or submersion in water dictates they be removed for inspection as required. If removed they should be thoroughly cleaned and prelubed with wheel bearing grease before reinstalling. Check oil seals and replace if necessary.

Brakes: Brake linings should be checked at regular intervals for wear. If vehicle is driven in water, as when launching a boat, brakes should also be inspected for rust and corrosion. Keep rubbing points between brake shoes and backing plates well lubricated with a light coating of recommended brake lubricant. When replacing linings, use the best grade obtainable for maximum performance. Keep brakes adjusted.

Vehicles with self-adjusting brakes, also used to launch boats, will give better service if the self-adjusting mechanisms are removed. When linings get wet they have a tendency to get spongy and swell up and may easily get over-adjusted.

Wheels and Tires: Keep tires inflated to the specified pressures for the loads you are carrying. Don't overinflate, underinflate or overload. Check frequently, especially after off-road trips, for cuts and ruptures. Do this before you get back up to highway speeds.

For best service rotate tires every 6000 miles.

Check lug nuts frequently when traveling.

One final word about tires: Know your total vehicle weight and check out the load capacity of your tires. If you are overloaded or even right on the borderline, buy larger tires, even if it means also going to larger wheels. From a safety standpoint, tires are your most important piece of equipment.

For extended off-road use it's a good idea to carry a good tire pump and a repair kit. We recommend tubes in the tires for extended off-road driving.

Electrics: Check chassis wiring for breaks, chafing and tightness. It's a good idea to carry extra fuses and extra stop light and turn indicator bulbs–especially when towing a trailer of any kind. The gendarmes probably hand out more tickets for lighting violations than any other kind.

Don't forget headlight adjustment. As you load up the vehicle, hook on a trailer, change the attitude of the car, adjustment is going to change.

BODY

Exterior: A good wash and wax job does wonders for any car. The critical area is underneath the car. Especially if you get into areas where they use salt solutions to keep streets clear of ice and snow. Under this condition, it's a good idea to use a high pressure hose as frequently as possible on the underside. Pay particular attention to those hard to get at areas. It doesn't take too long for accumulation of salts to completely rust away body panels.

Interior: Most owner's manuals cover the application of soap, water, cleaning fluid and elbow grease quite thoroughly for this area.

Don't forget to lubricate door and hood hinges and latches at regular intervals. This means before they start squeaking.

Trailer Hitches

Most hitches are built like part of a battleship and as a result some people are apt to put them on and forget about them.

Even battleships sink, so it's a good idea to look at your hitch from time to time, preferably just before you use it.

On the car side, check the attachment points. Make sure all mounting bolts are tight. If it's welded on, make sure no cracks are developing in the welds. Check the ball for tightness and for excessive wear.

On the trailer side, check all welds for cracks. Make sure the safety chains haven't been dragging and several of the links are about to wear through. If there's a built-in screw jack for raising the front of the trailer, keep a light film of water resistant grease applied to the threads for ease of operation. The latch, or locking mechanism, should work freely and if it's supposed to lock in place, it should. The hitch should be kept painted with a good rust retardant paint. This is especially necessary when used with a boat trailer.

Camper Units and Trailers

Exterior: Body materials currently being used in these units range from steel and aluminum to plastic and fiberglass. Each has its own characteristics as far as care and maintenance are concerned. Generally speaking, all may be cleaned with mild soap and cold water.

All will benefit from an occasional waxing to preserve the finish—whatever it is. However, don't use wax with a built-in abrasive cleaner on any body except a steel one.

Other than general cleaning there is very little maintenance involved in the exteriors. If the windows are set in rubber, it is a good idea to have a supply of natural silicone lubricant rubber seal on hand to treat ıt with. Spread the lubricant evenly with a brush or the finger and work it into the surface. This will keep the rubber fresh and flexible and maintain a good weatherproof seal.

Owners of units made of aluminum sheets pop-riveted together would do well to invest in a pop-rivet gun and a supply of rivets. These rivets have been known to loosen up under hard usage and, if they aren't attended to, can allow seams to pull loose. Check for loose rivets and when found drill them out with the proper size drill and replace with a fresh rivet. Pop-rivet guns are simple to use and can be picked up for $5 or less at the local hardware store.

A tube of calking compound is also a good investment and should be included on every list of spare equipment. Camper units have been known to leak and this compound is a quick, easy way to cure the problem.

Interiors: The interiors of these units are just like those of a house only on a slightly smaller scale. As such, they require the same type of maintenance, using the same type of equipment: dust cloths, soap and water, cleaning solvents, vacuum sweepers, dust pan and broom.

There is one big difference. Unless your house is located in an area of unusually frequent and severe earthquakes, it isn't subjected to the same stresses and strains that your camper unit or trailer is.

In your home, when a door starts to fall off a cabinet, you can wait as long as you like before getting around to repairing it.

Don't try that in a camper or a trailer. Things like loose cabinet doors or spreading joints need almost immediate attention or one finds himself with a floor full of splintered woodwork.

Trailer Chassis

Suspension: Very similar to that outlined in the paragraphs on vehicles. The same attention must be paid to spring bushings, seats and attaching hardware as on the tow vehicle.

Wheel Bearings: Trailer wheel bearings must be inspected and re-packed at regular intervals using the same procedure and materials mentioned in the tow vehicle wheel bearing paragraph. Wheel bearings on boat trailers are critical due to the continued dunkings they get. They should be checked frequently to make sure the grease hasn't washed out.

Brakes: Trailer brakes are quite similar to car and truck brakes. The main difference is that they are electrically operated instead of hydraulically operated. Adjustment of the brakes is accomplished the same as with a hydraulic brake.

Linings should be checked periodically and replaced when thickness gets to an eighth-inch or less.

Wheels and Tires: Keep tires inflated to recommended pressures. Tires designed for trailers require higher pressures than do car and most truck tires. Check your owner's manual for specified pressures.

Tires should be rotated in accordance with the procedure recommended in the owner's manual for long life.

When parked between trips, maintain recommended air pressure in all tires at all times. Try to park in shaded areas so tires are not exposed to the direct rays of the sun.

If parking for extended periods of time, put the trailer on blocks so tires do not touch ground. In areas where sunshine prevails, tires should be covered to protect them from ozone deterioration from the sun.

Electrics: If your camper unit or trailer is equipped with auxiliary batteries, they should undergo the same periodic checks and service as the battery in the tow vehicle.

Regularly check all trailer wiring for signs of wear or chafing and for tight connections. It is a good idea to carry extra interior and exterior lamp bulbs.

Accessories

Water Systems: Water storage tanks and lines should be drained periodically and flushed with fresh water. If staleness is detected in the system, this can usually be cured by washing a mild baking soda solution through the system.

Holding Tanks: The modern trailer or camper sewage system is practically maintenance free. All you have to do is drain it as required. If you have trouble, call a plumber.

All fittings and connections in both the fresh water system and sewage system should be checked periodically when traveling to insure tightness.

LP Gas or Butane Appliances: Most well-equipped camper units, trailers, vans and motor homes use either liquid propane gas or butane gas as a power source for stoves, refrigerators and hot water heaters. Like the gas appliances in your home they are virtually maintenance free. The important things are to keep the burner heads clean, and periodically check all fittings, connections and mounting bolts for tightness.

Storage

Storage is mainly a matter of common sense. Whatever type of unit you have, it should undergo a thorough cleaning first. Some protection from the weather should be provided. The storage area should be ventilated and it won't hurt to leave one or two of the unit's windows cracked open just slightly to provide interior ventilation.

Wheeled units should be put on blocks with the tires not touching the ground. If in an exposed area tires should be covered to prevent weathering.

Water and sewage systems should be thoroughly drained and flushed using air pressure if possible. Make sure all lines are completely drained, especially necessary if you live in a cold climate where freezing is a danger.

Special attention must be given to batteries. They must be kept charged at regular intervals because an uncharged battery will freeze.

A specific gravity reading of 1.225 is as low as you should let the battery get. A normal battery will discharge itself in thirty to forty-five days, so it should be checked about every two weeks in cold weather.

Ice boxes and refrigerators should be cleaned before storage and the door left open slightly to prevent ice box odor. Always be certain little children have no access to empty ice boxes or even stored campers. They could be suffocated.

Trail Cycles

Engine: Service intervals on equipment like this are not so much a matter of miles and months as hours of operation. Even that isn't too easy to keep track of. Best thing to do is get in the habit of checking most things after each time you use it.

This would include engine oil level, air cleaner and transmission oil level. If the engine has valves with mechanical lifters, the lash should be checked and set to specification at regular intervals every other time you use it. The same goes for clutch adjustment.

Distributor or magneto points should be checked for condition and adjustment, as well as cleanliness, after each fourth outing. Always carry a spare spark plug and be ready to change it as required.

Chassis: Not much to do here either. Keep tires to recommended pressures and check spoke tightness periodically. The mechanically operated front and rear brakes should be adjusted as required.

Check chain tension from time to time and adjust as required. Invest in a hand grease gun and use it on what few lube fittings there are after each outing. This helps keep the dirt flushed out.

Every four months or so, depending on length and severity of usage, both front and rear wheels should be disassembled and the wheel bearings cleaned and repacked.

After each outing the bike should be thoroughly cleaned. The chassis parts can be washed down with mild soap and water. The engine and transmission case as well as chrome wheels will respond best to a commercial cleaner such as Gunk. Just brush it on, let it soak a while, then flush it off with cold water.

When storing a trail bike for extended periods of time, remove the spark plug, squirt a little engine oil in the cylinder, then put the spark plug back in.

Put it in a protected area, cover it with a tarp and it is good for as long as you want to leave it. It might be a good idea to drain all the fuel out of it before storing. Gasoline will get stale with age and this might cause starting problems when you unwrap it.

Outboard Motors

Engine and Accessories: Before each outing visually check all fuel lines for tightness. Check all wiring for tightness, signs of chafing or areas that might be getting too much engine heat.

Also check mounting bolts of all accessories such as starting motor, generator, distributor and carburetor. The reason this should be done before each outing with the motor mounted on the boat and the boat ready for the water is that trailering induces quite a bit of vibration and any of these parts or pieces could have come loose.

If engine has an oil sump, check oil level. Spare spark plugs should be carried at all times and replaced as required, which is usually frequently.

After each outing, and after you get home, it's a good idea to flush out the engine cooling system with fresh water. Hook up a garden hose to the water inlet and turn it on. Start the engine and let it idle.

When you are sure engine is flushed, remove fuel supply and let the engine run itself clean. This insures that fuel lines and carburetor bowl are completely drained. Turn off garden hose and let water drain from engine.

Complete engine should be cleaned after use by wiping down with solvent-dampened rag. Exterior may then be waxed using a non-abrasive type wax.

Periodically check accessory drive belts for proper tension and for signs of wear. Replace if needed.

Distributor or magneto contact points should be checked for condition and proper gap at regular intervals.

Gear Train and Prop: Lubricant level in gear case should be checked after each outing. Use only specified lubricant and don't overfill.

Check prop for nicks, scratches and straightness after each time out. Small nicks and scratches can be repaired using a small file and crocus cloth. Prop straightening is best handled by an expert. Don't try and run one that's bent even slightly.

Between outings, keep an eye on battery condition. As mentioned earlier, a normal battery will discharge by itself in thirty to forty-five days. Keep the charge level up as a battery that discharges completely too many times has a short life. Some people like to use the same type and size battery in their boat as they do in their cars. They switch them every two weeks or so and figure it's worth the trouble.

Storage: When storing an outboard motor for the season, follow the cleaning, flushing and draining procedures mentioned above. Then all you have to do is wrap it in a tarp or some other suitable dust proof cover, set it in an out of the way place, and forget it until you're ready to use it again.

Body Damage

Some motor homes exteriors are of fiberglass on a steel frame, and to repair the damage the service man cuts out the broken area, matches a new piece to fit and glues it back in.

Others are made of sheet aluminum on aluminum or wood struts.

Peel off the damaged piece, examine for structural damage, lay on a new sheet and screw or rivet it in place. It's that easy.

Rollie Swain was in Tennessee one day when a fellow came into the shop, with a chassis mount camper.

"He had misjudged a low underpass and he had really clobbered the front of the cab over section.

"They had him out of there in two hours. Pulled the skin off, replaced a couple of ribs and laid on a new skin.

"They only charged him $35 for the aluminum and $25 for putting it on.

"It's all in knowing what you are doing."

14. *RV Service*

☐ Dodge Division felt a need some time ago, explained truck operations chief Joe James, "not just for good reliable service for our chassis and engines, which are our prime responsibility, but also from the standpoint of our company name plate being on the motor homes."

The auto/truck makers are not in the camper/motor home business.

Their dealers sell trucks to RV builders and the auto/truck dealers often sell campers to their retail customers.

Regardless, the fellow who buys an RV is quite apt to look to the auto dealer who sells that particular brand of engine and chassis for his service requirements.

Although there is a divided area of responsibility here, the auto/truck factory men realized they had to solve a customer relations problem.

Joe James continued: "You are out in Keokuk, Iowa and drive one of these motor homes into the middle of a dealer's shop and you might just fill up the whole shop.

"The service manager gets a little shook up, because he never even saw a Monomatic toilet, let alone know how to fix it.

"Or the customer says, 'The refrigerator won't make ice cubes!'

"So the dealer tells the customer, 'My mechanics are truck mechanics, not electricians, not gas men, not plumbers. You'll have to drive across town to the XYZ Company which is the warranty service center for that appliance.'

"Now you have a distraught customer," James continued. "He bought this RV from a Dodge dealer and by golly a Dodge dealer should service it.

"Dealers are equipped to handle all engine and chassis requirements, but when you get to the exotic equipment inside, quite frankly a boat outfitter could repair it better than a car operation.

The refrigerator, the stove, the air conditioner—any one of these can be an aggravation if not working properly, and can threaten to ruin an otherwise pleasant vacation, especially if you have a van load of hot, restless, thirsty, hungry kids.

Faced with the necessity of filling an existing service void, Dodge has instituted the first network of recreational vehicle service centers from coast to coast. The network is being expanded to cover all areas of the country. These centers are especially qualified to service RVs of all types. They have qualified technicians, tools, equipment and parts to assure customer satisfaction. These facilities are indicated with an open triangle (Δ) in the service directory on the following pages.

Another first from Dodge: A fleet of Tradesmen vans specially equipped to handle most highway emergency situations. Because these vans have tools and parts, they will be particularly valuable in areas with high concentrations of recreational vehicles. The vans will provide courtesy service or arrange for assistance on a disabled vehicle. They will be equipped with C.B. radios which will monitor channel 9 to provide contact with R V owners who can reach them by radio.

This directory of Dodge medium and heavy duty truck service facilities provides a ready guide for RV and motor home owners to on-the-road service. Only those dealers qualified to handle medium duty or larger units are listed. However the many other Dodge passenger car and light truck facilities throughout the country, although they are not listed, may provide service when an owner so desires.

ALABAMA

Andalusia
J.M. Merrill Motor Co., Inc.
238 S. Cotton St.
Phone: (205) 222-1161 ●★

Anniston
Hodges Dodge City, Inc
916 S. Quintard Ave.
Phone: (205) 237-0331 ●

Bay Minette
Hadley Motor Co.
112 Hoyle Ave.
Phone: (205) 937-2271 ●★

Birmingham
Liberty Truck Sales, Inc.
912 N. 31st St.
Phone: (205) 322-6695 ▲■★○Δ

Blountsville
King Motor Co., Inc.
116 W. Main St.
Phone: (205) 429-2371 ●★

Brent
Dailey-Faucett Motor Co.
Main St.
Phone: (205) 926-3291 ●★

Cullman
Norell-Fields Dodge, Inc.
1302 Second Ave. West
Phone: (205) 734-0721 ●

Dothan
Robert Malone Motors, Inc.
817 S. Oates St., P.O. Box 1767
Phone: (205) 792-9217 ▲★

Enterprise
City Auto Sales, Inc.
123 Dothan Rd.
Phone: (205) 347-8906 ▲★

Florala
Burgess-Harrison Motors, Inc.
North 6th St.
Phone: (205) 858-3485 ●★

Gadsden
Crown Dodge, Inc.
712 Forrest Ave.
Phone: (205) 546-5276 ●★

Guntersville
Guntersville Motor Co.
North Broad St.
Phone: (205) 582-3252 ●★

Huntsville
Huntsville Dodge, Inc.
705 Wheeler Ave.
Phone: (205) 536-8513 ▲★

Mobile
Mobile Dodge, Inc.
3118 Highway 90 West
Phone: (205) 478-5252 ▲★ Δ

Selma
Hooper Motor Co.
1411 Water Ave.
Phone: (205) 872-2304 ●★

● Medium Truck ▲ Heavy Truck ■ Diesel ★ Road Service ○ Night Service Δ Motor Home/Recreational Vehicles

Sheffield
Zelke Dodge, Inc.
1301 E. Second St.
Phone: (205) 381-2300 ●★

Talladega
Jim Preuitt Chrysler-Plymouth-Dodge
Battle & Tinney Sts.
Phone: (205) 362-4106 ●

Tuscaloosa
Warrior Dodge, Inc.
410 Bridge Ave.
Phone: (205) 345-4545 ●△

ARIZONA

Casa Grande
G.B.F. Motors
841 W. Gila Bend Hwy.
Phone: (602) 836-8289 ●

Flagstaff
Flagstaff Dodge
1200 Switzer Canyon Rd.
Phone: (602) 774-5293 ●△

Phoenix
Freeway Dodge
2331 W. Camelback
Phone: (602) 264-9741 ●△

Valley Dodge, Inc.
4240 W. Glendale
Phone: (602) 939-6555 △

Tucson
Bill Breck Dodge, Inc.
3030 E. Speedway
Phone: (602) 327-7462 ●▲■★△○

ARKANSAS

Harrison
Cecil Motor Co.
322 E. Rush St.
Phone: (501) 372-6161 ●★

Jonesboro
Abernathy Motor Co.
906 Gee Street
Phone: (501) 932-2246 ●★△

Lake Village
Burnside Motors
Hwy. 65 & 82 So.
Phone: (501) 265 5574 ●△

Little Rock
Little Rock Dodge, Inc.
5809 S. University
Phone: (501) 562-7200 ●△

Pine Bluff
Wooley-Gandy Motors, Inc.
Highway 67S
Phone: (501) 535-1288 ●▲

Pocohontas
Powell-Sims Motor Co.
Hwy. 67
Phone: (501) 892-3432 ●★

Rogers
Floyd Cox Dodge
Hwy. 71 South
Phone: (501) 636-4769 ●

Springdale
Jim Bryant Motors Co., Inc.
Hwy. 71 S.
Phone: (501) 751-4563 ●★△

Waldron
Denton Motor Co.
516 S. Main St.
Phone: (501) 637-2771 ●★

CALIFORNIA

Anaheim
Anaheim Dodge
1120 S. Anaheim St.
Phone: (213) 639-1208
Phone: (714) 776-0333 ●▲

Bakersfield
S.A. Camp Motor Co.
1815 24th St.
Phone: (805) 323-7961 ▲▲

Burbank
Joe Phillips Dodge
549 S. San Fernando Rd.
Phone: (213) 849-2838 △

Chico
Sierra Dodge Motors, Inc.
293 E. 2nd St.
Phone: (916) 343-3765 ●△

Concord
Concord Dodge, Inc.
1700 Orion Ave.
Phone: (415) 687-9000 ●▲

Covina
Covina Dodge
345 S. Citrus
Phone: (213) 331-0041 △

Crescent City
Bob Mathews Motors
1301 Northcrest Drive
Phone: (707) 464-3790 ●△

Downey
Dodge Trucks, Inc.
7878 E. Telegraph Rd.
Phone: (213) 773-7771 ●▲■★○△

Downey Dodge, Inc.
9655 E. Firestone Blvd.
Phone: (213) 862-8121 △

El Centro
Imperial Valley Dodge, Inc.
Imperial Hwy. & Ira Aten Rd.
Phone: (714) 352-8832 △

El Monte
El Monte Dodge, Inc.
3650 N. Tyler
Phone: (213) 448-9819 △

Eureka
John Ehret Dodge
21 West 4th St.
Phone: (707) 442-0731 ●△

Fair Oaks
Edgett Motors, Inc.
10123 Fair Oaks Blvd.
Phone: (916) 967-5727 △

Fremont
Fremont Dodge
4300 Peralta Blvd.
Phone: (415) 792-2570 ●△

Fresno
Fresno Dodge, Inc.
650 Fulton
Phone: (209) 264-9711 ●△

Fullerton
Jerry Goodwin Dodge, Inc.
1110 W. Orangethorpe Ave.
Phone: (714) 879-6880 △

Garden Grove
Brookhurst Dodge
10151 Garden Grove Blvd.
Phone: (714) 537-8220 ●△

Huntington Beach
Beach City Dodge
16555 Beach Blvd.
Phone: (714) 540-2660 △

Inglewood
Earle Ike Dodge, Inc.
1175 S. LaBrea
Phone: (213) 671-0411 ●△

LaMesa
Carl Burger Dodge
Hwy. 80 at Jackson Dr.
Phone: (714) 463-9321 ●△

Lancaster
H.W. Hunter
44733 Sierra Hwy.
Phone: (805) 942-0451 ●

Long Beach
Glenn E. Thomas
340 E. Anaheim
Phone: (213) 437-6491 ●△

Los Gatos
West Valley Dodge, Inc.
16212 San Jose Ave.
Phone: (408) 356-3131 ●△

Merced
Marasti Motors
1629 W. 16th St.
Phone: (209) 722-7407 ●△

Modesto
Bill Hughes Dodge
722 "I" St.
Phone: (209) 524-6811 ●▲■★○△

Monterey
Cypress Motors, Inc.
724 Abrego St.
Phone: (408) 735-4196 △

National City
Stanley Dodge, Inc.
2829 National Ave.
Phone: (714) 474-1531 ●▲△

Novato
Nave Dodge
1029 First St.
Phone: (415) 897-4137 △

Oakland
Dodge Trucks, Inc.
2121 Peralta St.
Phone: (415) 835-5800 ●▲■★○△

Pasadena
Wegge Dodge
1021 Colorado St.
Phone: (213) 681-6327 ▲★△

Redwood City
Dodge Center
640 Veterans Blvd.
Phone: (415) 365-6000 ●△

Richmond
Cortese Dodge
160 - 23rd St.
Phone: (415) 234-0596 ●△

Riverside
Moss Motors
8151 Auto Drive
Phone: (714) 688-6200 ●★△

Sacramento
Swift Dodge
6250 Florin Road
Phone: (916) 422-4300 ●△

San Bernardino
Inland Center Dodge, Inc.
666 S. "E" St.
Phone: (714) 884-8255 ●△

San Diego
Howard Taylor Dodge
3740 Rosecrans
Phone: (714) 297-3721 ●▲△

Padre Dodge
3550 El Cajon Blvd.
Phone: (714) 283-4455 △

San Jose
Bob Hiam Dodge, Inc.
1611 N. First St.
Phone: (408) 298-4571 ●△

Santa Ana
Santa Ana Dodge, Inc.
1401 N. Tustin
Phone: (714) 835-3691 ●△

Santa Monica
Claude Short Dodge
1127 Santa Monica Blvd.
Phone: (213) 870-3922 ●△

Santa Rosa
Chiaroni Dodge
930 South "A" St.
Phone: (707) 542-3331 △

Stockton
Stockton Dodge, Inc.
540 N. Hunter
Phone: (209) 466-0901 ●△

Sunnyvale
Sunnyvale Dodge, Inc.
1095 W. El Camino Real
Phone: (408) 738-0410 ●△

Van Nuys
Ottie Alburn Sales & Service
5546 Sepulveda Blvd.
Phone: (213) 787-2200 △

COLORADO

Colorado Springs
Bill Breck Dodge, Inc.
3200 Hwy. 24E.
Phone: (303) 632-8812 ●▲■★△

Cortez
G & H Motor Co.
126 E. Main St.
Phone: (303) 565-3461 ●

Denver
Denver Dodge Truck Center
5135 York St.
Phone: (303) 266-2151 ●▲■★△

Windish-Old R/V Service Center
11225 West 6th Ave.
Phone: (303) 238-8591 △

Durango
Durango Dodge, Inc.
902 Second St.
Phone: (303) 247-1212 ●★

Ft. Morgan
Morgan Auto Co.
230 State St.
Phone: (303) 243-1562 ●★

Grand Junction
Ed Eisenhauer Motor Co.
2122 North Ave.
Phone: (303) 243-1562 ●▲★△

Greeley
Hitt-Graham Dodge, Inc.
3501 W. 10th St.
Phone: (303) 352-7246 △

Walt Sparrow Dodge
1108 8th Ave.
Phone: (303) 352-7246 ●★

Lamar
Reese Motor Co.
412 E. Olive
Phone: (303) 336-2231 ●

Littleton
Dodge Country U.S.A., Inc.
5445 S. Broadway
Phone: (303) 794-4274 △

Montrose
Hartman Brothers, Inc.
531 Main St.
Phone: (303) 249-3434 ●

Salida
Salida Motors, Inc.
300 F St.
Phone: (303) 539-2567 ●

Sterling
Ray Smith Motor Co.
330 N. 3rd St.
Phone: (303) 522-1962 ●★

CONNECTICUT

Ansonia
Cavallaro Motors, Inc.
41 Clifton Ave.
Phone: (203) 735-6468 ●★

Danielson
S.E. Poludniak, Inc.
Westcott Rd.
Phone: (203) 774-3578 ▲★○

Hartford
Schechtman Motors, Inc.
265 Murphy Rd.
Phone: (203) 527-8246 ▲

Middletown
Al's Auto Sales, Inc.
Saybrook Rd.
Phone: (203) 346-9637 ●★○

Milford
Milford Dodge, Inc.
579 Bridgeport Ave.
Phone: (203) 878-5971 ●★

Naugatuck
Bosco Dodge
799 New Haven Rd.
Phone: (203) 729-4564 ●★

New London
Linder Motors, Inc.
409 Broad St.
Phone: (203) 443-8335 ●★

New Milford
Couch Brothers
Rt. 25
Phone: (203) 254-4429 ●★

Norwalk
Shorehaven Dodge, Inc.
124 Westport Ave.
Phone: (203) 846-1601 ●△

Putnam
Dag Motors
RR 1, Upper School St.
Phone: (203) 928-4842 ●★

Rockville
O'Dell Dodge, Inc.
Route 83
Phone: (203) 646-2333 ●

Willimantic
Smith Motors, Inc.
1150 Main St.
Phone: (203) 423-4558 ●★

Windsor Locks
Allen Motors, Inc.
6 Stanton Rd.
Phone: (203) 527-5107 ●★

DELAWARE

Newark
Rittenhouse Motor Co.
P.O. Box 204
Phone: (302) 368-9107 ▲★○

Viola
Chambers Dodge Truck Center
Route 13
Phone: (302) 284-4555 ▲■

Wilmington
Kirkwood Motors
4800 Kirkwood
Phone: (302) 999-0141 ●△

FLORIDA

Bradenton
Jim Boast Dodge, Inc.
4827 14th St. W.
Phone: (813) 755-8585 ●△

Callahan
Keen Motor Co.
U.S. Highway 1
Phone: (904) 879-3636 ▲★

Clearwater
Kenyon Dodge
1300 U.S. Hwy. 19 South
Phone: (813) 531-3521 ●★▲△

Daytona Beach
Rossmeyer Dodge, Inc.
721 Ballough Road
Phone: (904) 255-0571 ●△

Eustis
Eustis Dodge, Inc.
237 Bay St.
Phone: (305) 357-4108 ●★○

Ft. Lauderdale
Massey-Yardley Dodge, Inc.
1600 N. Federal Highway
Phone: (305) 566-7541 ●○△

Fort Myers
Stan Dobbs Dodge, Inc.
4300 South Cleveland Ave.
Phone: (813) 936-4118 ●★△

Ft. Pierce
Jacobson Dodge, Inc.
3019 S. U.S. 1
Phone: (305) 461-4770 ●△

Ft. Walton Beach
Bud Wooley's Dodge City
314 Eglin Parkway
Phone: (904) 242-2102 ●

Gainsville
Poole-Gable Motors
119 S. E. First Ave.
Phone: (305) 372-4343 ●★

Homestead
Roberts & Kelley C-P, Inc.
29200 S. Federal Hwy.
Phone: (305) 248-0510 △

Jacksonville
Massey Dodge, Inc.
3333 North Main St.
Phone: (904) 353-7411 ●▲★△

Regency Dodge, Inc.
9875 S. Atlantic
Phone: (904) 725-3050 ●△

Kissimmee
Fred Drake Dodge
2880 N. Orange Blossom Trail
Phone: (305) 423-2471 ●△

Lakeland
Bunker Hill, Inc.
325 S. Lake Parker Ave.
Phone: (813) 688-5535 ●

Leesburg
Mag-Low Motors, Inc.
1390 N. Blvd. West
Phone: (904) 787-1452 ●

Melbourne
Riverside Dodge
2200 N. U.S. Hwy. 1
Phone: (305) 723-5661 ●△

Merritt Island
Cape Cars, Inc.
1775 E. Merritt Causeway
Phone: (305) 636-2246 ●△

Miami
Dadeland Dodge, Inc.
8455 S. Dixie
Phone: (305) 621-3667 ●

Miami Truck & Motor Co.
301 N.W. 171st Street
Phone: (305) 621-3667 ▲■△

Trail Dodge, Inc.
2900 S. W. 8th St.
Phone: (305) 642-5100 ●

Naples
Robins Dodge, Inc.
850 9th Street N.
Phone: (813) 642-7058 ●★○△

Ocala
Marion Motor Co.
112-120 N. Magnolia St.
Phone: (904) 629-0306 ●★

Orlando
Art Grindle Dodge, Inc.
4101 Colonial Drive W.
Phone: (305) 299-1120 ▲△

Panama City
Dixie Dodge, Inc.
1001 East Hwy. 98
Phone: (904) 785-1591 ●★

Pensacola
Hill-Kelly Dodge, Inc.
5771 N. Pensacola Blvd.
Phone: (904) 476-9078 ●▲★△

Plant City
Jack Ramsey Motors
1204 E. Baker St.
Phone: (813) 752-5151 ●

Pompano Beach
Vic Frances, Inc.
2390 N. Federal Hwy.
Phone: (305) 390-1010 ●△

Quincy
Quincy Dodge, Inc.
916 W. Jefferson Ave.
Phone: (904) 627-7135 ●

St. Petersburg
Colonial Dodge, Inc.
2323 34th St. N.
Phone: (813) 895-1661 ●▲△

Tallahassee
Bob Drake Dodge, Inc.
1401 N. Monroe St.
Phone: (904) 222-3134 ●★△

Tampa
Brooks Massey Dodge
2966 N. Dale Mabry Hwy.
Phone: (813) 872-6645 ●

Venice
Wolfer Motors, Inc.
915 S. Tamiami Trail
Phone: (813) 488-6150 ●★

Vero Beach
Dependable Dodge, Inc.
2370 Commerce Ave.
Phone: (305) 567-5214 ●

West Palm Beach
Palm Beach Dodge, Inc.
2101 Okeechobee Blvd.
Phone: (305) 683-1511 ●★△

Winter Park
Luke Potter Dodge, Inc.
1050 N. Orlando Ave.
Phone: (305) 644-1919 ●▲△

GEORGIA

Albany
Irv Wolf Dodge, Inc.
801 E. Oglethorpe Exp.
Phone: (912) 432-5361 ●△

Athens
Ivy Truck Sales, Inc.
2194 West Broad
Phone: (404) 549-7555 ▲★

Atlanta
Dodge Trucks, Inc.
1661 Stewart Ave., S.W.
Phone: (404) 758-9561 ▲■★○

Holton Dodge, Inc.
2461 Stewart Ave. S.W.
Phone: (404) 761-7121 ●★○

Major Dodge, Inc.
3097 Piedmont Rd., N.
Phone: (404) 261-5130 ●△

Augusta
Bill Jones Dodge City
1886 Gordon Hwy.
Phone: (404) 736-8414 ●★

Bainbridge
Willis Motor Sales, Inc.
Broad at Calhoun Sts.
Phone: (912) 246-2886 ●

Brunswick
Gordon MacGregor
26 Glynn
Phone: (912) 265-1160 ●★

Canton
Canton Dodge
275 Marietta St.
Phone: (404) 479-4402 ●★

Clarksville
Stewart Motors
West Louise St.
Phone: (404) 754-2143 ●★

Dalton
Pye Dodge, Inc.
3809 Chatsworth Road
Phone: (404) 278-6859 ●△

Decatur
City Dodge, Inc.
2650 N. Decatur Road
Phone: (404) 292-3220 ●△

Douglas
Jardine Auto Co.
501 S. Peterson St.
Phone: (912) 384-3721 ▲★○

Glennville
Dixie Chry-Ply-Dodge
U.S. 301, Rt. 2
Phone: (912) 654-2511 ●★

Jesup
Clanton Motors
448 N. First St.
Phone: (912) 427-3794 ●★

Lakeland
Banks-Lake Motor Co.
110 N. Mill St.
Phone: (912) 482-3786 ●★○

Macon
Macon Dodge, Inc.
3068 Riverside Dr.
Phone: (912) 743-8963 ●△

Marietta
Marietta Dodge, Inc.
701 S. 4-Lane Hwy.
Phone: (404) 427-9446 ▲△

McRae
Griffith Motor Co.
Oak St., U.S. 23
Phone: (912) 867-3521 ●

Millen
Parker Motor Co.
Highway 25 S.
Phone: (912) 982-2945 ●★

Newnan
Gentry Dodge, Inc.
65 Jefferson St.
Phone: (404) 253-5771 ●

Ocilla
Ocilla Truck & Implement Co.
U.S. 129 N.
Phone: (912) 468-7461 ●

Rome
Marshall Jackson Motor Co.
809 Martha Berry Blvd.
Phone: (404) 232-0844 ●★

Savannah
Karp Motors
45 W. Broad St.
Phone: (912) 236-6121 ●★

Summerville
Turpin Motors, Inc.
Lyerly Rd.
Phone: (404) 857-5661 ●★

Sylvania
Jones Chrysler Plymouth Co.
Hwy. 301, S.
Phone: (912) 564-2048 ●★

Thomson
Hunts Chrysler Plymouth
Augusta Highway
Phone: (404) 595-1244 ●★

Valdosta
Oliver Motors, Inc.
1103 N. Ashley
Phone: (912) 244-1653 ●△

Vidalia
Dyal Crosby Motors, Inc.
410 W. First St.
Phone: (912) 537-7318 ●

Washington
Nash-Willis Motor Co.
E. Robert Tombs Ave.
Phone: (912) 678-2425 ●★

IDAHO

Boise
Valley Dodge Center
1601 Fairview Ave.
Phone: (208) 345-5800 ●△

Bonners Ferry
Corner Garage
313 Main St.
Phone: (208) 267-3265 ●

Burley
Bonanza Motor Co.
1137 Overland
Phone: (208) 678-9486 ●▲★△

Coeur D' Alene
Sunset Dodge
750 W. Appleway
Phone: (208) 664-4746 ●△

Emmett
Joy Motor Sales
419 N. Washington
Phone: (208) 365-4475 ●

Idaho Falls
Ellsworth Bros., Inc.
490 North Yellowstone
Phone: (208) 522-2610 ●▲★△

Lewiston
Lewiston Dodge, Inc.
1005 Main St.
Phone: (208) 743-5554 ●

Moscow
Reynolds Dodge, Inc.
922 Troy Rd.
Phone: (208) 882-2132 ●

Nampa
Dobbs Motor Co.
909 S. Third St.
Phone: (208) 466-2483 ●△

Orofino
Hanson Garage, Inc.
218 First St.
Phone: (208) 476-4549 ▲

Pocatello
Pocatello Dodge, Inc.
555 East Center St.
Phone: (208) 232-4721 ●★△

Sandpoint
Lakeshore Motors
105 Pine St.
Phone: (208) 263-2129 ●

Twin Falls
Bob Reese Motors
500 Blk. 2nd. Ave. South
Phone: (208) 733-4564 △

ILLINOIS

Belleville
Oliver C. Joseph, Inc.
223 W. Main Street
Phone: (618) 233-8140 △

Belvidere
Burton Motor Sales
201 N. State St.
Phone: (815) 544-3911 ●

Brimfield
Brimfield Motor Co.
U.S. Route 150
Phone: (309) 446-3291 ●★

Bushnell
Parker-Speer Dodge, Inc.
145 W. Hurst
Phone: (309) 772-2153 ●

Carlyle
Siever Bros.
8th & Washington
Phone: (618) 594-2624 ●

Carrolton
Pruitt Motor Co.
420 South 5th
Phone: (217) 942-3412 ●★

Centralia
Jennings Dodge Sales
Hwy. 161 West
Phone: (618) 532-6728 ●

Charleston
Grimes Motor Sales
11th and Madison
Phone: (217) 345-4455 ●

Chicago
Cee Eddy Dodge, Inc.
6445 Northwest Highway
Phone: (312) 775-6616 ●

Colonial Dodge
6600 N. Western Ave.
Phone: (312) 465-3000 ●

● Medium Truck ▲ Heavy Truck ■ Diesel ★ Road Service ○ Night Service △ Motor Home/Recreational Vehicles

Dodge Trucks, Inc.
815 Pershing Rd. W.
Phone: (312) 927-4949 ▲★■△

Grand Spaulding Dodge, Inc.
3300 W. Grand Ave.
Phone: (312) 227-3300 ●

North Cicero Dodge, Inc.
2662 N. Cicero
Phone: (312) 889-6400 ●

Olympia Dodge, Inc.
20937 S. Western Ave.
Phone: (312) 481-5700 ●△

Collinsville
Bitzer-Schmacker Motors, Inc.
120 W. Clay
Phone: (618) 344-0202 ●

Danville
Koehn Motors, Inc.
319 N. Vermillion
Phone: (217) 446-0936 ●★

Decatur
Kilborn Motors, Inc.
201 W. Wood
Phone: (217) 428-4476 ▲★○

De Kalb
North Central Motors
427 E. Lincoln Hwy.
Phone: (815) 756-9752 ●△

Edwardsville
Cassens & Sons
121 Hillsboro
Phone: (618) 656-6070 ●

Effingham
Goeckner Bros. Sls. & Service
403 E. Fayette
Phone: (217) 342-3355 ●

Elgin
Horace Motors, Inc.
222 S. Grove Street
Phone: (312) 741-9400 ▲△

Elmhurst
Elmhurst Dodge, Inc.
750 York Rd.
Phone: (312) 833-6700 ●

Evanston
Evanston Dodge City, Inc.
111 Chicago
Phone: (312) 491-9111 ●△

Fairfield
Stephens & Weaver Motors
West Hwy. 15
Phone: (618) 842-2177 ▲

Galva
Galva Auto Sales
216 N.W. 1st
Phone: (309) 932-3290 ▲★

Glen Ellyn
Don Miller Dodge
285 Roosevelt Rd.
Phone: (312) 469-6600 ●△

Harrisburg
B.W. Rude Motor Co.
100 S. Main St.
Phone: (618) 253-7858 ●

Hillsboro
Lingle Motor Co.
130 E. Seward
Phone: (217) 532-3242 ●★

Jerseyville
Jersey County Motor Co.
217 North State
Phone: (618) 498-2143 ●★○

Joliet
Ted Benson Dodge, Inc.
606 N. Chicago
Phone: (815) 723-3435 ●

LaGrange
Grange Dodge, Inc.
5949 S. LaGrange Rd.
Phone: (312) 352-9250 ●

LaSalle
Comparon Motor Sales
836 Second St.
Phone: (815) 223-3350 ●★

Mason City
Brooks Motor Co.
125 N. Tonica
Phone: (217) 482-5629 ●★

Mattoon
Miller & Son Motor Co.
1401 Broadway
Phone: (217) 234-6461 ●

Mendota
R. C. Service Co.
903 Illinois Ave.
Phone: (815) 538-6311 △

Midlothian
Muncaster Dodge, Inc.
14510 S. Cicero Ave.
Phone: (312) 597-6200 ●△

Morrison
Eddie Schuler
Lincoln Way West
Phone: (815) 772-2196 ▲★△

Morton
Heiniger Motor Co.
W. Jackson St.
Phone: (309) 264-2291 ●

Morton Grove
Golfview Dodge
9009 Waukegan Rd.
Phone: (312) 966-0400 ●△

Mt. Carmel
Kamp Motor Sales, Inc.
630 Market
Phone: (618) 262-4233 ●★

Mt. Pulaski
Dick Schull Motor Co.
Cook and LaFayette
Phone: (217) 792-3314 ●★

Ottawa
Sierra Motors, Inc.
Rt. 6 & 71 E.
Phone: (815) 434-3240 ●△

Palatine
Arlington Park Dodge, Inc.
1400 E. Northwest Hwy.
Phone: (312) 392-6300 ●

Pana
B.C. King, Inc.,
8 N. Locust
Phone: (217) 562-3986 ▲★

Paris
Floyd Hegg Motor Co.
225 N. Central
Phone: (217) 465-0312 ●★

Peoria
River Oaks Dodge, Inc.
804 Main St. W.
Phone: (309) 676-0845 ▲★

Pittsfield
Benson Motor Co.
802-804 W. Washington
Phone: (217) 285-2139 ●

Rochelle
Blomberg Motors, Inc.
Hwy. 51 South
Phone: (815) 562-7576 ●★

Rockford
Dodge City Sales, Inc.
3929 Broadway
Phone: (815) 399-0269 ●★○■△

Salem
Blitzer Auto Sales
714 W. Main
Phone: (618) 548-0381 ●★

Shelbyville
Bitzer-Taggert Motor Co.
1012 W. Main
Phone: (217) 774-2143 ▲★

Springfield
Springfield Dodge Sales
412 S. 4th Street
Phone: (217) 523-5685 ▲

Steelville
Bockhorn Motor Sales
1014 W. Broadway
Phone: (618) 865-3419 ●

Sullivan
Gateway Motors
111 North Hamilton
Phone: (217) 728-4451 ●

Taylorville
Harrison Motor Sales
222 W. Main Cross
Phone: (217) 824-3377 ●★

Vandalia
Vandalia Motor Sales, Inc.
1127 N. 5th Street
Phone: (618) 283-3363 ●★

Waukegan
G.L. Miller Motor Sales
555 S. Genesee
Phone: (312) 662-0555 ●

Winchester
Taylor Motor & Implt. Co.
335 W. Cherry
Phone: (217) 742-3112 ●★

INDIANA

Anderson
Broadway Sales Corp.
633 Broadway
Phone: (317) 644-7715 ●★

Angola
L & M Motors, Inc.
U.S. 27 South
Phone: (219) 665-2125 ●

Attica
Barker Motors
106 W. Main
Phone: (317) 762-2488 ●

Auburn
Dailey Motor Sales
109 E. Fifth
Phone: (219) 925-4200 ▲★

Bluffton
John W. Gallman, Inc.
225 W. Wabash
Phone: (219) 824-1620 ●★

Cannelton
Malone's Garage
538 Seventh St.
Phone: (812) 547-2401 ●★

Chesterton
Buhman Dodge
401 N. Calumet Rd.
Phone: (219) 926-1610 ●

Clinton
Mike's Motor Co.
111 Elm St.
Phone: (812) 832-2411 ●★

Connersville
Riedman Motors
610 Grand Ave.
Phone: (317) 825-4341 ●★

Crawfordsville
O.K. Gallosway & Son
116 N. Water St.
Phone: (317) 362-0900 ●

Decatur
Phil L. Macklin Co.
107 S. First St.
Phone: (219) 724-7129 ●★

Dunkirk
Leon Etchison Motors, Inc.
145 E. Commerce St.
Phone: (317) 3811 ●

Elkhart
Lochmandy Dodge Sales, Inc.
1226 W. Bristol St.
Phone: (219) 264-1174 ●△

Evansville
Vandeveer, Inc.
500 Greenriver Rd.
Phone: (812) 477-9261 ▲

Flora
Flora Chrysler Plymouth
105 N. Main
Phone: (219) 967-4333 ●★

Fortville
Rash Motors, Inc.
231 S. Main St.
Phone: (317) 485-5151 ●★

Fort Wayne
Ft. Wayne Dodge, Inc.
100 W. 30 Bypass
Phone: (219) 484-1533 ●△

Frankfort
Zink Motors
1551 E. Wabash
Phone: (317) 654-5536 ●

Gary
Broadway Dodge, Inc.
5880 Broadway St.
Phone: (219) 887-9561 ●△

Goshen
Sorg Dodge, Inc.
U.S. 33 West
Phone: (219) 533-8605 ●△

Greencastle
Putman Motor Sales
118 N. Indiana
Phone: (317) 653-5156 ●★

Greenfield
M.E. Andis
U.S. 40 West
Phone: (317) 462-4478 ●

Hammond
Bohling Auto Sales
222 Douglas St.
Phone: (219) 933-0265 ●

Indianapolis
Capitol Dodge, Inc.
4343 W. 38th St.
Phone: (317) 293-6220 ●△

Indiana Truck Center
1404 W. Washington
Phone: (317) 635-6431 ▲★■○

McGinty Dodge
3419 East St. South
Phone: (317) 787-8361 ●

Palmer Dodge
3820 N. Keystone
Phone: (317) 545-3321 ●

Shadeland Dodge, Inc.
1630 N. Shadeland
Phone: (317) 357-8001 ▲

Jeffersonville
Vissings Dodge, Inc.
115 West 19th St.
Phone: (812) 283-3561 ●★

Kendallville
Hilkert & Pankop, Inc.
625 S. Main
Phone: (219) 347-2060 ●★

Knightstown
Goodwin's, Inc.
Main & Madison
Phone: (317) 345-2555 ▲★

La Grange
LaGrange County Dodge, Inc.
Road 9 North
Phone: (219) 463-2161 ●△

LaPorte
Rembold Motors, Inc.
607 J St.
Phone: (219) 362-7812 ●

Lebanon
Kincaid Auto Sales
200 S. Mendian
Phone: (317) 482-5180 ●★

Logansport
Logansport Dodge, Inc.
222 E. Melbourne
Phone: (219) 753-4811 ●★

Marion
Western Dodge, Inc.
3527 South Western Ave.
Phone: (317) 674-3394 ●★

Mishawaka
Brook Motor Sales, Inc.
916 E. McKinley
Phone: (219) 255-4751 ●△

Muncie
Champlin Dodge, Inc.
2450 N. Broadway
Phone: (317) 282-5907 ●

Newberry
Kuhlenschmidt Chrysler Products
Highway 57
Phone: (812) 659-2811 ●

Noblesville
Paul Goeke, Inc.
State Road No. 32 East
Phone: (317) 773-4447 ▲★

Oldenburg
Oldenburg Garage, Inc.
Vine St.
Phone: (812) 934-2033 ●★

Plainfield
Walt's Dodge Sales
310 W. Main
Phone: (317) 839-2506 ●

Princeton
McGarrah Sales & Service
Prince & Warnock
Phone: (812) 385-4811 ●

Rensselaer
Johnny Rusk, Inc.
Harrison and Van Rensselaer
Phone: (219) 866-3031 ●★

Richmond
Raper Sales, Inc.
N. W. 5th St., U.S. 35
Phone: (317) 962-3502 ●★

Roanoke
Hartley Garage
112 E. Second
Phone: (219) 672-2700 ▲

Rochester
Hammel Chrysler-Plymouth-Dodge
1702 S. Main
Phone: (219) 223-2711 ●★

Rockville
Jacks & Jacks Motor Co.
122 N. Jefferson
Phone: (812) 569-5419 ●

Rushville
Farthing Dodge Sales
253 Buena Vista Dr.
Phone: (317) 932-2541 ●

Shelbyville
Jerry Porter Dodge
326 East Broadway
Phone: (317) 392-2841 ●★

South Bend
Harold Medow, Inc.
222 N. Lafayette Blvd.
Phone: (219) 232-3368 ▲★●△

Terre Haute
Vigo Dodge, Inc.
4120 Dixie Bee Road
Phone: (812) 234-2615 ●△

Tipton
Clyde Overdorf Motors
State Road 28 East
Phone: (317) 675-7426 ●

Valparaiso
Grieger Motor Sales, Inc.
1415 E. Lincoln Way
Phone: (219) 462-1983 ●

Veedersburg
Myers Motor Sales
109 W. 2nd St.
Phone: (317) 294-2902 ●

Versailles
Walston Motors, Inc.
211 W. Perry
Phone: (812) 689-6101 ●

Wakarusa
Truex Auto Sales
114 N. Elkhart
Phone: (219) 862-2250 ●★

Winamac
Knebel Motor Sales
320 S. Monticello Ave.
Phone: (219) 946-3231 ●★○△

IOWA

Algona
Percival Motors, Inc.
800 S. Philips
Phone: (515) 295-2471 ●

Audubon
Jensen Motor Co.
411 Market St. (U.S. 71)
Phone: (712) 563-3464 ●

Burlington
Delzell Bros., Inc.
812-818 Washington St.
Phone: (319) 754-7505 ●

Cedar Rapids
Dean Powers Co.
455 Waconia Ave. S.E.
Phone: (319) 363-2663 ▲△

Cedar Rapids
Handler Motor Co.
712-728 2nd Ave. S.E.
Phone: (319) 363-3521 ●○

Cherokee
Petersons Cars, Inc.
515 West Main St.
Phone: (712) 225-5713 ●

Clinton
Car Carrier Motor Sales
1331 Roosevelt St.
Phone: (319) 243-2451 ●

Davenport
Davenport Dodge, Inc.
4100 Brady Street
Phone: (319) 391-4100 ▲△

Denison
Ehrich's Motor Co.
114-18 N. Main
Phone: (712) 263-4046 ●

Des Moines
Des Moines Dodge, Inc.
2103 Ingersol
Phone: (515) 283-2482 ▲△

De Witt
Peters Motor Co., Inc.
507 10th St.
Phone: (319) 659-5158 ●

Dubuque
Wilson Bros.
90 Dubuque Kennedy Rd
Phone: (319) 583-5781 ●▲

Forest City
Whiteis Auto Co.
125 West "K" St.
Phone: (515) 582-4040 ●★

Griswold
Griswold Auto Co.
615 Main St.
Phone: (712) 778-4555 ●★

Harlan
Harlan Auto Mart, Inc.
12th & Chatburn
Phone: (712) 755-1121 ●

Independence
Chrysler Lines
501 1st E.
Phone: (319) 334-2619 ●

Indianola
Heaivilin Dodge
600 S. Jefferson
Phone: (515) 961-2849 ●

Iowa City
Hertwig Motors, Inc.
629-711 S. Riverside Dr.
Phone: (319) 338-3611 ●★

Keokuk
McCredie Dodge
Main St. Rd.
Phone: (319) 524-2660 ●★

Lake City
Boyd's Inc.
110 E. Washington
Phone: (712) 464-7950 ●★

Lake Park
Lauscher Motors
Highway 219 So.
Phone: (712) 832-3642 ●

Le Mars
Neisius Motor Co.
22 Second St. N.E.
Phone: (712) 546-4151 ▲

Mason City
Hale-Phipps Mtrs.
215 15th Street, S.W.
Phone: (515) 424-2277 ●★△

Northwood
Boyd Implement Co.
8th Street North
Phone: (515) 324-1041 ●★

Red Oak
Bryan-Gates Auto Co.
1400-1410 Broadway
Phone: (712) 623-2565 ●

Shenandoah
MacMalloy Motor Co.
814 West Thomas
Phone: (712) 246-2576 ●

Sioux City
Sioux City Dodge, Inc.
2101 E. 6th St.
Phone: (715) 258-0691 ●★

Spencer
Asher Motor Co.
600 Grand Ave.
Phone: (712) 262-5730 ●★

Sumner
Wuttke Motors
206 W. 1st St.
Phone: (515) 224-3317 ●

Waterloo
Simpson Motor Co.
403 Franklin St.
Phone: (319) 234-7546 ●△

KANSAS

Arkansas City
Bill Fildes Motor Co., Inc.
412 So. Summit St.
Phone: (316) 442-3170 ●

Atchison
Lutz Bros. Auto & Truck Service
835 Commercial Street
Phone: (913) 367-2532 ●★

Atwood
C.W. Beamgard
210 State St.
Phone: (913) 626-3547 ●

Caldwell
Shoffner Motor Co.
538 N. Main
Phone: (316) 845-6915 ●

Chanute
Ellis Dodge, Inc.
120 N. Lincoln
Phone: (316) 431-2970 ●★

Clyde
George Motor Co.
315 Commercial St.
Phone: (913) 785-2731 ●

Coffeyville
Stewart Motors, Inc.
309 West 8th
Phone: (316) 251-2480 ●

Columbus
Mitts Motors
917-25 West Maple St.
Phone: (316) 429-2910 ●

Dighton
Star Garage
125 S. Main St.
Phone: (316) 397-5851 ●

Dodge City
Sellers Dodge City Motor Co.
305 Second St.
Phone: (316) 225-5561 ●

Emporia
Powell Motors, Inc.
819 Commercial St.
Phone: (316) 342-2473 ●★

Garden City
Five Points Motor Co.
712-20 Jones
Phone: (316) 276-3256 ●

Goodland
Jensen Motor Co., Inc.
E. Hwy. 24
Phone: (913) 899-6120 ▲△

Great Bend
Parrish Motor Co.
1410 Williams
Phone: (316) 793-3519 ●

Greensburg
Greensburg Equipment Co.
204 E. Kansas Ave.
Phone: (316) 723-2148 ●

Hutchinson
Downtown Dodge
311 West 2nd St.
Phone: (316) 662-1229 ●

Independence
Quality Chrysler - Plymouth, Inc.
2022 West Main
Phone: (316) 331-6090 ●

Kansas City
Quality Dodge, Inc.
846 State Ave.
Phone: (913) 371-3370 ▲△

Kinsley
Fravel Motor Co.
317 E. 6th St.
Phone: (316) 659-2641 ●

Larned
Rupp-Marconet Motors, Inc.
123 E. 5th St.
Phone: (316) 285-3183 ●

Lawrence
Jim Clark Motors
2121 West 29th St. Terr.
Phone: (913) 843-3055 ●★△

Levenworth
Zeck Motor Co., Inc.
225 Seneca
Phone: (913) 32-4544 ▲★

Liberal
Gould Motor Co.
2250 Highway 83 N.
Phone: (316) 624-3423 ●

Lyons
Sam Rickabaugh Motor Co., Inc.
1001 W. Main St.
Phone: (316) 257-2381 ●

Marysville
Barker Motor Co.
9th & Center St.
Phone: (913) 443-3616 ●

McPherson
Sid Bacon Motor Co.
109 S. Maple
Phone: (316) 241-0371 ●

Ness City
Schwartzkopf Sales & Service
805 West Sycamore
Phone: (913) 798-2215 ●

Norton
City Motors
101 S. Norton
Phone: (913) 927-3234 ●

Oakley
Oakley Motors, Inc.
118 W. 2nd St.
Phone: (913) 672-8611 ●

Pratt
Howard Moyer Motors
619 S. Main St.
Phone: (316) 672-2261 ●

Salina
Bacon & Clark, Inc.
253 N. Santa Fe
Phone: (913) 827-5522 ● △

Marshall Motor Co., Inc.
801-25 E. Crawford
Phone: (913) 827-9641 △

Scott City
Church Motors
902 West 5th St.
Phone: (316) 872-3580 ●

Stockton
Rooks County Implement Co., Inc.
116 S. Cedar St.
Phone: (913) 425-6541 ●

Topeka
Jim Clark Chrysler-Plymouth
3220 Topeka Blvd.
Phone: (913) 266-3333 ●△

Shortman Motor Company, Inc.
1000 Quincy
Phone: (913) 233-1366 ▲

Ulysses
Anderson Motor Co.
305 S. Main
Phone: (316) 356-1636 ●

Wakeeney
Harries Motor Co., Inc.
100 Sixth St.
Phone: (913) 743-6491 ●

Waterville
Waterville Motor Co.
208 W. Main
Phone: (913) 785-2731 ●

Wichita
Don Schmid Motors, Inc.
3205 S. Broadway
Phone: (316) 591-2253 ●△

Spencers Dodge
1200 E. Douglas
Phone: (316) 363-7261 ▲

KENTUCKY

Bardstown
W.H. Samuels Motor Co.
120 W. Stephen Foster Ave.
Phone: (502) 348-9292 ●

Booneville
Marshals Chrysler Products
Hwy. 28 East
Phone: (606) 593-5882 ●

Bowling Green
Harry Leachman Motors, Inc.
1001 Center
Phone: (502) 842-4881 ▲★

Carlisle
Buntins Garage
Elm & Market St.
Phone: (606) 289-5182 ●

Danville
Whitehouse-Humphrey
206 E. Main St.
Phone: (606) 236-3954 ▲★

Dry Ridge
Thomas Chrysler Products
25 Main
Phone: (606) 824-3339 ●

Elizabethtown
Swope Motors, Inc.
N. Dixie Hwy.
Phone: (502) 765-2181 ●★

Flemingsburg
Eldridge Ros., Inc.
Rt. 1
Phone: (606) 845-5601 ●★

Frankfort
Frankfort Auto Sales
Thornhill By-Pass
Phone: (502) 223-8223 ▲

Harlan
Pace Motor Sales
N. Main St.
Phone: (606) 573-2236 ●

Hopkinsville
Sisk Motor Co.
9th & Clay St.
Phone: (502) 885-9004 ●★△

● Medium Truck ▲ Heavy Truck ■ Diesel ★ Road Service ○ Night Service △ Motor Home/Recreational Vehicles

Jackson
Johnson Motors
U.S. Hwy. 52, RR No. 1
Phone: (606) 666-2476 ▲

Lawrenceburg
Hanks Motor Co.
201-203 E. Woodford
Phone: (502) 839-4577 ●

Lebanon
Pickerill Motor Co.
108 Depot St.
Phone: (502) 692-2126 ●★

Lexington
Lexington Dodge
1560 New Circle Rd.
Phone: (606) 266-1155 ●△

Lexington Truck Sales
1198 New Circle Road, N.E.
Phone: (606) 252-6705 ▲■★

Louisville
Falls City Dodge
5311 Dixie Hwy.
Phone: (502) 582-2492 ●

Murray
Taylor Motor Co.
303 S. 4th St.
Phone: (502) 753-1374 ▲★

Newport
Newport Auto Sales
125 E. 3rd St.
Phone: (606) 581-4455 ●

Pineville
Gambrel & Madon Motor Co.
Kentucky & Cumberland Avenues
Phone: (606) 337-2396 ●

Somerset
McAlpin Chrysler Products, Inc.
U.S. Highway 27, S.
Phone: (606) 679-1188 ▲

LOUISIANA

Abbeville
Raywood Motors, Inc.
708 W. Port St.
Phone: (318) 893-0306 ●★

Baton Rouge
Airline Dodge
5255 Airline Hwy.
Phone: (504) 356-3414 ●▲△○

Standard Motor Car Co.
2029 North St.
Phone: (504) 348-5121 ●▲△○■

Harvey
Hughes Dodge, Inc.
1660 Westbank Expressway
Phone: (504) 368-6900 ●▲★△■○

Houma
Southland Dodge, Inc.
505 Sunset Ave.
Phone: (504) 876-1817 ●

Lafayette
Dependable Dodge
1700 S.E. Evangeline
Phone: (318) 232-1430 ●▲■△

Lake Charles
Nelson Dodge, Inc.
3465 Ryan St.
Phone: (318) 477-8873 ●▲■★○△

Lockport
Autin Dodge
La. Highway No. 1
Phone: (504) 532-3374 ●

Metairie
Clearview Dodge, Inc.
4848 Veterans Memorial Hwy.
Phone: (504) 888-7150 ●▲■○

New Orleans
Gentilly Dodge, Inc.
6101 Chef Menteur Hwy.
Phone: (504) 242-6644 ●△

Rayne
Stamm Raymond, Inc.
219 N. Adams St.
Phone: (318) 334-3750 ●★

Shreveport
Hutton-Donaldson, Inc.
2511 Linwood Ave.
Phone: (318) 424-8341 ●▲△

Winnsboro
Lanier Motor Co.
305 Main St.
Phone: (318) 435-4290 ●★

MAINE

Biddeford
Harry B. Center, Inc.
321 Elm St.
Phone: (207) 284-4586 ●

Brunswick
Bodwell Motors
169 Pleasant St.
Phone: (207) 725-2664 ●★

Dexter
Hartley Motors
Corinna Road
Phone: (207) 924-7316 ●▲

Fort Kent Mills
Gilman Bouchard, Inc.
Market St.
Phone: (207) 994-5917 ▲★○

Kennebunk
Snowden Motor Co., Inc.
88 York St., U.S. Route
Phone: (207) 985-2022 ●★

Lewiston
Marcel Motors
1155 Lisbon St.
Phone: (207) 783-8553 ●▲★○△

Mexico
Joy's Sales & Service, Inc.
1 Bridge St.
Phone: (207) 364-7836 ●★

Millinocket
Moir Auto Sales
Balsam Drive
Phone: (207) 723-9774 ●

Portland
Henley-Kimball, Inc.
380 Forest Ave.
Phone: (207) 772-1955 ●▲★○

Presque Isle
Silvers Garage, Inc.
Houlton Rd.
Phone: (207) 769-2011 ●▲

Rockland
Ellery T. Nelson, Inc.
New County Rd.
Phone: (207) 594-4481 ▲★○

MARYLAND

Cumberland
Penn-Mar Mtr. Co.
1-8 National Hwy.
Phone: (301) 722-6340 ●★

Frostburg
Frostburg Auto Co.
114 W. Main St.
Phone: (301) 689-9935 ▲■★○

Hagerstown
Central Motor Dodge, Inc.
940 S. Potomac St.
Phone: (301) 739-7800 ●

Mt. Airy
The Jones Motors, Inc.
Routes 27 & 144
Phone: (301) 829-1440 ●

New Carrollton
Banning's Beltway Dodge
8100 Annapolis Road
Phone: (301) 459-6800 ●▲△

Oakland
Ralph Pritts & Sons
112 E. Liberty St.
Phone: (301) 895-5102 ▲★○△

Rockville
Reed Bros., Inc.
608 E. Montogomery Ave.
Phone: (301) 424-8200 ●

Towson
Towson Dodge, Inc.
1609 E. Joppa Rd.
Phone: (301) 825-3046 ●★△

MASSACHUSETTS

Attleboro
Arnold & Johnson, Inc.
42 County Rd.
Phone: (617) 222-2100 ▲★○

Auburn
Gross & Bracci, Inc.
916 Southbridge St.
Phone: (617) 832-2091 ▲★

Ayer
Gervais Inc.
39 Central Ave.
Phone: (617) 772-3187 ●

Belmont
Pleasant St. Garage
1000 Pleasant St.
Phone: (617) 484-5420 ●★

Beverly
Doolings Motor
81-85 Rantoul St.
Phone: (617) 922-4810 ●★

Boston
Commonwealth Dodge, Inc
971 Commonwealth Ave.
Phone: (617) 254-0404 ▲★○

Braintree
Cliff Handy, Inc.
19 Stedman Ave.
Phone: (617) 843-6000 ▲★○

Bridgewater
Wally Krueger Motors
456 Bedford St.
Phone: (617) 697-2200 ●★

Brockton
Brockton Dodge, Inc.
1906 Main St.
Phone: (617) 588-5110 ▲★○

Brookfield
Brookfield Motors, Inc.
Route No. 9
Phone: (617) 867-7473 ●★

Cambridge
Porter Square Dodge
820 Somerville Ave. Boston Area
Phone: (617) 491-8280 ●

Canton
Bonded Dodge
955 Tunpick St.
Phone: (617) 828-6200 ●★

Clinton
Meleen Motors, Inc.
359 High St.
Phone: (617) 365-6544 ●★

Dartmouth
New Bedford Dodge, Inc.
225 State Rd.
Phone: (617) 997-2200 ▲★○

Dudley
Lavoie Auto Co.
West Main St.
Phone: (617) 943-4400 ●★

East Boston
Neptune Motors, Inc.
480 Bennington St.
Phone: (617) 567-5800 ●★

Falmouth
Falmouth Dodge, Inc.
486 Main St.
Phone: (617) 548-2000 ●★

Greenfield
Hartwin Dodge
397 Federal St.
Phone: (413) 773-3696 ●★

Hingham
Whipple Motors, Inc.
315 Lincoln St.
Phone: (617) 749-2360 ●★

Hyannis
Central Cape Dodge, Inc.
Iyanough Rd.
Phone: (617) 775-8424 ●★

Kingston
John Hamilton, Inc.
45 Main St.
Phone: (617) 746-7200 ●★

Lawrence
Manzi Auto Sales, Inc.
10 Carver St.
Phone: (617) 683-9591 ●

Mansfield
Old Colony Motors, Inc.
77 West St.
Phone: (617) 339-8181 ●★

Marion
Hiller Company
Front St.
Phone: (617) 748-0019 ●★

Maynard
Great Road Garage
146 Great Road
Phone: (617) 897-8353 ●○

Millbury
Chabot Motors, Inc.
North Main St. Route No. 146
Phone: (617) 791-6231 ●

Natick
Natick Dodge Inc
1360 Worcester St.
Phone: (617) 655-1505 ▲★

Newton
Silver Lake Motors
444 Watertown St.
Phone: (617) 244-5880 ●★

North Adams
Windsor Motors
100 Union St.
Phone: (413) 663-8800 ▲

Norwood
Boch Dodge, Inc.
1201 Providence Hwy.
Phone: (617) 762-7200 ▲★

Pittsfield
Shapiro Motors, Inc.
631 North St.
Phone: (617) 448-8255 ●★

Quincy
Granite Motor Sales, Inc.
338 Washington St.
Phone: (617) 479-6700 ▲★○

Randolph
North Main St. Garage, Inc.
659 Main St.
Phone: (617) 963-3100 ●★

Scituate
Paul Young Motors
126 First Parish Rd.
Phone: (617) 545-1200 ●★

Somerville
Knox Bros. Motor Co., Inc.
645 Broadway St.
Phone: (617) 666-2200 ▲★

S. Duxbury
Cushing Bros.
5 Chestnut St.
Phone: (617) 934-2011 ●★

Springfield
Hampden Dodge, Inc.
648 State St.
Phone: (617) 734-8251 ●

Watertown
Crawford Motors, Inc.
15 Crawford St.
Phone: (617) 924-6700 ●

Westboro
J.L. Harris, Inc.
Turnpike Rd.
Phone: (617) 366-8221 ▲★

Whitman
Lloyd's Garage, Inc.
500 South Ave.
Phone: (617) 447-2441 ●★

Worchester
Worcester Dodge, Inc.
520 Park Ave.
Phone: (617) 753-4771 ▲★

MICHIGAN

Ann Arbor
College Dodge, Inc.
3365 Washtenaw
Phone: (313) 662-4485 ●★

Battle Creek
Dodge Center, Inc.
301 W. Michigan Ave.
Phone: (616) 965-2377 ▲★

Bay City
Bay City Motors, Inc.
4191 North Euclid Ave.
Phone: (517) 686-1503 ●△

Capac
K & L Dodge
131 N. Main St.
Phone: (313) 395-4505 ●★

Cheboygan
L.J. Ormsbee Motors, Inc.
U.S. 27 S. Main St.
Phone: (616) 627-5673 ▲★

Croswell
Bricker Motor Sales
13 Wells Street
Phone: (313) 679-3373 ●★

Detroit
Eastowne Dodge
11245 Gratiot
Phone: (313) 372-2100 ●★△

Great Lakes Dodge Truck Center, Inc.
3350 E. Jefferson Ave.
Phone: (313) 539-2420 ●▲

Husak Brothers, Inc.
8421 Michigan Ave.
Phone: (313) 582-5757 ●

Ken Brown
3350 Jefferson Ave.
Phone: (313) 568-0450 ●▲★○△

Raynal Brothers
9103 Chalmers
Phone: (313) 526-1300 ●★△

East Detroit
Colonial Dodge, Inc.
24211 Gratiot Ave.
Phone: (313) 778-1800 ●▲△

Farmington
Town & Country Dodge, Inc.
31015 Grand River
Phone: (313) 474-6750 ●△

Fenton
Kirk Sales & Service, Inc.
112 Silver Lake Rd.
Phone: (313) 629-0391 ●★

Ferndale
Fernwood Dodge
23000 Woodward Ave.
Phone: (313) 399-8100 ●△

Northwestern Dodge, Inc.
10500 W. 8 Mile Rd.
Phone: (313) 399-6700 ●▲★△

Flint
Flint Dodge, Inc.
5152 N. Clio Rd.
Phone: (313) 785-7801 ●▲★△

Frankenmuth
Schaefer & Bierlein
1015 Weiss St.
Phone: (517) 652-9965 ●▲★△

Garden City
Crestwood Dodge, Inc.
32850 Ford Rd.
Phone: (313) 421-5700 ●▲△

Grand Rapids
Northfield Dodge, Inc.
4100 Plainfield N.E.
Phone: (616) 363-9011 ●△

Wonderland Dodge
440 28th Street
Phone: (616) 452-3143 ▲★○△

Greenville
Jeff Branch Motor Sales, Inc.
6472 N. Greenville
Phone: (616) 754-3635 ▲★△

Hastings
Hastings Motor Sales
328 N. Michigan Ave.
Phone: (616) 945-2454 ●★

Hesperia
Gillett Auto Sales
61 N. Division
Phone: (517) 854-3935 ●

Hillsdale
Playford Dodge
Carleton Rd. W.
Phone: (517) 437-3394 ●★

Iron Mountain
Ken's Motor Sales, Inc.
North U.S. Highway 2
Phone: (906) 774-2120 ●★△

Jackson
Wolverine Dodge, Inc.
1910 E. Michigan Ave.
Phone: (517) 787-2400 ▲★

Kalamazoo
H.J. Cooper, Inc.
Michigan at Park
Phone: (616) 342-0101 ▲★△

Lakeview
R. & C. C. Bollinger, Inc.
208 Lincoln Ave.
Phone: (517) 352-7251 ●▲■★○△

Lansing
Capitol Dodge, Inc.
3011 E. Saginaw Street
Phone: (517) 351-3200 ▲★

Livonia
Terrina Company-Div. of Car Corp.
12011 Market St.
Phone: (313) 261-6990 △

Madison Heights
Oakland Dodge, Inc.
101 W. 14 Mile Road
Phone: (313) 585-8800 ●△

Marquette
Specker Motor Sales Co.
722 Washington West
Phone: (906) 225-1395 ●

Mt. Clemens
Mt. Clemens Dodge
43774 Gratiot N.
Phone: (313) 772-1130 ▲△

Muskegon
Lake Dodge, Inc.
3146 Henry Street
Phone: (616) 733-4401 ●△

Northville
G.E. Miller Sales & Service
127 Hutton Street
Phone: (313) 349-0660 ▲★

Oxford
Jerry Hight Dodge, Inc.
14 N. Washington
Phone: (313) 628-4858 ●

Paw Paw
R. A. Imus, Inc.
201 Commercial
Phone: (616) 657-3124 ●

Petoskey
Brown Motor Sales, Inc.
212 E. Mitchell St.
Phone: (616) 347-2568 ▲★

Pigeon
Pigeon Motor Sales
7392 W. Michigan Ave.
Phone: (517) 453-3621 ●★

Pontiac
Motor City Dodge, Inc.
855 Oakland Ave.
Phone: (313) 338-9222 ●△

Port Huron
Don R. Brewer Dodge, Inc.
4080 24th Ave.
Phone: (313) 385-4481 ▲■△

Rogers City
A-P Super Service
338 N. Third St.
Phone: (517) 734-2941 ●★

St. Louis
Paul Cameron
1024 E. Washing Ave.
Phone: (517) 681-2194 ▲

Saginaw
Saginaw Dodge, Inc.
5355 State St.
Phone: (517) 752-8168 ▲△

Saline
Steeb Dodge Sales, Inc.
147 W. Michigan Ave.
Phone: (313) 429-9431 ▲

Sault Ste. Marie
S & S Motors
2601 Ashmun St.
Phone: (906) 632-8621 ●

Scottville
Steingraber Auto Sales
104 W. Broadway
Phone: (616) 757-4706 ●

Southfield
Tel-Twelve Dodge, Inc.
24625 Twelve Mile Rd.
Phone: (313) 354-6600 ●△

Sterling Hgts.
Sterling Heights Dodge
40111 Van Dyke
Phone: (313) 939-3900 ●

Sturgis
Dan's Motors, Inc.
1139 S. Centerville Rd.
Phone: (616) 651-5459 ●★

Tawas City
Ottawa Equipment Co.
840 E. Lake St.
Phone: (517) 362-5429 ▲★

Taylor
South Pointe Dodge, Inc.
13500 Telegraph Road
Phone: (313) 946-9450 ●

Tecumseh
Les Dallas, Inc.
2805 W. Monroe Rd.
Phone: (313) 423-2147 ●

Three Rivers
Boeschenstein Motor Sales
1008 W. Michigan Ave.
Phone: (616) 278-7085 ●★

Traverse City
Charron Chrysler of Traverse City, Inc.
2625 North Memorial Highway
Phone: (616) 946-2556 ▲★

Vassar
Bob McKee Sales & Service
960 W. Saginaw Rd.
Phone: (517) 823-2061 ●★

Walled Lake
McMan Dodge, Inc.
1010 W. Maple
Phone: (313) 624-1572 ●▲△

Warren
Van Dyke Dodge, Inc.
28400 Van Dyke
Phone: (313) 755-0600 ●△

Wayne
Carpenter Truck Center, Inc.
3850 Howe Rd.
Phone: (313) 565-7214 ●■▲★○

Ed Carpenter Sales
33640 Michigan Ave.
Phone: (313) 721-6600 ●★

West Branch
Sherm's Sales & Service, Inc.
503 E. Houghton St.
Phone: (517) 545-2216 ▲★

White Pigeon
J.H. Kash, Inc.
500 W. Chicago Rd.
Phone: (616) 483-2685 ●

Wyandotte
Jim Vince Dodge
2319 Fort St.
Phone: (313) 386-2800 ▲★

Yale
Eilber & Barth
17 S. Main St.
Phone: (313) 387-3271 ●★

MINNESOTA

Albert Lea
Evans Motor Sales
Highway 65 South
Phone: (507) 373-4164 ●★

Alexandria
Saars Motor Sales
2000 S. Broadway
Phone: (612) 763-6646 ●

Anoka
River Motors
650 E. Main St.
Phone: (612) 421-3330 ●

Austin
Holiday Dodge
109 4th St. S.E.
Phone: (507) 433-8877 ●

Bemidji
Saar Motor Co.
314 Minnesota Ave.
Phone: (218) 751-4230 ●★

Benson
Quinn's Inc.
Hwy. 12 East
Phone: (612) 842-6601 ●

Bloomington
Freeway Dodge, Inc.
8011 Penn Ave. S.
Phone: (612) 888-8891 ●

Brainerd
Piggott Motors, Inc.
901 W. Washington St.
Phone: (218) 829-4133 ●

Cambridge
Fredlund Bros., Inc.
234 S. Main St.
Phone: (612) 689-3131 ●

Cloquet
Seaway Motor Co.
24 8th St., N.
Phone: (218) 879-7233 ●★

Crookston
Main Street Motor Sales
216-218 N. Main St.
Phone: (218) 281-1161 ●★

Duluth
Plaza Dodge, Inc.
1400 London Rd.
Phone: (218) 728-3695 ●△

Ely
Mike Motors
908 E. Sheridan St.
Phone: (218) 365-4038 ●

Faribault
Dingmann Motor Co.
119 N.W. 4th St.
Phone: (507) 334-8616 ●★

Fergus Falls
Fergus Dodge, Inc.
119-121 Washington Ave., W.
Phone: (218) 736-6911 ●△

Glenco
Johnson Motor Co., Inc.
401 W. 10th St.
Phone: (612) 864-5115 ▲★

Grand Rapids
Clusiau Sales & Rental, Inc.
815 W. 4th St.
Phone: (218) 326-9421 ●

Granite Falls
Lyle Monson Motors
Hwy. 212
Phone: (612) 564-2528 ●★

Hopkins
Brellenthin Hopkins Dodge, Inc.
701 Excelsior
Phone: (612) 935-3371 ●

Howard Lake
Howard Lake Motors, Inc.
West U.S. Hwy. No. 12
Phone: (612) 543-4481 ▲★

Hutchinson
Frank Motor Co., Inc.
Fair Ave. & Adams St.
Phone: (612) 897-2455 ●

Inner Grove
Trail City Dodge, Inc.
4665 S. Robert Trail
Phone: (612) 455-2201 ●

International Falls
Wherley Motor Sales
309 5th St.
Phone: (218) 283-8486 ●★

Little Falls
Guild Equipment Co., Inc.
118 West Broadway
Phone: (612) 632-5717 ●★

Mankato
Beutz Motors, Inc.
2000 N. Front St.
Phone: (507) 387-3113 ▲★

Marshall
Chas. H. Lutz Co.
107-109 S. 5th St.
Phone: (507) 532-4930 ●

Milaca
North Star Garage, Inc.
125 S. Central
Phone: (612) 983-6236 ●★

Minneapolis
Anderson Bros. Motor Co.
1201 E. Lake Rd.
Phone: (612) 721-5085 ▲★

North Star Dodge, Inc.
6800 Osseo Rd.
Phone: (612) 560-8000 ●△

Moorhead
Balmer Motor Co.
15 N. 8th St.
Phone: (218) 233-1573 ●★

Mora
Tinker & Johnson, Inc.
124 N.W. Railroad
Phone: (612) 679-3533 ●★

Ortonville
Amberg Motor Co., Inc.
Hwy. No. 12 W.
Phone: (612) 839-2536 ●★

Pine City
Holetz Motor Co.
Phone: (612) 629-2955 ●★

Pipestone
C.J. Amdahl & Sons, Inc.
515 E. Main St.
Phone: (507) 825-4525 ●★

Rosemount
Rosemount Dodge
Highway No. 3
Phone: (612) 423-2246 ●★△

St. Cloud
Otto Bros., Inc.
301 5th Ave. S.
Phone: (612) 251-4765 ●

St. Paul
Wilkins Dodge, Inc.
1013 University Ave.
Phone: (612) 646-4011 ●▲■★△

Sauk Center
Dan Welle Motors
414-420 Main St.
Phone: (612) 352-2000 ●★

● Medium Truck ▲ Heavy Truck ■ Diesel ★ Road Service ○ Night Service △ Motor Home/Recreational Vehicles

Savage
George Allen Garage
226 Minnesota E.
Phone: (612) 890 2400 ●★

Sherburn
Eisenmenger Motors
Hwy. 16
Phone: (507) 764 5621 ●★○

Tower
Arrowhead Garage
Phone: (218) 753-4200 ●

Two Harbors
Bacon Sales & Service
629 7th Ave.
Phone: (218) 834 2257 ●★

Virginia
Dependable Motors, Inc.
101 Chestnut St.
Phone: (218) 741 9242 ●★

Wadena
Uselman's Inc.
Hwy. U.S. 10E.
Phone: (218) 631 3505 ●

Waseca
Lewer Auto Co.
118 S. State St.
Phone: (507) 835 1940 ●★

Wheaton
C & P Sales
Hwy. 75
Phone: (616) 563-4788 ●★

White Bear Lake
White Bear Dodge, Inc.
3430 Hwy. No. 61
Phone: (612) 484-8521 ●★○△

Willmar
Town & Country Motors, Inc.
U.S. Hwy. No. 71 N.
Phone: (612) 235-0818 ●

Windom·
Van Nest Motors
307 9th St.
Phone: (507) 831-1639 ●★

Winthrop
Conklin Auto Co.
Hwy. 19 E.
Phone: (507) 647-5342 ●★

Worthington
Buysse Motors of Worthington, Inc.
1518 Oxford St.
Phone: (507) 376-2175 ●

MISSISSIPPI

Bay Springs
Abney Motor Co.
2nd St. & 5th St.
Phone: (601) 764-3035 ●

Cleveland
Crutcher Motor Co.
417 E. Sunflower Rd.
Phone: (601) 843-3648 ●

Corinth
Corinth Auto Exchange
515 Childs
Phone: (601) 286-3351 ●★

Forest
Marler Auto Co.
476 W. Third St.
Phone: (601) 469-2732 ●▲★

Greenville
Holland Mtr. Co.
1622 Highway 82 E.
Phone: (601) 335-2311 ●★

Gulfport
Turnbough Motor Co.
Pass Road & Hewes Ave.
Phone: (601) 864-6411 ●★

Hattisburg
Harry Dole Dodge
Highway 49 South
Phone: (601) 582-4448 ●★

Jackson
Capitol Dodge Truck Center
I-20 Exit - No. 19 North
Phone: (601) 939-7922 ●▲■★○

Service Motor Co.
Hwy. 80 West
Phone: (601) 352-4483 ●

Kosciusko
Duke & Hunt Dodge
Hwy. 12 East
Phone: (601) 289-2812 △

Meadville
James Wentworth Motor Service
Hwy. 84
Phone: (601) 384-2374 ●★○

Natchez
A-B Motor Co., Inc.
212 Shields Lane
Phone: (318) 442-2847 ●★

Pascagoula
Harry Dole Dodge
205 W. Live Oak St.
Phone: (601) 762-7061 ●

Senatobia
Brown & Gulledge Motor Co.
419 W. Main St.
Phone: (601) 562-8234 ●★

Waynesboro
Walker Dodge Sales
717 Court St.
Phone: (601) 735-2302 ●★

Yazoo City
Coleman Motor Co.
Highway 3 By-Pass
Phone: (601) 746-2953 ●★

MISSOURI

Boonville
Stonfield Chrysler, Plymouth
1226 11th St.
Phone: (816) 882-6617 ●

Bowling Green
Shaon Motor Co.
Hwy. 61 & 161
Phone: (314) 324-2278 ●

Brookfield
Wolfe Auto Sales, Inc.
321 Helm St.
Phone: (816) 258-3361 ●

Camdenton
Williams Motors
E. Hwy. 54
Phone: (314) 346-2293 ●

Cape Girardeau
Harris Truck & Trailer
2145 Independence
Phone: (314) 436-3353 ●▲■

Cassville
J.C. Kenney Motors
205 South Main St.
Phone: (417) 847-2112 ●★

Chillicothe
Adams Motor Co.
708 S. Washington
Phone: (816) 646-1978 ●

Florissant
Florissant Dodge, Inc.
2175 N. Hwy. 140
Phone: (314) 831-3300 ●

Independence
Frontier Dodge, Inc.
1700 S. Noland Rd.
Phone: (816) 833-2100 ▲△

Jefferson City,
Capitol Dodge, Inc.
2500 Missouri Avenue
Phone: (314) 636-7153 ●

Joplin
Frank Scott, Inc.
"A" & Main Sts.
Phone: (417) 624-4915 ▲★△

Kansas City
Midwest Motors
601 Truman Rd.
Phone: (816) 221-3060 ●

Kirksville
Updyke Motor Co.
1515 S. Baltimore
Phone: (816) 665-2828 ●★

Lebanon
J. Ward Owen Garage
260 W. Elm St.
Phone: (417) 532-6124 ▲★○

Lee's Summit
Burton Motors
126 E. Third St.
Phone: (816) 524-4330 ●

Marshfield
Tarr's Garage
547 W. Jackson
Phone: (417) 468-2171 ●★

Mehlville
Signal Dodge, Inc.
7127 S. Lindbergh
Phone: (314) 487-2600 ●△

Nevada
Richardson Motor Co.
118 S. Main St.
Phone: (417) 667-3368 ●

Poplar Bluff
Jackson
422 Pine Blvd.
Phone: (314) 785-5769 ▲★

St. Ann
St. Ann Motors, Inc.
10805 St. Charles Rock Rd.
Phone: (314) 739-8800 △

St. Louis
King Dodge, Inc.
3300 S. Kingshighway
Phone: (314) 832-7200 ●
Ray Rixman, Inc.
7915 N. Broadway
Phone: (314) 381-3500 ●▲△

Savannah
McCarty Motors
Hwy. 71 N
Phone: (816) 324-3138 ●

Sedalia
Bryant Motor Co.
2nd & Kentucky
Phone: (816) 862-2700 ●★○

Springfield
Central Dodge, Inc.
1200 St. Louis St.
Phone: (417) 862-9272 ●★

Sweet Springs
Hall Motor Co.
Highway 40
Phone: (816) 335-6315 ●

Tipton
Garber Motors, Inc.
Highway 50
Phone: (816) 433-5547 ●★

Washington
Krumsick Motor Co.
16 West 5th St.
Phone: (314) 239-4775 ●★

Wellsville
Arens Dodge
115 N. First St.
Phone: (314) 684-2357 ●★

MONTANA

Anaconda
Anaconda Chrysler Center
600 E. Park
Phone: (406) 563-7400 ●△

Baker
Randash Motors
119 S. Main
Phone: (406) 778-2227 ●▲△

Billings
Midland Dodge, Inc.
2605 First Ave. N.
Phone: (406) 245-4131 ●

Bozeman
Rolfe & Wood, Inc.
25 North Wilson
Phone: (406) 586-5438 ●

Butte
Wilson Motor Co.
8 S. Montana
Phone: (406) 723-3271 ●

Chinook
Jamieson Motors, Inc.
100 Penn Street
Phone: (406) 357-2470 ●

Columbus
Lethert Motor & Implement
First Ave. & Fourth St.
Phone: (406) 322-5351 ●

Cut Bank
Palmer Implement
123 W. Main Street
Phone: (406) 938-2402 ●△

Fort Benton
Fort Benton Motor Co.
1207 Front St.
Phone: (406) 622-5131 ●

Great Falls
Frontier Dodge, Inc.
1017 10th Ave. S.
Phone: (406) 761-6300 ●△

Hamilton
Mellott Motor Co.
300 S. Second St.
Phone: (406) 363-2323 ●

Hardin
Triangle Motor Co.
22 East Third St.
Phone: (406) 665-2104 ●

Havre
Hi-Line Auto Center
331 West First St.
Phone: (406) 265-4326 ●△

Helena
Dodge City, Inc.
534 N. Main St.
Phone: (406) 442-1903 ▲

Kalispell
Big Valley Dodge
102-114 First Ave. E.
Phone: (406) 756-4335 ●△

Malta
Dobson Motors, Inc.
5 North First W.
Phone: (406) 654-1632 ●

Miles City
Provost Motor Co.
600 Bridge St.
Phone: (406) 232-3320 ●

Missoula
Wakley Motors
1600 Stephens
Phone: (406) 543-5137 ●△

Ronan
Ronan Auto Body
Sales & Service, Inc.
New Hwy. 93, North
Phone: (406) 676-3961 ●

Sidney
Action Auto, Inc.
220 East Main
Phone: (406) 482-2312 ●

Wolf Point
Camrud Motors
113 Fallon St.
Phone: (406) 653-1160 ●△

NEBRASKA

Alliance
Dobson Motor Co.
502 Box Blutte
Phone: (308) 762-2950 ●★

Arnold
Forrester's Garage
Phone: (308) 848-2288 ●

Aurora
Vetter Brothers
1313 "L" St.
Phone: (402) 694-2687 ●★

Central City
Haith Motor Co.
E. Hwy. 30
Phone: (308) 946-3011 ★○

Columbus
Columbus Motors
2903 13th St.
Phone: (402) 564-8176 ●★

Deshler
Deshler Motor Co.
712 4th Street
Phone: (402) opr. 107 ●★

Dodge
Farmers Garage
Phone: (402) 693-2190 ●

Exeter
Erdkamp Motors
Seneca Street
Phone: (402) 266-5181 ●

Falls City
Armbruster Motor Co.
307 W. 17th St.
Phone: (402) 245-2471 ▲★

Fremont
H & H Motors
6th & H Street
Phone: (402) 721-6090 ●

Grand Island
Grand Island Dodge
South Highway 281
Phone: (308) 382-4546 ●

Lexington
Dawson Country Motor Co.
120 E. 6th St.
Phone: (308) 324-2336 ●★

McCook
Dodge City
West Hwy. 6 & 34
Phone: (308) 345-2790 ●

Milford
Subway Motors
Highway No. 6
Phone: (402) 761-6481 ●★

Norfolk
Norfolk Dodge, Inc.
1800 W. Omaha
Phone: (402) 371-2623 ●

North Platte
Brink Dodge
315 E. 4th St.
Phone: (308) 532-5920 ●

Omaha
Dodge Motor Trucks, Inc.
1721 Nicholas
Phone: (402) 341-1080 ▲★○△

Orchard
Thelander Auto Service
5th & Main
Phone: (402) 893-4105 ●

Scottsbluff
Gilman Motor Co.
27th & Avenue E.
Phone: (308) 632-4163 ●★

Sidney
Elwell Motors
901 Illinois
Phone: (308) 254-4547 ●★

Valentine
Raubach Motor Co.
Highway No. 20 W.
Phone: (308) 394-5658 ●

West Point
Vern W. Hagedorn
303 N. Main St.
Phone: (402) 372-3392 ●

Wilber
Altman's Garage
Phone: (402) 821-4861 ●

NEVADA

Elko
Wright Motor Co.
685 Idaho St.
Phone: (702) 738-3412 ●△

Henderson
Henderson Dodge, Inc.
460 Boulder Hwy.
Phone: (702) 564-1801 ●△

Las Vegas
Las Vegas Dodge, Inc.
3470 Boulder Hwy.
Phone: (702) 385-4321 ●△

Reno
Reno Dodge Sales, Inc.
700 Kietzke Lane
Phone: (702) 786-1211 ●△

NEW HAMPSHIRE

Amherst
Millward Motors, Inc.
Nashua St.
Phone: (603) 673-1220 ▲★

Berlin
Glen Motors, Inc.
38 Glen Ave.
Phone: (603) 752-1134 ▲★○

Exeter
Exeter Dodge, Inc.
92 Portsmouth Ave.
Phone: (603) 772-3727 ●

Newport
Chase & Avery
20 Sunapee St.
Phone: (603) 863-2333 ★○

Portsmouth
Portsmouth Dodge, Inc.
155 Greenleaf
Phone: (603) 436-1243 ●▲★△

Rochester
Copp's Dodge
Milton Road
Phone: (603) 332-2798 ▲★

NEW JERSEY

Belford
Werner's Automotive, Inc.
Highway No. 36
Phone: (201) 787-3600 ●

Boonton
Corigliano Motor Service, Inc.
213 Washington St.
Phone: (201) 334-3900 ▲★○△

Bricktown
Circle Dodge,, Inc.
781 Route No. 70
Phone: (201) 477-5555 ●

Cherry Hill
Cherry Hill Dodge
Marlton Pike
Phone: (609) 665-3980 ●★○

Cinnaminson
Cinnaminson Dodge, Inc.
2101 Rt. 130
Phone: (609) 829-9393 ▲★△

Clifton
Beloff Motors, Inc.
540 Lexington Ave.
Phone: (201) 478-2600 ●

Clinton
Wargo Motors
2-8 Easton Ave.
Phone: (201) 735-5711 ▲★○

Dover
Swartz Motors, Inc.
200 E. Blackwell St.
Phone: (201) 366-0224 ●★

Egg Harbor
Compton Motors, Inc.
2843 White Horse Pike
Phone: (609) 965-1494 ●★

Elizabeth
Elizabeth Dodge, Inc.
600 Newark Ave.
Phone: (201) 351-1155 ●

Fords
Woodbridge Dodge, Inc.
450 King George Rd.
Phone: (201) 826-1220 ●▲★○△

Freehold
Freehold Dodge, Inc.
South St.
Phone: (201) 462-6234 ●

Hammonton
Nick's Auto Sales
301 White Horse Ave.
Phone: (609) 561-5811 ●★

Hasbrouck Heights
Modern Traveler, Inc.
60 Railroad Avenue
Phone: (201) 288-2727 △

Hawthorne
Chet Decker Auto Sales
300 Lincoln Avenue
Phone: (201) 427-2100 ●

Highstown
Solomon Dodge
Rt. 130
Phone: (609) 448-1310 ●★

Lakewood
Lakewood Motor Center, Inc.
2101 Highway No. 9
Phone: (201) 363-7859 ▲★

Livingston
Livingston Dodge, Inc.
576 W. Mt. Pleasant Ave.
Phone: (201) 992-4800 ▲

Lodi
Modern Traveler, Inc.
Rt. 46
Phone: (201) 778-3553 △

Madison
Mikan Motors, Inc.
280 Main St.
Phone: (201) 377-6400 ●

Malaga
R. H. Vassallo
Delsea Dr.
Phone: (609) 691-4453 ▲★○

Mercerville
Barton F. Francis
2235 Nottingham Way
Phone: (609) 587-8080 ●★

Metuchen
Suburban Dodge, Inc.
87-99 Central Ave.
Phone: (201) 548-6260 ●★

Mt. Ephraim
Black Horse Dodge, Inc.
620 N. Black Horse Pike
Phone: (609) 933-1444 ▲★

Newark
Newark Dodge, Inc.
239 Central Ave.
Phone: (201) 623-0300 ▲★△

N. Plainfield
North Plainfield Dodge, Inc.
555 Somerset St.
Phone: (201) 754-5800 ●

Orange
De Maio Dodge, Inc.
36 Main St.
Phone: (201) 676-1025 ●★

Paramus

Paramus Dodge, Inc.
West Route 4
Phone: (201) 845-0704 ●▲

Paterson

Ed Kevil Motors, Inc.
969 Market St.
Phone: (201) 684-0900 ●

Piscataway

Central Jersev Dodge Truck Center
1570 S. Washington Ave.
Phone: (201) 752-8800 ●▲■△

Pleasantville

Geisel Motors
310 W. Verona Blvd.
Phone: (609) 641-7800 ●★

Point Pleasant

Tally's Sales & Service
2138 Bridge St.
Phone: (201) 892-4545 ●★

Ridgefield

Santangelo Motors, Inc.
660 Bergen Blvd.
Phone: (201) 945-2900 ●

Ridgewood

Station Motors, Inc.
44 Franklin Ave.
Phone: (201) 445-6040 ●

Roselle Park

Benick Motors
130 Westfield Ave.
Phone: (201) 245-7222 ●

Salem

Davis Dodge
500 Quinton Rd.
Phone: (609) 935-0455 ●★

South River

Knoblock Bros., Inc.
164 Prospect St.
Phone: (201) 257-1111 ●★△

Toms River

Dodge City
950 Hooper
Phone: (201) 244-1900 ●★

Totowa

Johnnine's Auto Center
148-160 Union Blvd.
Phone: (201) 274-7886 ●★

Trenton

Olden Avenue Dodge, Inc.
1635 N. Olden Avenue
Phone: (609) 393-4200 ●▲

Union

Betz Union Motors
1604 Stuyvesant Ave.
Phone: (201) 686-4114 ●△

Union City

Arrow Motors
4900 Kennedy Blvd.
Phone: (201) 867-0069 ●△

Waterford Works

Iannoco Motors
White Horse Pike
Phone: (609) 767-1687 ●▲

Wayne

Ed Van Ness Motors, Inc.
Route No. 23
Phone: (201) 694-1000 ●

Westfield

Westfield Dodge, Inc.
425 North Ave. East
Phone: (201) 232-0076 ●

Woodridge

Ridge Dodge, Inc.
85 Route 17
Phone: (201) 939-9400 ▲△

NEW MEXICO

Albuquerque

Big Country Dodge, Inc.
1200 Lomas Blvd. N.E.
Phone: (505) 242-2741 ●▲■★△

Belen

Auge Sales & Service
711 E. River Rd.
Phone: (505) 864-4482 ●★

Carlsbad

Sam Thomas Motors
521-527 S. Canal St.
Phone: (505) 885-4858 ●★

Gallup

Gallup Auto Sales
700 Aztec W.
Phone: (505) 863-9313 ●★

Las Cruces

Sandoval Dodge
955 S. Truck By-pass
Phone: (505) 524-7723 ●★

Lovington

Bill Hughes Dodge
123 S. Main St.
Phone: (505) 396-2007 ●★

Portales

Trader Horn Motors
601 S. Avenue "C"
Phone: (505) 356-4871 ●★

Roswell

Southwest Dodge, Inc.
P.O. Box 549
Phone: (505) 622-3180 ●★○

Santa Fe

Hancock Old Mtrs. Inc.
P.O. Box 4455
Phone: (505) 982-1956 ●★

Silver City

Ray Burchfield Motor Co.
402 E. Silver Heights Blvd.
Phone: (505) 538-2977 ●★

NEW YORK

Adams

Fulkerson Motors
Route 11
Phone: (315) 232-4564 ●

Adams

Goslin Chrysler Plym., Inc.
R.D. 1
Phone: (315) 232-4545 ★

Addison

Warren Stiker
East Front St.
Phone: (607) 962-4697 ●

Albany

Albany Dodge, Inc.
770 Central Ave.
Phone: (518) 438-8461 ●▲★△

Auburn

Ryerson Dodge, Inc.
Grant Ave. Rd. 6
Phone: (315) 253-9791 ●★▲

Avon

Frank Piraino, Inc.
110 West Main St.
Phone: (716) 926-2270 ●

Babylon

Herbee Motors, Inc.
260 E. Main St.
Phone: (516) 669-0670 ▲

Batavia

Hawley Motors, Inc.
306 West Main
Phone: (716) 343-1780 ●★▲

Binghamton

Miller Motor Car Corp.
4455 Vestal Parkway E.
Phone: (607) 797-1221 ●★▲△○

Brooklyn

Bay Ridge Motors, Inc.
254 Bay Ridge Ave.
Phone: (212) SH-8-5100 ●

Mid County Dodge, Inc.
1640 Bedford Avenue
Phone: (212) 778-8838 ●

Buffalo

Crest Dodge, Inc.
1510 Orchard Park Rd.
Phone: (716) 674-8500 ▲●○

Pioneer Dodge, Inc.
3445 Delaware Ave.
Phone: (716) 876-6900 ●

Canandaigua

Finger Lakes Motors, Inc.
2555 Rochester Road
Phone: (315) 394-0570 ●

● Medium Truck ▲ Heavy Truck ■ Diesel ★ Road Service ○ Night Service △ Motor Home/Recreational Vehicles

Catskill
C & P Motors, Inc.
Route 9W
Phone: (315) 943-4440 ●

Chafee
James R. Shaw Co.
Olean Rd.
Phone: (716) 496-7312 ●★▲

Chatham
Chatham Motors, Inc.
17 Austerlitz St.
Phone: (518) 892-5251 ●★

Cheektowaga
Mid-City Dodge, Inc.
2185 Walden Ave.
Phone: (716) 685-1000 ●▲△

Cohoes
Newell Brothers, Inc.
169-171 Ontario St.
Phone: (518) 237-2204 ●

College Point
Recon Car Corp. of New York
112-03 14th Avenue
Phone: (212) 762-6800 △

Cooperstown
Mohawk Chrysler Plymouth
115 Chestnut St., Rt. 28
Phone: (607) 547-9262 ●

Cornwall
Johnson's Garage
45 Academy Ave.
Phone: (914) 534-3680 ●★

Croghan
Donaldson Dodge
Phone: (315) 346-1315 ●

Crown Point
Vincent S. Jerry & Sons, Inc.
S. Main Street
Phone: (518) 597-3339 ●

Delhi
Delhi Motor Company, Inc.
4 Meredith St.
Phone: (607) 746-2181 ●

Dexter
Eveleigh Motor Sales, Inc.
518 Williams St.
Phone: (315) 639-6245 ●★○

Elmira
Carroll Motor Co., Inc.
251 Baldwin St.
Phone: (607) 773-9108 ●★

Elmira Chrysler Plymouth, Inc.
2000 Lake St.
Phone: (607) 734-2254 △

Fredonia
Farrell Chrysler Plymouth, Inc.
258 W. Main St.
Phone: (716) 673-1371 ●

Fulton
Longley Bros.
E. River Rd. S.
Phone: (315) 593-2135 ●★○

Geneva
Geneva Automobile Co., Inc.
145 Castle St.
Phone: (315) 789-2662 ●★

Glens Falls
Ford Garage Co., Inc.
109 Warren St.
Phone: (518) 793-2571 ▲★

Gouverneur
Gouverneur Motor Sales, Inc.
385-387 East Main Street
Phone: (315) 287-1380 ●★

Hamburg
Fairway Dodge Sales, Inc.
395 Buffalo St.
Phone: (716) 649-6200 ●

Hempstead
Hempstead Dodge
257 Main St.
Phone: (516) 485-2222 ●△★

Hyde Park
Hyde Park Motor Co.
Post Road
Phone: (914) 229-2185 ●

Jackson Heights N.Y.C.
Stapleton & Schneider Mtr. Sales, Inc.
74-17 Northern Blvd.
Phone: (212) 446-6500 ●★

Jamaica
Queensboro Auto Sales
150-40 Hillside Ave.
Phone: (212) 297-1500 ●

Jamestown
Cusimano Bros. Garage, Inc.
616 Buffalo St.
Phone: (716) 484-7125 ▲●

Johnstown
Howell and Pierson, Inc.
224 West Main St.
Phone: (518) 762-3183 ●▲

Kenmore
Kenton Dodge, Inc.
3445 Delaware Ave.
Phone: (716) 876-6900 ▲

Lakeland
Val's Motors, Inc.
756 State Fair Blvd.
Phone: (315) 468-6201 ▲★○

Lancaster
Delacy Motors, Inc.
5229 Broadway
Phone: (716) 683-1200 ●

Lawyersville
Head Sales & Service
Route 145
Phone: (518) 234-3528 ●★

Little Valley
A.L. Sibley Motors, Inc.
520 Rock City St.
Phone: (716) 938-2441 ★

Lockport
Schmid Motors, Inc.
5869 S. Transit Rd.
Phone: (716) 434-2811 ●

Long Lake
Day's Garage
Rt. 30 North
Phone: (518) 624-3111 ●★

Madison
Madison Dodge, Inc.
Main Street
Phone: (315) 893-6074 ●

Mahopac
Mahopac Dodge
Rt. 6
Phone: (914) 628-3201 ●

Malone
S & S Motors
West Main St. Rd.
Phone: (518) 483-2500 ●

Manhasset
Cy Greene Motors, Inc.
1170 Northern Blvd.
Phone: (516) 627-6221 ●

Manlius
A.F. Ryan & Sons, Inc.
102 E. Seneca St.
Phone: (315) 682-2761 ●★

Maspeth
Dodge Trucks, Inc.
58-80 Borden Ave.
Phone: (212) 894-3430 ●▲■★○△

Massena
North Country Dodge, Inc.
E. Orvis Street
Phone: (315) 769-2428 ●

Mohawk
Holt Bros., Inc.
94 W. Main St.
Phone: (315) 866-2120 ●★

Moravia
James E. Ryerson, Inc.
55 Main St.
Phone: (315) 497-1030 ●★

Newark
Arcadia Oil Co., Inc.
515 N. Main St.
Phone: (315) 331-4774 ●

Niagara Falls
Falls Dodge, Inc.
2380 Military Rd.
Phone: (716) 297-5800 ▲★

Norwich
Nearing Dodge
Hale St. Ext.
Phone: (607) 334-3131 ●★

Oakfield
Zigrossi Motors
109-111 Main St.
Phone: (716) 948-5532 ●

Olean
Paul Brown Motors, Inc.
1145 E. State St.
Phone: (716) 372-0080 ▲★●

Oneida
A. F. Ryan & Sons, Inc.
122 Cedar St.
Phone: (315) 363-2400 ●★

Oneonta
Burr's Dodge, Inc.
316-318 Chestnut St.
Phone: (607) 432-1254 ●

Penn Yan
Keuka Dodge Inc.
Rd5, Rt. 14A
Phone: (315) 536-8931 ●★○

Perry
McClurg Chrysler Plymouth, Inc.
125 N. Center Street
Phone: (716) 237-6131 ●

Plattsburgh
E.S. Mason, Inc.
Upper Cornelia St.
Phone: (518) 563-0500 ▲★

Port Richmond Staten Island
Memoly Dodge
18-93 Richmond Terr.
Phone: (212) 442-8903 ●

Pulaski
Dick Goslin, Inc.
Rt. 11-N
Phone: (315) 298-5131 ●★

Randolph
Randolph Motors, Inc.
91 Jamestown St.
Phone: (716) 358-4825 ●★

Richfield Spr.
Frank Patterson Sons
Main St.
Phone: (315) 858-1430 ●★

Ridgewood
S & W Sales Co., Inc.
350 St. Nicholas
Phone: (212) 821-3060 ▲

Rochester
Culver Dodge, Inc.
1733 Ridge Rd. E.
Phone: (716) 482-3500 ▲●△

McEvoy Dodge, Inc.
2400 W. Henrietta Rd.
Phone: (716) 271-1900 ▲●△

McEvoy Dodge West-Ridge, Inc.
4477 Ridge Road West
Phone: (716) 352-6600 ●▲△

Weller Motors, Inc.
Stutson St. & Thomas Ave.
Phone: (716) 342-5000 ▲★

Rome
A.J. Ryan Motors
601 W. Dominick
Phone: (315) 336-8300 ●★

St. Johnsville
Capece Motors, Inc.
Main & Center Sts.
Phone: (518) 568-4541 ●★

Savannah
Tiberio Motors
W. Church St.
Phone: (315) 365-5283 ●

Schenectady
Wedekind Motors, Inc.
1595 State St.
Phone: (518) 374-4167 ●

Scottsville
Gray-Raycheff, Inc.
69 Rochester St.
Phone: (716) 889-3583 ●★

Sidney
Fendick Chrysler Plymouth, Inc.
27 Smith Street
Phone: (607) 563-4651 ●

Silver Creek
Damon Motors
120 Central Ave.
Phone: (716) 934-2141 ●★

South Salem
George T. Tator & Sons, Inc.
Spring St.
Phone: (914) 763-3136 ●★

Springville
Bob Johnson Motors
195 W. Main
Phone: (716) 592-2881 ●★

Syracuse
Sam Dell's Dodge Corp.
1011 W. Genesee St.
Phone: (315) 472-6633 ▲★●△

Theresa
Bickelhaupt's Garage
211 Main St.
Phone: (315) 628-4421 ●★

Troy
Ken Goewey Dodge, Inc.
360 Fifth Ave.
Phone: (518) 235-7700 ●

Watertown
Lathan's, Inc.
Outer Washington St.
Phone: (315) 782-2890 ●▲★○△

Watkins Glen
Learn Motor Company, Inc.
502 N. Franklin St.
Phone: (607) 535-2776 ●★

Wellsville
Pfuntner Sales & Service, Inc.
120 Railroad Ave.
Phone: (716) 593-2249 ●▲★

Westfield
Westfield Dodge City, Inc.
E. Main Rd.
Phone: (716) 326-2025 ●

Williamsville
Transitowne Dodge, Inc.
7408 Transit Rd.
Phone: (716) 634-8000 ▲★○△

Yonkers
Merit Motors, Inc.
132-136 So. Broadway
Phone: (914) 965-8900 ●

Yorkville
Dodge City of Utica, Inc.
Truck Route 5A
Phone: (315) 736-3371 ●▲★△

NORTH CAROLINA

Asheville
Dorato Motors, Inc.
860 Tunnel Rd.
Phone: (704) 298-4911 ●★

Burlington
Burch & Simmons Dodge, Inc.
1258 S. Church St.
Phone: (919) 227-4221 ▲★

Charlotte
City Dodge of Charlotte, Inc.
1220 S. Tryon St.
Phone: (707) 334-7263 ●△

Dodge Country, Inc.
4800 E. Independence Blvd.
Phone: (704) 536-4800 ●△

Concord
DeWitt Motor Co., Inc.
726 N. Church St.
Phone: (704) 782-8611 ●★

Elizabethtown
Clark Bros., Inc.
Poplar St.
Phone: (919) 862-2091 ●★

Fayetteville
Royal Dodge, Inc.
1045 Bragg Blvd.
Phone: (919) 485-4151 ●★○

Franklinton
J.O. Green Motor Co.
104 Main St.
Phone: (919) 494-2245 ▲

Gastonia
Craig Motor Co.
211-213 N. Chestnut St.
Phone: (704) 864-7786 ●★

Hendersonville
Bud Egolf Motors
447 South Main St.
Phone: (704) 692-9671 ●★

Hickory
Hickory Motor Sales, Inc.
345 First Ave., S.W.
Phone: (704) 345-3211 ▲★

High Point
Horace G. Ilderton, Inc.
701-709 S. Main St.
Phone: (919) 885-4091 ●△

Jacksonville
Padgett Motors, Inc.
2043 Lejeune Blvd.
Phone: (704) 353-1515 ●

Kannapolis
Bill Dove Motor Co., Inc.
Chestnut at "C" St.
Phone: (704) 933-2158 ●★

Laurinburg
Burgess Corbett Motors, Inc.
N. Main
Phone: (919) 276-1451 ●★

Lumberton
Freeman Motor Co., Inc.
1501 W. 5th St.
Phone: (919) 739-3224▲★△

Monroe
Helms Bros., Motor Co., Inc.
1900 Skyway Extension
Phone: (704) 283-8971 ●★

Morganton
Tux Bowers Motor Co.
304 S. Green St.
Phone: (704) 437-0671 ●★

Mt. Airy
Burton Dodge, Inc.
825 Lebanon St.
Phone: (919) 786-5841▲

New Bern
The Auto Mart
Hwy. 70 East
Phone: (919) 638-1304▲

Plymouth
Dixie Motor Co. of Plymouth
Hwy. 64 By-Pass
Phone: (919) 793-2415 ●★

Raleigh
Raleigh Dodge, Inc.
716 Downtown Blvd.
Phone: (919) 828-7461▲★

Rocky Mount
Bandy Dodge
602-616 N. Church St.
Phone: (919) 442-4111▲★

Shelby
Tedder Motor Co., Inc.
311 E. Marion St.
Phone: (704) 487-6334 ●★

Sylva
Cogdill Motor Co., Inc.
71 E. Main St.
Phone: (704) 586-2618 ●★

Whiteville
Whiteville Carolina Motors, Inc.
701 By-Pass South
Phone: (919) 642-3196 ●★

Williamston
Dixie Motor Co.
Hwy. 64 By-Pass
Phone: (919) 792-2154 ●★

Wilmington
D & E Car Exchange
6220 N. Market St.
Phone: (919) 799-4210 ●★

Winston Salem
Carolina Garage
201 Waughtown St.
Phone: (919) 784-7380●▲■

Yadkinville
Mendenhall Motors, Inc.
E. Main St.
Phone: (919) 679-8811 ▲★

NORTH DAKOTA

Bismark
Missouri Valley Motors
501 Main
Phone: (701) 223-2190 ●★

Carrington
Nicolson Carr, Inc.
968 S. First St.
Phone: (701) 652-3191 ●★

Cavalier
Erwin Motors
Hwys. 5 & 18
Phone: (701) 265-8355 ●

Cooperstown
V & W Motors, Inc.
10th & Rollin Ave.
Phone: (701) oper. 2461●★

Crosby
Crosby Motors, Inc.
124 S. Main
Phone: (701) 965-6332 ●

Devils Lake
Dodge Towne, Inc.
5th & 3rd Ave.
Phone: (701) 662-2141 ●

Edgeley
Anderson Bros., Inc.
311 Main
Phone: (701) oper. 5411●★

Grand Forks
Valley Motor Co.
1518 State Mill Rd.
Phone: (701) 775-4648 ▲★

Harvey
Nelson Auto & Implement Co.
119 West 9th St.
Phone: (701) 324-2273 ●

Hazen
West End Shop
411 W. Main St.
Phone: (701) 748-2470●

Jamestown
Midwest Motors
305 First Ave. N.
Phone: (701) 252-0980▲★

Lisbon
Hanson Motors, Inc.
624 S. Main
Phone: (701) 683-4791●★

Mandan
Mandan Chrysler-Plymouth, Inc.
110 5th Ave., N.W.
Phone: (701) 663-9584▲△

Mayville
Tastad Motor Co.
39 & 43 West Main
Phone: (701) 786-2351●

Minot
Don Moe Dodge, Inc.
102 3rd St. S.E.
Phone: (701) 838-9151▲★

Oakes
James Valley Auto & Imp.
203 W. Main St.
Phone: (701) 742-2196●

Petersburg
Petersburg
U.S. Hwy. No. 2
Phone: (701) 345-3271●

Valley City
Miller Motors
Hwy. 94 W.
Phone: (701) 845-2780●★

Washburn
Hoffmann Motors Sales
527 Main Ave.
Phone: (701) 462-3569●★

Williston
Crighton Distributors, Inc.
223 E. Broadway
Phone: (701) 572-2147●★

OHIO

Akron
Southwest Dodge, Inc.
406 W. Exchange St.
Phone: (216) 836-7941 ●△

Town 'N Country Store
3567 Copley Rd., Box 4206
Phone: (216) 666-8818 △

Amherst
Sliman's Sales & Service, Inc.
Cor. Rt. 58 & Elyria Ave.
Phone: (216) 988-4484 ●△

Andover
Swezeys Garage, Inc.
200 West Main St.
Phone: (216) 293-3666 ●

Archbold
Liechty Motors
Lugbill Subdivision
Phone: (419) 445-2576 ●★○

Ashland
Harolds Motor Co., Inc.
333 Orange St.
Phone: (419) 323-1569 ●

Barberton
Barberton Motor Sales
865 Wooster Road
Phone: (216) 745-1176 ●★

Barnesville
Kinney Motor Co.
Corner Main & Gardner
Phone: (614) 425-2915 ●★

Batavia
Anstaett Dodge
140 W. Main St.
Phone: (513) 732-2575●★

Bedford
Frank G. Elliott, Inc.
245 Broadway Ave.
Phone: (216) 232-2121 ●△

Bellaire
McClain Motor Co.
34th & Noble St.
Phone: (614) 676-1221 ●★

Bellevue
Firelands Motor Co.
1111 Castalia St.
Phone: (419) 483-7990 ●

Berlin
Stutzman Motor Sales, Inc.
Main Street
Phone: (216) 893-2041 ●△

Bethel
Crawford Chrysler-Plymouth
Main & Concord Sts.
Phone: (513) 763-2432 ●

Blanchester
Hollon Sales & Service
511 N. Broadway
Phone: (513) 783-2436 ▲★

Bowling Green
Bob Sams Dodge
1053 N. Dixie Hwy.
Phone: (419) 353-8721 ●★

Brookville
Westbrook Dodge
11140 Westbrook Rd.
Phone: (513) 833-2501 ●

Brunswick
Brunswick Dodge, Inc.
1700 Pearl Rd.
Phone: (216) 225-9131 ▲

Bucyrus
Studer-Perrin Dodge, Inc.
321 North Sandusky
Phone: (419) 562-7882 ●

Cadiz
Long Motors, Inc.
350 Jarvis Ave.
Phone: (614) 942-3676 ●★○

Caldwell
Worl Thompson Dodge & Chrysle
510 Cumberland St.
Phone: (614) 732-2332 ●★

Cambridge
Jefferis Mtrs., Inc.
704 Turner Ave.
Phone: (614) 439-1327 ●★

Canfield
Frederick Motors, Inc.
16 Lisbon St.
Phone: (216) 533-3307 ●△

Canton
Kempthorne Motors, Inc.
1449 Cleveland N.
Phone: (216) 452-6511 ▲△

Celina
Buschor Motor Sales
1015-17 W. Logan St.
Phone: (419) 958-3294 ●★○

Chardon
Junction Auto Sales, Inc.
Jct. U.S. 322 at Ohio 44
Phone: (216) 286-6161 ▲△

Chillicothe
Shawnee Dodge, Inc.
1600 N. Bridge St.
Phone: (614) 773-5451 ●

Cincinnati
Colerain Dodge, Inc.
8700 Colerain Ave.
Phone: (513) 522-7200 △

Hirlinger Truck Sales
3426 Spring Grove Ave.
Phone: (513) 541-4213 ▲★○△

Kenmont Dodge, Inc.
7788 Montgomery Rd.
Phone: (513) 793-2600 ●

Tom Kneer Dodge, Inc.
6475 Glenway Ave.
Phone: (513) 661-7373 ●★

Tri-County Dodge, Inc.
135 Northland Blvd.
Phone: (513) 771-5701 ●

Circleville
Wes Edstrom Motors
150 E. Main St.
Phone: (614) 474-3550 ▲★○

Cleveland
Porach Dodge City
15600 Lorain Ave.
Phone: (216) 941-4111 ●★

Spitzer Motor City, Inc.
13001 Brookpark Rd.
Phone: (216) 267-2100 ▲★△

Columbus
Earl's Truck Sales & Service
1515 Frank Road
Phone: (614) 276-6514 ●▲■

Northland Dodge, Inc.
1889 Morse Road
Phone: (614) 267-7401 ●△

Spitzer Columbus, Inc.
5100 E. Main
Phone: (614) 861-0250 ●

Westside Dodge, Inc.
4000 W. Broad St.
Phone: (614) 272-0000 ●△

Dalton
G.G. Grim Co.
Highway 30 & 94
Phone: (216) 828-2228 ●△★

Dayton
Dayton Truck, Inc.
3339 North Dixie Drive
Phone: (513) 278-4821 ▲■★

Dixie Dodge
3201 S. Dixie Hwy.
Phone: (513) 294-4900 △

Delphos
Sheeter Motor Sales
502 N. Main Street
Phone: (419) 695-2072 ●★△

E. Cleveland
East Cleveland Dodge
14401 Euclid Ave.
Phone: (216) 451-5300 ●△

Edgerton
Casebere Motors
Indiana St.
Phone: (419) 298-2631 ●★

Elyria
Spitzer Motors of Elyria, Inc.
140 E. Bridge St.
Phone: (216) 323-3311 ▲△

Englewood
Englewood Trailer Sales
547 S. Main St.
Phone: (513) 836-2691 △

Findlay
Willard Garage, Inc.
124 W. Crawford St.
Phone: (419) 423-1715 ●

Fostoria
Bill Bishop Motor Co.
155 E. South St.
Phone: (419) 435-6692 ●△

Fremont
Fremont Motor Sales
1940 W. State St.
Phone: (419) 332-5502 ●

Galion
Galion Dodge, Inc.
126 N. Washington St.
Phone: (419) 468-1270 ●

Gallipolis
Carroll Norris Dodge
50-52 State Street
Phone: (614) 446-0842 ●

Gibsonburg
Helle Garage
113 N. Webster
Phone: (419) 637-2116 ●★△

Jackson
Coll Auto Sales
301 Main St.
Phone: (614) 286-2184 ●

Kent
University Dodge
1338 W. Main St.
Phone: (216) 673-0200 ●

Kinsman
I.L. Hine Motor Sales
P.O. Box 6
Phone: (216) 876-2775 ●

Lakewood
Podway Motors, Inc.
14400 Detroit Avenue
Phone: (216) 226-7500 ▲★

Lancaster
James Motors
1250 N. Memorial Dr.
Phone: (614) 654-0460 ●

Lebanon
Bercaw Chrysler-Plymouth Sales
518 W. Main St.
Phone: (513) 932-4831 ●★

● Medium Truck ▲ Heavy Truck ■ Diesel ★ Road Service ○ Night Service △ Motor Home/Recreational Vehicles

Logan
Tansky Motors, Inc.
297 E. Main St.
Phone: (614) 385-5678 ●★

Mansfield
Spitzer Motors of Mansfield
744 Park Ave., West
Phone: (419) 524-2511 ●★△

Marietta
Pottimeyer Auto Sales, Inc.
3rd & Green Sts.
Phone: (614) 382-1168 ▲★

Marion
Race Motor Sales, Inc.
646 N. Main St.
Phone: (614) 382-1168 ●▲★△

Maumee
Maumee Valley Dodge, Inc.
725 Illinois Ave.
Phone: (419) 893-0241 △

Mayfield Heights
Spitzer Motor Center, Inc.
6060 Mayfield Road
Phone: (216) 461-6400 ●★△

McConnelsville
K.M. Coole Auto Sales
E. Main St.
Phone: (614) 962-4111 ●○

Mentor
Coleman-Young Motors, Inc.
7272 Mentor Ave.
Phone: (216) 951-2900 ●△

Mt. Victory
Hardin Motors, Inc.
S. Main St.
Phone: (513) 354-2681 ▲★○

Newark
Ray Merchants Motors, Inc.
55 West Church St.
Phone: (614) 345-2653 ●

New Lexington
The Newton-Foraker Co.
215 S. Main St.
Phone: (614) 342-1979 ●

New Philadelphia
Harry Humphries Auto City, Inc
Rt No. 21 South at I-77
Phone: (216) 343-4455 △

Niles
Bonaquist Motor Sales, Inc.
331 Robbins
Phone: (216) 652-6901 ●△

North Olmstead
Len Derin Dodge, Inc.
26100 Lorrain Ave.
Phone: (216) 777-6000 ●△

Norwalk
Downtown Dodge, Inc.
33 E. Seminary St.
Phone: (419) 668-8241 ●

Oak Harbor
Spangler-Nau Motor Sales
121 Locust St.
Phone: (419) 898-2431 ●

Oxford
George H. Kyger & Sons
4999 College Corner
Phone: (513) 523-5566 ●

Painesville
Village Dodge, Inc.
2115 Mentor Ave.
Phone: (216) 354-4368 ▲△

Pandora
Steiner Motor Sales
108 S. Jefferson St.
Phone: (419) 384-4631 ●★

Peebles
Bob Malcom Chrysler Plymouth
213 Rarden Rd.
Phone: (513) 587-3733 ●★○

Poland
Pyramid Motors, Inc.
143 W. McKinley Way
Phone: (216) 757-1521 ●△

Portsmouth
Henry Oberling Motor Co.
1202 Offnere
Phone: (614) 353-3136 ●

Ravenna
Martin Motors
983 East Main St.
Phone: (216) 296-6455 ● △

Russellville
Brown County Motor Sales
Columbus St.
Phone: (513) 377-4701 ▲

St. Marys
Baker Auto, Inc.
117 N. Front St.
Phone: (513) 394-2392 ▲★○

Salem
Sam Brown Dodge, Inc.
909 W. State Street
Phone: (216) 332-1571 ▲

Sidney
H.R. Van Tilburgh Sales
R.R. No. 4, N. Dixie Hwy.
Phone: (513) 492-9282 ●

Springfield
Copes Travel Rama
810 Bechtle Ave.
Phone: (513) 323-9163 △

North Motors
Murray & North
Phone: (513) 325-7021 ●

Steubenville
Pietro Di Novo & Son
232 North Third St.
Phone: (614) 282-2793 ●

Strongsville
Ed Goldie, Inc.
11800 Pearl Road
Phone: (216) 238-8100 ●△

Struthers
McIntee Motors, Inc.
480 Poland Rd.
Phone: (216) 755-9831 ●△

Toledo
Westgate Dodge, Inc.
4750 Monroe St.
Phone: (419) 478-2241 △▲★

Toronto
Hutchison Sales & Service
311 Findley St.
Phone: (614) 537-1561 ●

Upper Sandusky
John H. Neate, Inc.
305 N. Sandusky Ave.
Phone: (419) 294-1953 ●

Van Wert
Frederick Dodge, Inc.
1003 W. Main St.
Phone: (419) 238-3944 ●★

Vermillion
Walker Brothers, Inc.
5652 Liberty Ave.
Phone: (216) 967-3222 ●

Wadsworth
Hardman & Rudey
900 Broad St.
Phone: (216) 334-1596 ●

Warren
Sanzenbazher Motors
760-770 E. Market St.
Phone: (216) 399-1831 ●★

Westerville
Gene Gould, Inc.
320 S. State St.
Phone: (614) 882-7448 ●

Wilmington
Patton Motors
127 E. Main St.
Phone: (513) 382-2518 ●

Youngstown
W.O. Strausbaugh Motor Co.
1097 Wick Ave.
Phone: (216) 743-1131 ●▲△

Zanesville
Balderson Motor Sales
2770 Maple Ave.
Phone: (614) 453-0558 ●△

OKLAHOMA

Alva
Earl Brunstetter Motors
427 Barnes
Phone: (405) 327-0150 ●

Clinton
Williamson Chrysler-Plymouth Co.
315 Gary Freeway
Phone: (405) 323-3720 ●

Cushing
Bartel Motors, Inc.
121-123 West Moses
Phone: (918) 225-2864 ●

Enid
Dean Pearson Dodge, Inc.
215 S. VanBuren
Phone: (405) 237-1216 ●★

Guthrie
Scrutchfield Motor Co.
323 N. Division
Phone: (405) 282-2758 ●

Guymon
Pierce-Barnett, Inc.
409 Hwy. 54, W.
Phone: (405) 338-3530 ●

Hobart
McNutt Motor & Implement Co.
404 S. Jefferson
Phone: (405) 726-2358 ●

Holdenville
Bob Stafford Motor
123 S. Broadway
Phone: (405) 379-2234 ●

Kingfisher
Hauser Motors
109 N. Main St.
Phone: (405) 375-4450 ●

McAlester
Kelley Motor Co.
Hwy. 69 S.
Phone: (918) 423-5291 ●★

Muskogee
Parker Motor City
Hwy. 69 North
Phone: (918) 682-6653 ▲★○△

Oklahoma City
Jack Clark Dodge
Main at Shartel
Phone: (405) 235-1461 ●★△

May Avenue Dodge, Inc.
4025 N. May Ave.
Phone: (405) 946-0601 ●

Okmulgee
Bryant Bros. Motor Co.
210 N. Grand
Phone: (918) 736-3070 ●

Purcell
Boston-Kindblade
Chrysler-Plymouth-Dodge
115 N. Green
Phone: (405) 527-6575 ●

Stillwater
Paul L. Burch Dodge
113 E. 9th St.
Phone: (405) 372-6487 ●

Stroud
Hale Hays Motors
220 S. 8th St.
Phone: (918) 968-3017 ▲

Tulsa
Parrish & Clark
1001 S. Boston
Phone: (918) 584-1481 ▲

Tink's Auto Mart
4400 S. Sheridan
Phone: (918) 622-8000 △

Vinita
C. R. Moore Co. of Vinita
228 S. Wilson
Phone: (918) 256-4455 ●

Wagoner
Green Country Dodge, Inc.
601 W. Cherokee
Phone: (918) 485-3643 ●

Wewoka
Filson Motor Co.
122 W. 3rd St.
Phone: (405) 257-3562 ●

Woodward
Vasser-Armstrong Motor Co.
302 E. Oklahoma Ave.
Phone: (405) 254-4511 ●★

OREGON

Albany
Ralston Motor Co.
630 S. Lyon St.
Phone: (503) 926-2288 ●

Baker
Valley Motor Co.
1950 Auburn St.
Phone: (503) 523-4492 ●△

Beaverton
Beaverton Dodge, Inc.
9500 S.W. Canyon Rd.
Phone: (503) 292-3545 ●△

Burns
Teague Motor Co.
1223 Hines Blvd.
Phone: (503) 573-2863 ●△

Enterprise
Courtney Motors
311 W. Main St.
Phone: (503) 426-3167 ●△

Eugene
Eugene Dodge
77 W. 11th Ave.
Phone: (503) 345-3311 ●△

Gladstone
Jack Livingston Dodge
1255 S.E. McLoughlin
Phone: (503) 655-2591 ●△

Hillsboro
Bunge Motor Co.
First and Washington
Phone: (503) 648-3171 ●△

Hood River
Knoll Motor Co., Inc.
1105 12 St.
Phone: (503) 386-3011 ●

Klamath Falls
Sureoz Motors
424 S. 6th Street
Phone: (503) 882-6668 ●△

Madras
Thomas Sales & Service
342 Fifth St.
Phone: (503) 475-2279 ●△

McMinnville
Triangle Motors, Inc.
Fourth and Baker
Phone: (503) 472-2154 ●△

Medford
Lithia Motors, Inc.
324 E. 5th
Phone: (503) 779-3300 ●△

Newport
Coast Chrysler Center, Co.
Hwy. 101 Between 4th & 5th Sts.
Phone: (503) 867-4664 ●△

Ontario
Treasure Valley Motors
11 S. West First
Phone: (503) 889-9603 ●△

Pendleton
Keith Farley Chrysler Plymouth, Inc.
1400 S.W. Court
Phone: (503) 276-7341 ●△

Portland
Sandy Blvd. Dodge, Inc.
2510 N.E. Sandy Blvd.
Phone: (503) 234-0771 ●△

Roseburg
Northtown Dodge, Inc.
1400 N.E. Stephens
Phone: (503) 672-6555 ●

Salem
Teague Motor Co.
2650 Commercial
Phone: (503) 364-0184 ●▲△

The Dalles
C.H. Urness Motors Co.
200 Union St.
Phone: (503) 296-2284 ●

PENNSYLVANIA

Allentown
Bill Peoples Dodge, Inc.
2340-52 South Lehigh St.
Phone: (215) 791-0300 ●▲★△

Bangor
Joseph C. Reagle, Inc.
R. D. No. 3
Phone: (215) 863-6900 ●

Bedford
Shaffer Motors
Rd. No. 2, Rte. 220
Phone: (814) 623-5977 ●

Bellevue
Corsello Sales & Service, Inc.
500 Lincoln Ave.
Phone: (412) 766-8900 ●○

Berwick
Gay Car Sales
1892 W. Front St.
Phone: (717) 752-4592 ▲★○

Bethel Park
Jack Miller's Garage
4740 Library Road
Phone: (412) 563-0106 △

Boyertown
Quigley Motors
Rt. 100 North
Phone: (215) 367-2191 ●★

Brackenridge
Highland Dodge
10th Ave. at Penn St.
Phone: (412) 226-2900 ●

Braddock
Avenue Motor Co.
205 Braddock Ave.
Phone: (412) 271-1886 ●

Bradford
Harold C. Bauschard
170 Seaward Ave.
Phone: (814) 362-5541 ▲★

Bridgeville
Burgunder Motors, Inc.
Rts. 50 & 519
Phone: (412) 221-4422 ●

Brodheadsville
H.A. Rodenbach & Son
Rt. 209
Phone: (717) 992-4827 ▲★

Butler
Nickles Dodge
1631 N. Main St.
Phone: (412) 287-2734 ●★△

Carlisle
"K" Street Motors
Pitt & "K" Streets
Phone: (717) 243-3512 ●▲★

Carmichaels
Bailey's Garage
332 S. Vine St.
Phone: (412) 966-7000 ●★

Chambersburg
Shivley Motors, Inc.
801 Lincoln Way West
Phone: (717) 264-7134 ●★

Clairton
Clairton Auto Sales
701 7th St.
Phone: (412) 233-8182 ●

Clarion
Laughlin Freas Motor Co.
1074 E. Main St.(U.S. 322 East)
Phone: (814) 226-9550 ●

Clearfield
City Auto Sales
216 N. Third St.
Phone: (814) 765-6541 ●★○

Clifford
Clifford Motors, Inc.
Main St.
Phone: (717) 222-3155 ●▲★△

Coatesville
Ernie Patton Motors, Inc.
2945 E. Lincoln Hwy.
Phone: (215) 384-7515 ●★

Conshohocken
Bowe's Dodge Truck Center, Inc.
1600 Fayette St.
Phone: (215) 247-1242 ▲○

Cresson
Summit Motors, Inc.
2nd St. & Wm. Penn
Phone: (814) 886-2360 ●★

Dallas
L.L. Richardson
50 Lake St.
Phone: (717) 675-5882 ●

Duncannon
Forrers Garage
High and Cherry St.
Phone: (717) 834-3135 ●★○

Duncansville
Suburban Dodge
1407 Third St.
Phone: (814) 695-5688 ●★

Dunmore
Valley Dodge Truck Center
400 Calvin St.
Phone: (717) 344-6126 ●▲■★

Elizabethtown
Petticoffer Dodge
Rt. 230 E.
Phone: (717) 367-1808 ▲★

Erie
Meadowcroft Dodge City, Inc.
1505 Pittsburg Ave.
Phone: (814) 453-4641 ●▲★△

Girard
Girard Auto Sales
808 Main St.
Phone: (814) 474-3411 ●

Gordon
Seitzinger Motors
E. Buddle St.
Phone: (717) 875-1210 ●★

Greensburg
Greensburg Motor Co.
660 E. Pittsburgh St.
Phone: (412) 834-2121 ●▲■★△

Greenville
J. W. Wolfe Motor Sales, Inc.
14 N. Race St.
Phone: (412) 588-4750 ●△

Grove City
Broad Street Garage
104 Broad St. N.
Phone: (412) 458-7040 ●★

Hanover
Kuhn Motors
735 Carlisle St.
Phone: (717) 637-3707 ●★

Harrisburg
Pennsylvania Dodge Truck Center
1812-30 Paxton St.
Phone: (717) 232-4271 ▲★○△

Havertown
McGarrity & Moser
625 W. Chester Pk.
Phone: (215) 528-6161 ●★

Hazelton
Stephen Butcher, Inc.
761 W. Broad St.
Phone: (717) 454-6683 ●★

Honesdale
B & B Dodge
125 Grandview Avenue
Phone: (717) 253-1290 ●

Houston
I.C. Patsch & Sons, Inc.
Pike & Haft Sts.
Phone: (412) 745-7000 ●

Indiana
McGregor Motor Co., Inc.
404 N. Fourth St.
Phone: (412) 463-3553 ●★

Irwin
Turnpike Dodge
224 Center Hwy.
Phone: (412) 271-2400/7735 ●★

Jeannette
Central Service Station
10 S. Second St.
Phone: (412) 523-5581 ●△

Jenkintown
Jenkintown Dodge
900 Old York Rd.
Phone. (215) 887-6900 ●★

Johnstown
H.E. Wagner Motor Sales Co.
850 Horner St.
Phone: (814) 536-3504 ●★

Kingston
Kingston Dodge, Inc.
303 S. Wyoming Ave.
Phone: (717) 287-3125 ▲

Lebanon
Lebanon Valley Dodge
232-40 S. Ninth St.
Phone: (717) 273-1632 ▲★○△

Lehighton
Hahn & Sons, Inc.
619 Iron St.
Phone: (215) 377-0470 ●★

Lewistown
Lash Motor Co.
425-500 Eelectric Ave.
Phone: (717) 248-0119 ●

Lima
Weathers Dodge
Baltimore Pike
Phone: (215) 566-7575 ●★

Lititz
J. B. Zatman, Inc.
423 Furnance Hill Pk.
Phone: (717) 626-8551 ●★

Lock Haven
Adam C. Dickey Co.
418 N. Vesper St.
Phone: (717) 748-2521 ●△

McConnellsburg
Richards Auto Sls.
810 Lincoln Way East
Phone: (717) 485-3113 ▲★

McKeesport
Paul W. Jones, Inc.
396-400 Eden Park Blvd.
Phone: (412) 462-7654 ●△

McKees Rocks
W. A. Burgunder, Inc.
1101 Charters Ave.
Phone: (412) 311-3636 ●★

Meadville
Griffin Dodge
1123 Park Ave.
Phone: (814) 336-2164 ●★

Meshoppen
Commonwealth Garage
Main Street & Rt. No. 6
Phone: (717) 833-5559 ●

Millville
W.O. Diehl & Sons
Eyers Grove Rd. No. 1
Phone: (717) 458-6421 ▲★

Monroeville
Monroeville Dodge, Inc.
3633 William Penn Hwy.
Phone: (412) 824-7000 ●▲△

Muncey
Vince Stein, Inc.
Main and New Sts.
Phone: (717) 546-3146 ▲★

New Castle
Palmer Motor Company
1500 Butler Ave.
Phone: (412) 658-4597 ●★

New Holland
Horning Dodge, Inc.
501 E. Main St.
Phone: (717) 354-2184 ▲★○

North East
Mackay Swift, Inc.
135 West Main St.
Phone: (814) 725-4574 ●

Oil City
Southside Motors, Inc.
204 E. Second St.
Phone: (814) 676-6597 ▲★

Olyphant
Lewis Bros.
R.D. No. 1
Phone: (717) 587-4355 ▲

Patton
Patton Motor Sales, Inc.
500 McIntyre Ave.
Phone: (814) 674-3663 ●★

Pennsville
Dalessio Motors, Inc.
South Broadway
Phone: (609) 678-3111 ●

Philadelphia
Burholme Mts., Inc.
7253 Rising Sun Ave.
Phone: (215) 725-4200 ●★

Northeast Dodge
6101 Frankford Ave.
Phone: (215) 754-5000 ●★

Penrose Dodge, Inc.
6815 Essington Ave.
Phone: (215) SA 4-7405 ●▲★△

Phoenixville
Hrivnak Motor Co.
Schuylkill & Rapps Dam
Phone: (215) 933-8941 ●★○

Pittsburgh
Baum Boulevard Dodge, Inc.
Baum Blvd. & Liberty Ave.
Phone: (412) 681-9800 ●▲★△

St. Clair Dodge, Inc.
2945 Banksville Rd.
Phone: (412) 343-0800 ●

Vern Staley Dodge, Inc.
4981 McKnight Rd.
Phone: (412) 931-5801 ●△

Quarryville
Winnie Hogg
N. Church St.
Phone: (717) 786-2175 ▲★○

Saxton
Giornesto Motor Co., Inc.
6th & Main
Phone: (814) 635-2944 ●★

Sayre
Penn-York Valley Motors
310 N. Keystone Ave.
Phone: (717) 855-0295 ●★○

Schnecksville
Krause Dodge, Inc.
2244 Main St.
Phone: (215) 799-3166 ●

Scottdale
Martinsek Motor Sales
301 Broadway
Phone: (412) 887-7800 ●★

Scranton
Scranton Dodge, Inc.
1146 Wyoming Ave.
Phone: (717) 344-1261 ●

Shamokin
Harner Motor Company
300 Center St.
Phone: (717) 648-5724 ▲★

Shanksville
Shanksville Auto Co.
Johns Street
Phone: (814) 267-5762 ▲★○

Shillington
Suburban Dodge, Inc.
Lancaster Pike at Thomas Dr.
Phone: (215) 777-7881 ▲★△

Shippensburg
Ed Naugle
608 King St. W.
Phone: (717) 532-4136 ●★○

E. Smethport
East Side Garage
Route 6
Phone: (814) 887-5731 ●

Somerset
Saylor Motor Co.
301 N. Center Ave.
Phone: (814) 445-7923 ▲■★△

Souderton
Souderton Motor Co.
2nd & Chestnut Sts.
Phone: (215) 723-4555 ●★○

Springfield
Springfield Dodge
770 Baltimore Pk.
Phone: (215) 554-7800 ●★○

Stroudsburg
E.M. Reinhart, Inc.
1875 N. Main St.
Phone: (717) 421-2440 ▲

Summer Hill
E.L. Jones Dodge, Inc.
Route 53
Phone: (814) 495-4691 ●★

Tamaqua
Milt Ziff Motors, Inc.
201 Cedar St.
Phone: (717) 668-1800 ●★

Titusville
Northwest Motors Corp.
416 S. Perry St.
Phone: (814) 827-6111 ●

Troy
Calkins Motor Sales, Inc.
510 Elmira Street
Phone: (717) 297-2115 ●

Tunkhannock
Ralph B. Sheldon & Son
Bridge & Harding St.
Phone: (717) 836-4071 ●★

Tyrone
Shopes' Garage
1216 Penna Ave.
Phone: (814) 684-2900 ●★

Union City
Truscuits, Inc.
85 Waterford St.
Phone: (814) 438-3875 ●

Uniontown
Thurby Motors
447 Connellsville St.
Phone: (412) 438-7991 ●

Warren
Warren Honda Rec. Center, Inc.
1089 Market Street
Phone: (814) 723-5400 △

Washington
George Stewart Motor Co.
42 E. Maiden St.
Phone: (412) 222-0500 ●★

W. Catasauqua
Berk Motor Co.
First Ave.
Phone: (215) 264-1384 ●★

● Medium Truck ▲ Heavy Truck ■ Diesel ★ Road Service ○ Night Service △ Motor Home/Recreational Vehicles

Wexford
North Hills Dodge, Inc.
10355 Perry Hwy.
Phone: (412) 935-3791 ●★

Williamsport
Van Campen Motors
601 W. Third St.
Phone: (717) 326-0567 ●★

Windber
Baumgardner Motors, Inc.
402 17th St.
Phone: (814) 467-7458 ●

Wysox
Dave Snell Chrysler Plymouth, Inc.
Route 6
Phone: (717) 265-2109 ●

RHODE ISLAND

Apponaug
William's Corner Garage, Inc.
3126 Post Road
Phone: (401) 737-6105 ●★

Cranston
Cann Motor, Inc.
1152 Park Ave.
Phone: (401) 944-7600 ●★

East Providence
Rima White Truck Center, Inc.
860 Waterman Ave.
Phone: (401) 438-6330 ●▲■★○△

North Kingstown
Kingstown Motor Company
6600 Post Road
Phone: (401) 884-3300 ●▲★△

Wakefield
Fred W. Smith, Inc.
36 Tower Hill Rd.
Phone: (401) 789-6500 ●

Warren
Bristol County Dodge, Inc.
205 Childs St.
Phone: (401) 245-2303 ▲★

West Warwick
West Warwick Dodge, Inc.
705 Main St.
Phone: (401) 828-2600 ●★△

Woonsocket
Jay Motors, Inc.
657 Social St.
Phone: (401) 769-6800 ●★

SOUTH CAROLINA

Chester
City Chrysler Plymouth, Inc.
Hwy. 72, By-Pass
Phone: (803) 385-3103 ●★

Columbia
Burnside Truck Center, Inc.
1500 Bluff Rd.
Phone: (803) 779-5942 ▲■★△

Greenville
Dodge City of S. C., Inc.
2645 Laurens Road
Phone: (803) 288-3000 ●△

Kingstree
East Side Motors
Warsaw Hwy.-P.O. Box 299
Phone: (803) 354-6174 ●★

Lancaster
Sonny Bowers Dodge, Inc.
Hwy. 200 South
Phone: (803) 285-1546 ●★

Lexington
Addy Dodge, Inc.
521 Columbia Ave.
Phone: (803) 359-2501 ▲★○△

Orangeburg
D.D. Salley & Co., Inc.
626 Russell, S.E.
Phone: (803) 534-6956 ●★

Rock Hill
Welch Motors, Inc.
125 Oakland Ave.
Phone: (803) 328-3886 ●★

Spartanburg
City Motor Car Co., Inc.
226 W. Main St.
Phone: (803) 583-1425 ●★

Sumter
General Dodge, Inc.
14 W. Canal St.
Phone: (803) 775-7333●★

SOUTH DAKOTA

Aberdeen
Martyn-Edwards Co.
301 S. Lincoln St.
Phone: (605) 225-9350▲★△

Brookings
LeFevre Motor Co., Inc.
312 Third Ave.
Phone: (605) 692-2922●△

Chamberlain
Wilmodt Motor Co.
115 S. Cortland
Phone: (605) 734-5211●

Deadwood
LeMar Motors Co.
Hwy. 85
Phone: (605) 578-2691●

Dell Rapids
Dells Motors Co.
301 4th St.
Phone: (605) 428-5460●

Huron
Jones Co.
118 Third St., S.E.
Phone: (605) 845-2934●★

Kadoka
Hemmingson Auto Service
Main St.
Phone: (605) 837-2204●

Mobridge
Kramer-Korbyn Auto, Inc.
121 Grand Crossing Blvd., E.
Phone: (605) 845-2934●★

New Holland
Van Zee Motor Sales
Phone: (605) 243-5201●

Pierre
Halst Motors, Inc.
200 W. Dakota
Phone: (605) 224-5811●

Rapid City
Dodge Town, Inc.
704 5th St.
Phone: (605) 343-2896●

Sioux Falls
Duke Tufty Co.
2317 S. Minnesota
Phone: (605) 336-1235●▲★△

Sisseton
Brooks Motors
120 First Ave. E.
Phone: (605) 698-7633●

Watertown
Williamson Dodge
303 West Kemp
Phone: (605) 886-6734●

Yankton
Zimmerman Motor Co.
403 E. 4th St.
Phone: (605) 665-7441●

TENNESSEE

Bristol
Delta Dodge Sales & Service
Hwy. 11 West
Phone: (615) 323-5117▲■★○△

Chattanooga
Gateway Dodge
402 W. Ninth St.
Phone: (615) 267-6521 ●

Crossville
Warner Motor Company
102 Rockwood St.
Phone: (615) 484-6630 ▲★○

Knoxville
Burgin Dodge, Inc.
4500 Clinton Hwy.
Phone: (616) 688-3620 ●○

Commercial Truck & Trailer Sales, Inc.
612 Dale Avenue
Phone: (615) 522-9696 ●▲★■○△

Madisonville
Harvey Motor Co.
Niles Ferry Hwy.
Phone: (615) 442-2485 ▲★

Memphis
Tom Hutton Co.
1710 E. Brooks Rd.
Phone: (901) 396-3960 ●▲△

Nashville
Key Chrysler-Plymouth, Inc.
1200 South Gallatin Road
Phone: (615) 227-7350 △

Music City Dodge
710 Murfreesboro Rd.
Phone: (615) 244-6666 ●△

Neely Coble Co.
1111 Polk Ave.
Phone: (615) 255-0561 ●▲■★○

Ripley
Jeff Davis Dodge
Hwy. 51 South
Phone: (901) 635-1822 ●△★

TEXAS

Abilene
Big Country Dodge, Inc.
So. First & Winters Freeway
Phone: (915) 698-2222 ●△

Alice
Yawn Dodge
1259 E. Main St.
Phone: (512) 664-7339 ●★

Amarillo
Hedgecoke Motor Co.
416 W. 6th St.
Phone: (806) 372-8355 ●★△

Andrews
Martin's Motors
200 S.W. 1st St.
Phone: (915) 523-2619 ●

Athens
Davis Motor Co.
118 S. Palestine
Phone: . (214) 675-2261 ●

Austin
Dependable Motors, Inc.
7309 Interrgnl. Hwy.
Phone: (512) 478-9621 ▲★△

Baytown
Lumus Baytown Dodge
2800 Market St.
Phone: (713) 427-7474 ●★△

Beaumont
Holly Motor Co.
700 Calder
Phone: (713) 835-5933 ●★

Beeville
Hardy Motors
P.O. Box 398
Phone: (512) 358-3020 ▲★○

Brady
Shuffield-Townsend
114 West Lockhart
Phone: (915) 597-3456 ●

Breckenridge
McCathren Motor Co.
220 West Elm
Phone: (817) 449-4448 ●★

Bryan
Halsell Motor Co.
1411 Texas Ave.
Phone: (713) 823-8111 ●★

Burnet
Fry Motors, Inc.
206 W. Polk
Phone: (512) 756-2128 ●

Carrizo Springs
Dimmit Motor Sales
W. Alamo & Highway 83
Phone: (512) 876-5028 ●★○

Coleman
Taylor Motor Co.
216 Live Oak
Phone: (915) 625-4111 ●★

Conroe
Standard Motor Co.
802 N. Frazier
Phone: (713) 756-4407 ▲★

Corpus Christi
Creveling Motor Co.
4313 S. Staples
Phone: (512) 854-3131 ●★△

Corsicana
Hervey Motors, Inc.
Jct. S. Hwy. 75 & 287
Phone: (214) 874-6548 ★△

Crane
Crane Motor Co.
606 South Gaston
Phone: (915) 558-3578 ●

Dallas
Dodge Trucks, Inc.
4200 Irving Blvd.
Phone: (214) 637-1960 ▲■★

Downtown Dodge, Inc.
5431 Lemmon Ave.
Phone: (214) 526-4600 ●

R. O. Evans Motor Homes
12113 Garland Road
Phone: (214) 328-9806 ★△

Lone Star Dodge, Inc.
12000 N.W. Hwy. E
Phone: (214) 328-3584 ●

Oak Cliff Dodge
111 N. Marsalis
Phone: (214) 943-4623 ●★

Preston Road Dodge
13130 Preston Rd.
Phone: (214) 239-5371 ●

Snuffy Smith Motor Homes
12424 North Central Expressway
Phone: (214) 234-2465 ★○△

Elcampo
Miller Motor Co.
101 W. 1st St.
Phone: (713) 325-5804 ▲★

El Paso
McKeon Dodge, Inc.
1363 Airway Blvd.
Phone: (915) 772-5261 ▲★●

Fort Stockton
Riggs Motor Co.
221 N. Main
Phone: (915) 336-5216 ●★

Ft. Worth
Longhorn Dodge, Inc.
2401 W. 7th St.
Phone: (817) 335-9367 ●△

Southside Dodge, Inc.
4500 South Fwy.
Phone: (817) 926-8111 ●△

Fredericksburg
Standard Service Co.
116 Main St.
Phone: (512) 997-2120 ●

Harlingen
Fergurson Motor Co., Inc.
602 W. Jackson
Phone: (512) 423-1685 ●★△

Hearne
K & B Dodge
600 Brown St.
Phone: (713) 546-3161 ●★

Hondo
Breiten Dodge
1214-1216 18th St.
Phone: (512) 426-3103 ●★

Houston
Burkett Motors, Inc.
1617 San Jacinto
Phone: (713) 222-0321 ▲★

Gulf Coast Dodge, Inc.
7250 Golf Freeway
Phone: (713) 644-5421 ●▲★△

Northline Dodge, Inc.
4638 Airline Dr.
Phone: (713) 692-6081 ●

Sharpstown Dodge Sales, Inc.
6890 S. W. Fwy.
Phone: (713) 783-6500 ●△

Karnes City
Karnes City Motor Co.
Calvert & Brown Sts.
Phone: (512) 459-2495 ▲★○

Kermit
McGuire Motors
123 N. Oak
Phone: (915) 586-2553 ●★

Kingsville
Richie Harris Dodgetown
800 S. 14th St.
Phone: (512) 592-4324 ●★

Lagrange
Meiners Motor Co.
304 E. Travis
Phone: (713) 968-3119 ▲★○

Laredo
Guajardo Motor Co.
1300 Houston
Phone: (512) 723-8293 ●

Levelland
Frontier Dodge
Ave. "H" & 11th St.
Phone: (806) 894-7373 ●△▲★

Littlefield
Garland Motor Co.
720 E. Third St.
Phone: (806) 385-4454 ▲★○

Lubbock
University Dodge Sales
1702 Texas Ave.
Phone: (806) 765-7741 ▲△

Marfa
Webb Brothers
102 East San Antonio
Phone: (915) 729-4341 ●★

Marshall
Carrington Motor Co.
1803 E. Grand
Phone: (214) 935-9355 ●

Mason
Leslie Motor Co.
328 Ft. McKavitt
Phone: (915) 347-5656 ●

Midland
Nickel Chrysler-Plymouth-Dodge
3705 West Wall
Phone: (915) 694-6661 ●△

New Braunfels
Becker Motor Co.
547 S. Seguin
Phone: (512) 625-3463 ●

Ozona
Stuart Motor Co.
Highway 290
Phone: (915) 392-3110 ●

Pasadena
Pasadena Dodge, Inc.
1831 S. Richey
Phone: (713) 473-9431 ●▲

Pecos
Grogan Motors
202 Cedar St.
Phone: (915) 445-3878 ●★

Pharr
El Centro Dodge
1213 W. Expressway
Phone: (512) 682-4356 ●

Plainview
McBeth Dodge
2408 W. 5th St.
Phone: (806) 223-2661 ●

Port Arthur
Gulfway Dodge
2949 Gulfway Dr.
Phone: (713) 983-3357 ●★

Rosenberg
Perkins Motor Co.
4800 Ave. H
Phone: (713) 662-2879 ●

San Antonio
O.R. Mitchell Motors
1130 Broadway
Phone: (512) 427-2281 ●

North Star Dodge, Inc.
7230 San Pedro
Phone: (512) 341-2251 ●★△

Snyder
Thomas Chrysler Plymouth
2103 25th St.
Phone: (915) 573-9386 ●★○

Temple
Ira Young Auto Co., Inc.
3207 General Bruce Blvd.
Phone: (817) 773-4556 ●

Tyler
Holley Motor Co.
236 S. Broadway
Phone: (214) 594-3321 ●★

Waco
Waco Dodge Sales, Inc.
1220 N. Valley Mills Dr.
Phone: (817) 772-8120 ▲★

Weslaco
Weslaco Dodge Truck Center, Inc.
E. State Highway
Phone: (512) 968-2158 ●★△

Witchita Falls
Morgan Motor Co., Inc.
2910 Jacksboro Hwy.
Phone: (817) 767-9271 ●★△

UTAH

Cedar City
Lunt Motor Co.
39 South Main
Phone: (801) 586-6591 ●★

Ogden
Robert H. Hinckley, Inc.
2810 Washington Ave.
Phone: (801) 394-8844 ●▲★

Price
Bunnell Dodge
154 E. Main St.
Phone: (801) 637-0284 ●★

Salt Lake City
Hinckleys Truck, Inc.
2309 S. State St.
Phone: (801) 484-8755 ●▲■★△

VERMONT

Burlington
C. H. Goss Co.
237 North St.
Phone: (802) 864-4521 ●▲★△

Fair Haven
Fair Haven Motors
20 Liberty St.
Phone: (807) 265-4964 ●★

Rutland
Killington Motors
270 S. Main St.
Phone: (802) 775-5597 ●

West Hartford
Clifford's Garage
Rt. 14
Phone: (802) 295-3013 ●★

VIRGINIA

Big Stone Gap
Keely Motor Co.
E. 5th Ave.
Phone: (703) 523-0085 ●

Blackstone
Hammock Rand Motors, Inc.
310 North Main St.
Phone: (703) 292-7271 ●★○

Christiansburg
Curtis Motor Sales & Service, Inc.
600 Roanoke St.
Phone: (703) 382-2178 ●

Covington
Dressler Motors
Monroe & Cherry Sts.
Phone: (703) 962-2291 ●★

Franklin
Blythe Dodge, Inc.
W. Franklin St. & Third Ave.
Phone: (703) 562-5477 ●★

Fredericksburg
Carl D. Silver, Inc.
2216 Princess Ann St.
Phone: (703) 373-8221 ●

Hampton
Poquoson Motors, Inc.
4116 Mercury Blvd.
Phone: (703) 826-1100 △

King William
Taylor Motor Co., Inc.
Phone: (703) 769-7564 ▲★

Lynchburg
John P. Hughes Motor Co, Inc.
800 Commerce St.
Phone: (703) 845-4511 ▲★

Marion
Holston Motor Co., Inc.
112 Broad St.
Phone: (703) 783-5126 ▲

Newport News
Shackelford Auto Co., Inc.
327 25th St.
Phone: (703) 244-1466 ●★

Tysinger Motor Co., Inc.
11061 Warwick Blvd.
Phone: (703) 595-7663 △

Norfolk
Tidewater Dodge, Inc.
6440 Military Hwy., N.
Phone: (703) 855-2091 ▲★○△

Petersburg
Triangle Dodge, Inc.
2833 Crater Rd., S.
Phone: (703) 733-4664 ●★

Portsmouth
King Dodge, Inc.
1313 High St.
Phone: (703) 397-3431 ●★

Richmond
Lawrence Motor Co, Inc.
Blvd. off Broad St.
Phone: (703) 358-1536 ●★○

Roanoke
Antrim Motors, Inc.
510 McClanahan St., S.W.
Phone: (703) 344-5126 ●△

Salem
Beach Brothers Motors, Inc.
1259 East Main St.
Phone: (703) 389-8137 ●

Suffolk
Tri County Dodge, Inc.
800-802 W. Washington St.
Phone: (703) 539-9958 ●★○

Virginia Beach
Bay Camping, Inc.
3757 Bonney Road
Phone: (703) 486-1211 △

Thompson Royal Dodge, Inc.
3443 Va. Beach
Phone: (703) 340-4900 ●★○

Waverly
Waverly Motors, Inc.
U.S. Hwy. 460
Phone: (703) 834-2500 ●★

WASHINGTON

Aberdeen
Bob Ahrendt Motors Co.
408 E. Market
Phone: (206) 532-0883 ●▲■△

Auburn
Valley Motors, Inc.
2925 Auburn Ave.
Phone: (206) 833-2485 ●▲△

Bellevue
Bellevue Dodge, Inc.
316 116th Ave., N.E.
Phone: (206) 454-7995 ●△

Bremerton
Jim Traveller Motors, Inc.
11th & Callow
Phone: (206) 373-2501 ●

Brewster
Goehry's, Inc.
11 Bridge St.
Phone: (509) 689-2531 ●△

Camas
Camas Motors
518 N.E. Birch
Phone: (206) 834-4463 ●

Centralia
Al's City Motors, Inc.
500 N. Tower Street
Phone: (206) 736-3369 ●△

Colville
Dallas Garage
230-250 N. Main
Phone: (509) 684-4401 ●

Ephrata
Robinson Thomas Motors
514 Basin St., N.W.
Phone: (509) 754-2476 ●△

Everett
Walsh-Platt Motors
Hewitt & Rucker
Phone: (206) 252-2157 ●

Ferndale
Jeffcott Motors
Main St.
Phone: (206) 384-1311 ●

Goldendale
Radke Motors, Inc.
300 Main St.
Phone: (509) 773-4555 ●

Kennewick
Tri-City Dodge, Inc.
124 W. Kennewick Ave.
Phone: (509) 582-5189 ●

Kent
Valley Garage, Inc.
1145 W. Meeker St.
Phone: (206) 852-0150 △

Lynnwood
Doug's Lynnwood Dodge, Inc.
20612 Hwy 99
Phone: (206) 774 3551 ●

Moses Lake
C & V Auto Sales & Service
520 E. Pioneer Way
Phone: (509) 765-3461 ●

Mt. Vernon
McDowell C-P Dodge
2020 Freeway Drive N.
Phone: (206) 424-7986 ●△

Newport
Rindels, Inc.
117 S. Washington
Phone: (509) 447-3513 ●△

Oak Harbor
Oak Harbor Garage
1333 West Pioneer Way
Phone: (206) 675-2264 ●△

Omak
Don Bryan Motors, Inc.
130 North Main St.
Phone: (509) 826-0540 ●

Port Angeles
Murray Motors, Inc.
302 E. First St.
Phone: (206) 457-6345 ●

Renton
Renton Dodge, Inc.
12601 Rainier Ave., N.
Phone: (206) 772-5070 ●△

Seattle
Dodge City
821 Lenora
Phone: (206) 624-8400 ●△

Snoqualmie
Moller Motors, Inc.
State Highway 2
Phone: (206) 888-0805 ●

Spokane
Dishman Dodge, Inc.
E. 7700 Sprague
Phone: (509) 924-3250 ●▲△

Tacoma
Tacoma Dodge, Inc.
4101 S. Tacoma Way
Phone: (206) 475-7300 ●▲△

Toppenish
Sig-Carlson, Inc.
201-03 Washington
Phone: (509) 865-3185 ●

Vancouver
Pederson Motors, Inc.
7th & Broadway
Phone: (206) 695-3431 ●

Walla Walla
Tex Brotherton, Inc.
401 W. Main St.
Phone: (509) 525-2350 ●△

Wenatchee
Valley Auto Co., Inc.
210 South Wenatchee
Phone: (509) 662-2121 ●

Yakima
Yakima Dodge
1712 South First St.
Phone: (509) 453-7173 ●△

WEST VIRGINIA

Barboursville
Louie Fonduk, Inc.
6018 Rte. 60—Box 216
Phone: (304) 736-5226 △

Buckhannon
Bud Bennett Motors
P. O. Box 230
Phone: (304) 472-1400 ●★

Charleston
Patrick Plaza Dodge, Inc.
4th Ave. at Patrick Plaza
Phone: (304) 343-5623 ●△★

Clarksburg
Auto Sales & Service
Second St. & Washington
Phone: (304) 624-6341 ●★○

Fairmont
Michael Motors, Inc.
317 Jackson St.
Phone: (304) 363-9300 ●★○

Kingwood
Snyder Motor Co.
208 Tunnelton St.
Phone: (304) 329-0850 ●★

Martinsburg
Union Sales Company
119 E. Race St.
Phone: (304) 267-8908 ●★

● Medium Truck ▲ Heavy Truck ■ Diesel ★ Road Service ○ Night Service △ Motor Home/Recreational Vehicles

Morgantown
Layman Motor Co. of Morgantown
949 University Ave.
Phone: (304) 296-4411 ●★○

Newell
Newell Central Service, Inc.
400 Washington St.
Phone: (304) 387-2955 ●

Parkersburg
Mullen Motor Co.
13th at Liberty Sts.
Phone: (304) 485-5555 ●★

Pineville
City Auto Service, Inc.
Route No. 10
Phone: (304) 732-2381 ●★○

St. Marys
Davis Motors, Inc.
419 Second St.
Phone: (304) 684-2451 ●★

Weston
Rogers Motor Co.
373 E. 3rd St.
Phone: (304) 269-5727 ▲★

Wheeling
Hopkins Motor Co.
430 U.S. Route 40
Phone: (304) 233-2300 ●★

WISCONSIN

Antigo
Kenyon Motors , Inc.
527 Clermont
Phone: (715) 623-3796 ●△

Appleton
Royal Dodge, Inc.
1610 Wisc. Ave.
Phone: (414) 739-6381 △

Ashland
Wallie Motor Co.
819-823 W. 2nd St.
Phone: (715) 682-2902 ▲★

Baraboo
Berning Motors, Inc.
S. Boulevard & Parkway
Phone: (608) 356-3968 ●★

Berlin
Johnson & Fortnum, Inc.
163-169 Park St.
Phone: (414) 361-1616 ●

Black River Falls
Don Kislinger Motor Sales
Route 4
Phone: (715) 284-4339 ●

Boscobel
Nelson & Brindley Motor Co.
Highway 61 & 132
Phone: (508) 375-4545 ●★

Burlington
Miller Motor Sales, Inc.
688 Milwaukee Ave.
Phone: (414) 763-2343 ●★

Cadott
Corner Motors, Inc.
Highway 27
Phone: (715) 289-3290 ●△

Cumberland
Cifaldi Motors
1020 2nd Ave.
Phone: (715) 822-4931 ●★

Darlington
Ostby Motors
125 E. Alice St.
Phone: (608) 776-2417 ●★

Durand
Bauer Bros. Mtr. Co., Inc.
119 W. Madison Ave.
Phone: (715) 672-8764 ●★

Eau Clair
A.E. Rogers Co.
707 S. Barstow
Phone: (715) 834-4186 ● ○

Fair Water
Card Motor Co.
Phone: (414) 346-5693 ●★△

Fond Du Lac
Crown Sales & Service, Inc.
33 Third St.
Phone: (414) 922-2450 ●★ △

Green Bay
John Ryan, Inc.
725 Main
Phone: (414) 437-5436 ▲ ●△

Green Leaf
Morrison Garage
RR No. 2
Phone: (414) 864-7441 ●★○

Hartford
Williams Motor Chrysler-Ply.
R.R. 2, Hwy. 60 East
Phone: (414) 673-3480 ●★○

Hayward
Gillis Motors, Inc.
316 E. First St.
Phone: (715) 634-2615 ●

Horicon
Guptill's Dodge Sales & Service
113 Washington St.
Phone: (414) 485-4765 ▲★

Kaukauna
Van Lieshout Motor Sales
225 Dodge St.
Phone: (414) 766-3771 ●★

Ladysmith
Rite-Way Oil Co.
204 Miner Ave. E.
Phone: (715) 532-5480 ●

Lancaster
Milt Funk Motors
104 S. Monroe St.
Phone: (608) 723-4234 ●★

Madison
Madison Motors
332 W. Johnson St.
Phone: (608) 257-1414 ▲★

Manitowoc
Bouril Auto Co.
916 S. 10th St.
Phone: (414) 682-7711 ●

Marinette
Chevalier Motors
2009 Hall Ave.
Phone: (715) 735-3361 ●★△

Marion
Mayne Auto Sales
121 Garfield Ave.
Phone: (715) 754-4211 ●★

Medford
Strebig Auto Co., Inc.
312 Wisconsin Ave.
Phone: (715) 748-4969 ●★○

Menomonie
Flick Motor Sales
422 Crescent St.
Phone: (715) 235-2101 ●★

Merrill
Park City Motors, Inc.
611 E. 2nd St.
Phone: (715) 536-7311 ●★

Milwaukee
Milwaukee Truck Center, Inc.
10521 W. Layton Ave.
Phone: (414) 425-4880 ▲○△

North Shore Dodge, Inc.
1433 W. Silver Spring Rd.
Phone: (414) 370-7050 ●

Monroe
Dearth Motors, Inc.
520 W. Hwy. 11
Phone: (608) 325-3181 ●★

Mt. Calvary
Abholds Garage, Inc.
Main Street
Phone: (414) 753 2141 ●△

Neillsville
Rychnovsky Bros.
306 W. 5th St.
Phone: (715) 743-3737 ●★

New London
Freiburger's Inc.
206 N. Pearl St.
Phone: (414) 982-4350 ●△

New Richmond
Bernard's Super Service, Inc.
355 S. Main St.
Phone: (715) 246-2236 ▲★

Okauchee
John Quaden Dodge, Inc.
780 Wisconsin
Phone: (414) 567-4408 ▲★

Oshkosh
Phil Raddatz Dodge, Ltd.
2880 Jackson Drive, U.S. 45 N.
Phone: (414) 231-9262 ▲

Plymouth
Hub City Auto Sales
105 N. Highland Rd.
Phone: (414) 893-6591 ●

Portage
Jenkins Motor Sales, Inc.
1114 Silver Lake Dr.
Phone: (608) 742-4112 ▲★

Port Washington
West Side Auto Service
109 Park St.
Phone: (414) 284-2161 ●

Potter
The Central Garage
Main St.
Phone: (414) 853-3561 ●

Poy Sippi
Dahike Fraser, Inc.
502 Main St.
Phone: (414) 987-2141 ●

Prairie du Sac
Tarnutzer's
431 Water St.
Phone: (608) 643-3030 ●★

Racine
Bob Ahsinger
2044 Lathrop Ave.
Phone: (414) 637-7453 ●

Reedsburg
Berning Garage
100 Second St.
Phone: (608) 524-4112 ▲★

Rice Lake
South Lake Motors
1620 S. Main St.
Phone: (715) 234-3497 ●★

Richland Center
Buhmeyer's Sales & Service
244 West Mill St.
Phone: (608) 647-2233 ●★

River Falls
A.W. Lund Co.
201-17 South Main St.
Phone: (612) 436-7565 ●

Shawano
Lasch Motors
600 E. Green Bay Ave.
Phone: (715) 526-4504 ●

Sheboygan
Seefeld Dodge, Inc.
1322 North 13th St.
Phone: (414) 457-4861 ●△

Sturgeon Bay
Moeller's Garage
304 N. Third St.
Phone: (414) 743-2723 ●★

Superior
Kapus-Erickson, Inc.
1318 Ogden Ave.
Phone: (715) 392-8191 ●★

Suring
Ehlinger Garage
Main St.
Phone: (414) 842-2277 ●

Theresa
Beck Motors, Inc.
Milwaukee St.
Phone: (414) 488-4343 ●○

Watertown
Watertown Dodge, Inc.
301 W. Main St.
Phone: (414) 261-3870 ▲

Wauwatosa
Dodge City of Wauwatosa
11333 W. Burleigh St.
Phone: (414) 771-8810 △●

Wisconsin Rapids
Warsinske Motor Co.
411 Eighth St.
Phone: (715) 423-6200 ●★

WYOMING

Casper
Coliseum Motor Co.
131 E. 5th St.
Phone: (307) 237-8491 ●★△

Cheyenne
Cheyenne Dodge, Inc.
16th & Evans
Phone: (307) 634-5887 ●★△

Cody
Barney's Auto Sales & Service
Yellowstone Hwy. 14 & 20 St.
Phone: (307) 587-4519 ●★

Riverton
Riverton Equipment Co.
1601 N. Federal Blvd.
Phone: (307) 856-2205 ●★

Worland
Edwards Motor & Equip.
707 Robertson
Phone: (307) 347-3490 ●★

15. Future of Camping

☐ Your trailer converted, in minutes, to a cruising houseboat . . . your camper, lofted across continents in giant, low-fare cargo superjets, and set down–for family fun and adventure–in some of the world's most remote, exotic and campable places . . . camper buses whose sides expand to hand you a two-in-one bargain: a comfortable lakeside cottage when you want it and out-of-doors transport when you need it.

Glimpses such as these of camping's future–the nearer-than-you-may-think future–frame the picture of camping tomorrow as the experts see it. What they see is more of us camping more of the time in greater comfort, with more conveniences and more for the fun of it than ever before.

Not only for fun, but by psychological necessity, say such into-the-future gazers as Dr. Marion Clawson, outdoor economist and former director of the U.S. Bureau of Land Management, who calls our growing outdoor migration and mobility the "emerging American life-style."

For the 65 per cent of us who today live compacted into cities and the 75 per cent who will likely be city dwellers tomorrow, camping, foresees Dr. Clawson, will help us keep our cool, uncorking urban tensions and becoming, for the cities' elbow-to-elbow and bumper-to-bumper millions, the retreat of last resort and reality.

Big as the vehicular camping boom is, as a nation of campers we've scarcely got our wheels wet. Right now, twenty-five million of us, one in every eight, take to the out of doors, millions as vehicular campers, whether in the family car or wagon fitted for camping or snug in designed-for-camping vehicles, motor home, travel trailer, tent trailer, pickup camper, travel car or compact van converted to the comforts of home afield.

By 1975 outdoor's legions and its campers (risen to seventy-five million) will triple, predicts the Outdoor Recreation Resources Review Commission, set up by the U.S. Congress in 1958 to look to, and help plan, America's recreational future.

How, and how far afield, with what comforts and new conveniences and vehicles and why, will you and the millions more be camping tomorrow? Here's an exciting look into the exciting future:

All the World Your Campground. As the world in the coming era of the supersonic jet shrinks, the vehicular campers will expand to the far and campable corners of the globe.

Having camped America first, millions will drive into the yawning maws of huge vehicular jet ferries, to be whisked overnight, overseas.

To Europe, already a camper's delight. To South America, its fingering system of new roads opening to camping the orchid fringes of the Amazon, the highlands of the Andes and the outskirts of its throbbing cities. To emerging Africa, the camper's adventurous big game new frontier. To the Orient, especially Japan and the collar highlands of the Himalayas, where the camper is king. To Australia, which some correctly call the campground continent.

Getting your camper, yourself and the kids there and back again will be fast, efficient and relatively inexpensive. The vehicular jet ferries, cargo versions of the SSTs already well along toward production, may load on their double decks as many as 50 to 75 mobile homes and truck campers.

For the short three-hour hop overseas, you'll ride in your camper, the whole family riding free in fact.

The cost, probably no more one way to Europe for the whole family and its camper or trailer than the one way boat fare for automobiles today, about $300 or $400.

Family Camper—More Leisure for Less. As the experts view it, within something less than a decade, owning a camping vehicle will be an economic necessity for the average family.

It will, if you expect to enjoy and participate in America's new leisure, the shriveling work week (by 1976 less than thirty-six hours for most breadwinners) that promises to turn every weekend into a family fun affair, stretched out paid vacations (for many, upwards of four weeks every year) and already legislated three-day holidays, perhaps as many as a dozen of them scattered throughout the year by the mid-70s.

Even while most of us will be earning more than ever before (40 per cent of families will be earning $10,000 or more by 1976, compared to 14 per cent earning that much today), the average family's fun budget simply won't stretch across the 150 days or so of time-off-for-leisure unless it vacations in budget-priced mobile luxury. That will mean in a self-contained camping vehicle.

Even today's expanding leisure, abbreviated compared to tomorrow's, tips the economic scales toward home-on-wheels vehicular ownership as more necessity than luxury. You have only to analyze your last vacation expenses to understand why:

If yours was an average vacationing family of four, you spent $36 to $60 a day ($9 to $15 per person) for bed and board. For the money, you put up at good but probably not the best motels and hotels and ate at good but not the best restaurants. For a week of it on the road, overnighting in motels or hotels and eating out in restaurants, you spent $252 to $420.

By the mid-70s, with on the road expenses risen a foreseeable 30 per cent, you'll be spending at least $45 to $80 a day for food and shelter.

To take advantage even of 100 of the new leisure's recreational days off an average family would need to budget annually more than $5000. Even in higher income, more-leisure-time tomorrow, not many will be able to afford it.

Vehicular family campers will. Carrying their accommodations, plain or fancy, with them, and cooking in rather than eating out, they'll be on the forefront of America's 150-day leisure participants: those who, gifted with the new leisure, will make and take full recreational advantage of it.

By then, we shall have arrived in the decade of the three-car family, with one of them, out of recreational and economic necessity, being not a car at all, but a home-away-from-home-on-wheels.

Then, even more than now, the status symbol of leisure will be a camping vehicle, the wheels and wherewithal for getting away from it all on a whim or a weekend. Not only by road, but by water too.

Rise of the Convertible Camper. Is it a boat . . . a camper . . . a car? Tomorrow the camping vehicle is apt to be all three. Right now, in fact, you can rig your travel trailer, the 10 to 30 foot long, 6 to 6½ foot wide, tow-it variety with retractable pontoons. Come to water, you merely lower the floats, hook a modestly powered outboard motor astern and your trailer becomes a houseboat.

Convertibility will make the big difference in camping vehicles of the future.

"People," explains an eyes-ahead designer, "will simply demand it, the go-anyplace vacation cabin on wheels which, with scarcely any effort at all, transitions to water to become what it was on land, a campable, mobile shelter."

Convertible campers of the future are likely to be more complex and futuristic. Take tomorrow's motor home, the decade ahead kin of today's luxurious $11,000 to $18,000 bus camper.

It will have a hull-like body of fiberglass or lightweight plastic. Its wheels will retract to become serviceable paddle wheels, once in water.

A control console will enable its driver to change gear ratios and even the pattern of wheel drives with the push of a button, converting tomorrow's go anywhere motor home for high speed expressways, four-wheel-drive terrain or town driving.

As a vacation home afloat, the motor home will cruise, pushed by its retracted wheel paddles or water-jet propulsion, at today's houseboat speeds, up to twenty-five mph. While hardly a speedboat, nor intended to be, it'll be fast enough for the average river or lake cruising camping family.

Similar convertibility will turn amphibian almost every manner of recreational vehicle, from truck camper to trailer. For millions, camping will no longer stop at the water's edge.

Coming, the Caravans. In the decade just ahead, you and your camping vehicle will be joining caravans, not along world trade routes as in centuries past, but along routes which lead to recreational camaraderie on five continents.

Caravaning today and tomorrow is camping togetherness, hundreds of families and their recreational vehicles, guided by a caravan leader, making camp and fun together. Adventuring where few of them, either because of distance or terrain, barriers of language and custom or sheer timidity, would likely venture alone.

Father of caravan camping was the late Wally Byam. Towing tours, out-of-this-world excursions fitted to the pace, the interests and the communal spirit of trailerites.

What Byam pioneered for the trailer clan, perhaps the majority of them retired folk with the time and the yen to trailer together, will be the mode of tho younger set and their recreation vehicles.

Your passport to global caravaning? Nothing more than the family's pickup camper, motor bus, van camper or tent trailer.

Caravaning, you'll camp your way along the legendary Alaska Highway, past Milepost 1523 (Fairbanks) and beyond, push south along the Pan American through Mexico and Central America, or roll the Autobahn across Germany in the wheels away companionship of others as wedded to communal adventuring as yourself.

Caravaning tomorrow will be part and parcel of the new American life style as you and the kids break the bonds and boredom of the city in quest of adventure that lies everywhere just under wheel.

Tomorrow's Camping Components and Costs. Versatility, as much as convertibility, will be designed into tomorrow's camping vehicle.

Consider today's vexing problem of around campsite transportation, the fact that once encamped, owners of larger pickup and motor home campers often find themselves without ready transportation for exploring the near at hand countryside or foraging into closeby towns for forgotten necessities.

Rather than be without wheels, some pack along a lightweight motor bike or two, behind their larger camping vehicle, some auxiliary means of transport, be it only a dune buggy.

Tomorrow, your camper will contain your car. It'll serve as your motor home's detachable power unit, its power boosted for pulling the camping unit by torque converters and electric wheel motors.

Just as versatile will be tomorrow's pickup campers. Sidewall extensions, hydraulically lowered, will hand you a two-story camping cabin with plenty of room on the first deck to bunk the kids. With the camper self-supported, its truck becomes your camp car.

It won't be a truck by today's image, but rather a heavy duty sports car, heavy on elegance, utility and luxury. The trend in camper truck elegance to match any family's first car is already developing. Dodge's futuristic Deora pickup truck, displayed at some auto and truck shows, but not in production, only hints at the future.

Tomorrow's camper pickup truck, actually the average family's second or even first car, will, with the flick of a switch, convert to a four-passenger sedan, the rear cab wall moving backwards to be met by a retracted roof extension and two additional bucket seats popping up from the truck bed.

More exciting, it'll also be a fast cruising boat. So your camper's versatile power unit will, in a single vehicle, solve both the road and water transport problems now vexing camping families.

Moreover, you'll be buying a three-in-one bargain, camper motive power which, in town, becomes your second car and is a road and water taxi.

The camping wife is in for some happy surprises too. No more dishes to wash, no meals to prepare, no cooking to do. What has to be cooked (ready-prepared meals) will be cooked automatically in less than ten minutes, start to finish.

What promises to let the camping wife be just a camper, not a cook, are sized-down, low-cost versions of the amazing new electric galleys now going into the much heralded jet air buses.

These new design electric ovens cook pre-prepared meals (four to six course dinners) in from six to twelve minutes. Tomorrow's vehicular campers will be built in with similar galleys.

Headed afield, you'll merely order in advance from a camp meal commissary, an entire week's or even a month's menu, the food already prepared, individually portioned and frozen. Pack them away in your camper's freezer, kept at minus 20°F. by liquid nitrogen, and you're ready to roll.

Camped, with lunchtime approaching, your wife merely takes from the freezer the meals labeled "Lunch, Day #1," and pops them into the camper's ultra-fast aircraft-type electric oven.

Five minutes, and you and the kids will sit down to a lunch afield the equal of any served in high-priced restaurants. As for the dishes? There aren't any, just a few plastic trays and discarded foil wrappings. Chuck them into your camper's smokeless incinerator (by the mid-70s, incinerators will be standard equipment in most camper units) and you're set for fishing, hiking or just doing nothing.

Will tomorrow's new breed of vehicular campers and their new conveniences be beyond the budget of the average camping family? Not at all. At least some indications suggest that, relative to costs today, some may be less expensive.

Today, most families expect to spend $1000 for a fancy car top or tent camper; between $3000 and $6000 for a pickup camper, truck included; $2500 to $6500 for a compact van camper; $6000 to $10,000 for fancy trailers and motor homes and, for the most luxurious and largest of roadable motor homes, somewhere between $11,000 and $20,000.

The same relative pricing should prevail in the decade ahead. And while costs, generally, will be up 30 per cent, say some economists, so will wages and salaries.

Proportional to your income, a vehicular camper should cost no more tomorrow than right now. Far greater usage in the decade of the new leisure will tend to reduce by perhaps 50 per cent or more the daily use cost of your camper, based on its original cost and the number of days you'll use it.

The Camping '70s, Campsites for Every Camper. With perhaps as many as three to five million vehicular campers afield by the mid-70s, compared to less than 500,000 today, where in the world, let alone in the U.S., you may ask, will all of them find camping space?

In an attempt to show the possible future of the pickup truck, the Alexander Brothers of Detroit created the Deora (opposite page) from a standard Dodge A-100 pickup (above). Unique features include retractable front window, center-hinged front door and swing-away steering wheel to allow driver entrance from frontal area.

DODGE

The answer: in the vast uncamped, sparsely peopled reaches of the nation and the world set aside and planned for outdoor recreation, including camping.

It is not, concluded the Outdoor Recreation Resources Review Commission, a problem of too little land, but of too little planning. That, and an uneven distribution of much of the U.S.'s millions of acres of recreation-potential land, some 283 million acres of it owned and managed by the U.S. government, the remainder comprising privately owned farm, forest and ranch lands.

Distribution poses perhaps the single knottiest problem. For example, while only 15 per cent of our population resides in the West, that area contains 72 per cent of our recreational reserves. By contrast, 25 per cent of all Americans live in the densely populated Northeast, which has only four per cent of the nation's recreational acreage.

Shaping up is a crash program, participated in by cities, counties, states and the Federal government, to turn this vast recreational potential to reality.

The new Bureau of Outdoor Recreation, first government agency to deal exclusively with outdoor leisure and its demands, is close to finalizing its monumental Nationwide Outdoor Recreation Plan, the masterplan for fun lands development in the '70s and beyond.

In 1964 Congress voted a 25-year plan for outdoor recreation. From the newly created Land and Water Conservation Fund, the U.S. will annually spend about $200 million to acquire and develop recreational land. About 60 per cent of this annual grant for outdoor leisure will go, on a dollar for dollar matching basis, to states and local governments, helping them to finance thousands of new recreational sites.

Planned is a nine-fold increase in campsites alone. New York State, typically, has launched a ten-year, $400 million park and campsite development program. It'll add 10,000 new campsites to the state's already extensive camping facilities. Californians recently voted a $150 million bond for outdoor recreation. Other programs are underway in New Jersey, Pennsylvania, Wisconsin, Rhode Island and Washington.

Even the West's preponderance of leisure lands may, in the future, find one ready-made solution: a coast to coast system of no cost overnight camping places for vehicular campers headed West toward America's abundant camping grounds.

The system, in fact, is nearing completion, the thousands of campable rest stops built everywhere, often every fifty miles or so along the Interstate Highway System, 60 per cent of its total 41,000 miles already finished.

Thus emerges the out-of-doors kaleidoscope of the Camping '70s, when a vehicular camper will be every family's passport to the new leisure, to global adventure and to just plain fun everywhere under the sun.